Concrete®

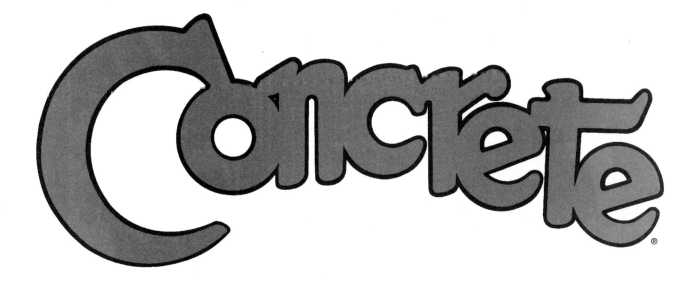

Concrete

Complete Short Stories 1986-1989

Paul Chadwick

With an introduction by
Archie Goodwin

DARK HORSE COMICS®

Mike Richardson • publisher
Neil Hankerson • executive vice president
David Scroggy • vice president of publishing
Lou Bank • vice president of sales & marketing
Andy Karabatsos • vice president of finance
Mark Anderson • general counsel
Diana Schutz • editor in chief
Randy Stradley • creative director
Cindy Marks • director of production & design
Mark Cox • art director
Sean Tierney • computer graphics director
Chris Creviston • director of accounting
Michael Martens • marketing director
Tod Borleske • sales & licensing director
Mark Ellington • director of operations
Dale LaFountain • director of m.i.s.

Published by
Dark Horse Comics, Inc.
10956 SE Main Street
Milwaukie, OR 97222

CONCRETE ®: COMPLETE SHORT STORIES 1986-1989
© 1986-1989, 1990 by Paul H. Chadwick
Foreword © 1990 by Archie Goodwin
Compilation © 1990 by Dark Horse Comics, Inc.
Cover image © 1993 by Paul H. Chadwick

ISBN: 1-56971-114-3
Second edition: August 1995

Printed in Canada

10 9 8 7 6 5 4 3 2 1

CONTENTS

INTRODUCTION

A lot of thinking goes in the average comic book.

Much of it takes place in thought balloons, although these have fallen somewhat into disfavor in recent years. More fashionable are first-person captions that function as a character's interior monologue. Whatever. It's still thinking and, by whichever stylistic device, a lot of it gets done in almost any comic book you choose to pick up. Especially if it's a comic about someone with extraordinary powers.

Something about having powers beyond human ken really turns a comic book character into a thought balloon or interior monologue magnet. Those things float around them like pilot fish around a shark. Too often they explain things. At their very worst they explain what the character's doing just in case you can't tell from looking at the picture. On a slightly higher level they explain what the character's feeling or they supply background information that the pictures can't.

Basically, thinking in comic books is exposition. Some writers do it far more artfully than others, but frequently even the well-written material is exposition. Trust me. As a writer who's foisted more than my share of expository thought balloons or captions (some artful, a fearful number probably not) on readers, I'm not speaking from a critical perch, just working experience. For your usual story to function, there are things that have to be explained. The thoughts of our readers provide a pretty convenient place for most of us to do that.

Paul Chadwick's *Concrete* is a rare and happy exception.

Oh, there's a lot of thinking going on in this collection of remarkable short stories. Paul employs a good many of the same comics conventions that the rest of us do. But the way he employs them . . .

By rights, *Concrete* should be pretty standard fare. Like too many other comic characters, Paul's protagonist, speechwriter Ronald Lithgow, has an origin worthy of a supermarket tabloid (SPACE ALIENS PUT MY BRAIN IN THE BODY OF A ROCK!). Except . . . once this happens, none of the other usual things happen. He doesn't suddenly start fighting crime; he isn't suddenly in conflict with world-dominating super villains (in fact true villains of any kind are pretty scarce in *Concrete*). Instead, Lithgow tries to find a thoughtful, reasonable way to lead a life given both the wonders and limitations of what's happened to him. And, through his art and writing, Paul Chadwick makes this fascinating.

And because he does it well, Paul also makes it appear simple and easy. It's not.

In early 1986, I was doing two things for Marvel Comics. I was editor of their imprint for creator-owned projects, Epic Comics, and, as a freelance writer, I was involved in helping to create characters for what would be another new Marvel line, the New Universe. The premise of the New Universe was that it would take place in "the real world" and examine how characters given extraordinary powers would learn to live and cope with their situations. Sounds familiar, yes?

To add to the irony, in my editor's hat I was trying to talk Paul into doing *Concrete* for Epic. As writer and artist we had worked together the previous year on another Marvel project, *The Dazzler*; Paul had gotten the assignment by showing sample pages of a personal project he had started.

The project was *Concrete* and, if the *Dazzler* experience did nothing else, it obviously made Paul confident and determined to go ahead with it next. With quibbles (hey, I'm an editor: nature of the beast), I liked *Concrete* very much and wanted Paul to do it with us. Unfortunately (for Epic: the good folks at Dark Horse who are bringing you this collection undoubtedly have no such feeling), I couldn't guarantee Paul everything he was looking for. Like being able to personally edit his book. I was too involved in other aspects of my job. And in the New Universe.

So, as an editor I didn't get to do *Concrete*. And, as one of the New Universe writers, I didn't get to do anything that even came close to it. Paul's work was a personal vision. The New Universe material wasn't. Some of our ideas were not bad, but in the end, most of us doing them couldn't get beyond the notion of regular comic-book melodrama, beyond the need for typical action or typical villains to fuel such action. There is nothing particularly wrong in this, except there were more than enough comic books already doing it.

There still are. And *Concrete* isn't one of them.

Which brings us back to all the thinking going on in comics. The characters in this collection, most particularly the main one, Concrete himself, are possibly the most thoughtful in comics. They may occasionally be guilty of thinking in exposition, but mostly they think about things. Their minds wander and take flight and move in logical yet refreshing directions, never quite winding up where you assume they're going to go.

A surprising number of the stories herein involve nothing but a character thinking. The end result may be whimsical, ironic, or melancholy, but through the inevitable humanity of the writing, the dream-like evoking of the environment in the art, it is always exciting. Not the standard comics excitement of punches thrown or worlds hurled into jeopardy, but the exhilarating and pleasurable excitement of a character finding something about himself — and by extension, us — that is true.

A lot of thinking goes on in the average comic book. Thanks to the thinking of Paul Chadwick, very little of it is like what you'll find here.

Archie Goodwin
New York, NY
July 1990

I originally had no plans to do Concrete short stories. So when Randy Stradley contacted me to suggest I take time off from the series proposal package I was preparing (which included the first three issues) to do a story for a comic he and Mike Richardson were putting together, *Dark Horse Presents*, I decided to politely decline. In the middle of my letter to him, however, a story idea hit me, and to my surprise I decided to do it.

It was a good move. *DHP* was a hit, and my story, "Lifestyles of the Rich and Famous" brought good notices from Don Thompson and (quite dramatically) Harlan Ellison. Those proved very helpful in selling the series and attracting the attention Concrete has gained, and I feel lucky and grateful they came when they did. It helps to have influential opinion-makers touting your work.

As my agent Mike Friedrich and I circulated the proposal and entered into negotiation with a number of publishers, I continued to do short stories for Dark Horse. They wanted to publish the regular *Concrete* book, but with offers from larger, established publishers in hand, I hesitated at going with an untried newcomer. However, generous terms, the knowledge I would be edited by an old friend, and the sheer enthusiasm Mike Richardson had for the series finally swayed me. I've never had reason to regret the decision.

A nice bonus of going with Dark Horse was that I could continue the short stories. I had taken to the form; it suited Concrete in a way I hadn't expected. While the main series followed the pattern I had originally envisioned — probably inspired by *Tintin* — of a quirky cast of characters going to an exotic locale and having an adventure, the short stories were good for stressing parts of the Concrete idea central to him. The warehouse domesticity, the bruising encounters with unsympathetic people, the frustrations of dealing with daily life in a freakish body — these fit well into smaller, modest 6- or 8-pagers. I have also been able to do vignettes that relate to the longer stories, but did not fit into them — as "Water God" relates to "The Transatlantic Swim," and "Goodwill Ambassador" relates to "In the Region of Snows."

The first story ("Lifestyles...") is the one most people tell me is their favorite — a compliment I receive with some dismay; has it been downhill from there? Of course, there's that cache of newness and untapped backstory in a first installment that can never be matched. By plunging into a story without the usual explanations, while still giving enough information (by implication) to understand the immediate events, I think I benefitted from readers' speculations and blank-filling. I recall Harlan Ellison's dismay at learning I had, after all, done a traditional "origin story" (Concrete #3). Why not retain the mystery and sense of strangeness? Well, I might well have stretched it out a bit, but I think you have to address central questions before too much time has passed. *Twin Peaks'* failure to reveal the murderer of Laura Palmer in its first season is a case in point; if there's no promise of ever knowing, there's no pleasurable tension about the mystery.

In this story is an example of the chilling effect of widely publicized censorship (or the call for it). Concrete's sublimated sexual feelings are redirected into his passion for collecting erotic art, and some of these paintings are visible in the first panel. However, for this story, I whited out some of the details in the paintings. This seems absurdly timid from today's standpoint, but it was a different time, then. The big news in the comics world was the quashing of Steve Gerber's Epic series, *Void Indigo*, partly because of the objections of a Christian comics distributor. America's religious right was at the height of its influence, and it seemed the pendulum would swing further that way before coming back. Fledgling Dark Horse had no standing in the field, and I certainly didn't. I was moved to (surely unnecessary) prudence out of the fear of wasting months of work (if this particular distributor didn't carry the book, it would fail). Funny to look back on a decision made out of deep insecurity.

"Under the Desert Stars" first exhibits what would become a mainstay of Concrete stories: the depiction of his imagined scenarios — here with panel borders drawn with a french curve, a showy device I dropped after a while. The first glimmering of my obsession with nature going unobserved by the characters amid it are here as well. "The Four-Wheeled Sleeping Pill" was an attempt at straightforward suspense — a clear problem to be solved with the tools at hand, with compounding complications. "The Gray Embrace" features one of my visual obsessions, the border between above and below the water. I grew up on Lake Washington and on Puget Sound in Washington State, and developed an enduring fascination for the unseeable world beneath the surface. Much of any artist's work, I suspect, is spent trying to recapture powerful feelings of childhood. The executive in the story is modeled on the producer of a film I worked on, *Pee-Wee's Big Adventure*.

"Burning Brightly, Brightly" expressed my feelings about doing art, all the good and bad reasons, pretty much. Painters who are self-directed enough to work on series of paintings with no outside parameters have always fascinated me. How do they muster the confidence to believe the world wants or needs what they're doing? I've always had more of an illustrator's mentality, trying to do my best for someone else's purpose. My *Concrete* work, I suppose, is the major exception. Still, sometimes, when looking through a Bud Plant catalog, I wonder what I can add that hasn't been done better before. Melissa Strangehands' speechlessness is also my usual reaction to meeting one of my heroes. Funny how that works.

"Little Pushes" is my favorite short story, and what I sent to Fantagraphics when they requested a Concrete story for their *Best Comics of the Decade* collection. It speaks to the heart of Concrete's dilemma, the humor works (I think), and I pulled off a fairly deft structural trick. As I write this, I am finally drawing up the story of Concrete's work on the film which forms the context of this story. Only took three years.

"Water God" features a couple of kids named David and Moose Hescox. My former studio mate, illustrator Richard Hescox, has a son named David. He has no daughter, though, so I named the girl after his cat. I named the boat, "Lady," after a broken-down old hound dog we had at the time. In "Straight in the Eye" I also slipped in some friends. Adam Munro resembles a filmmaker friend, Alan Munro. Laurie Newell, an illustrator and Adam's *covivant*, also plays a small part. I changed her first name to make the misunderstanding work. There's a moment in this story that has a quality that especially appeals to me: Concrete dropping hundreds of feet under a starry sky, watching to see if the plane will pull up in time, not knowing if he'll hit the water before he learns its fate. The strangeness, the danger, the natural beauty of the setting gave me special pleasure in imagining the sequence. This is the unsung pleasure of writing: the way it forces you to imagine experience with unusual vividness. Incidentally, though you might think so from this story, I have no particular phobia about bears.

"Next Best" is another story dealing with Concrete's aloneness, with a surreal opening dream. My reliance on dreams perhaps speaks of a frustration I have with the Concrete series; I like to draw fantastic, otherworldly things, and yet it's central to the strip that Concrete lives in our familiar, everyday world. Dreams allow me to let off a bit of that creative steam. "Now Is Now" led me to a pleasant afternoon sketching at the New Milford cemetery, causing me to evaluate some of the same issues Concrete does in the story. The names on the headstones have no special significance.

"With a Whimper" and "Quality Time" were, as you might guess from the artwork, done before I started *Concrete*. At the publisher's behest I added the framing devices with Concrete and Larry, thinking that the stories were similar enough in tone to the Concrete stories that nobody would be too disappointed. My illustrator friend Bryn Barnard narrates "Whimper," which is based on his experiences on the track team of Laguna Beach High School. His coach really did have them read *Psycho-Cybernetics* and chant before the meets as in the story. And he really knew a character like Steve Greave, although he didn't wind up in the Olympics. I was never able to work in Bryn's other teammate, "Snake." Snake got his nickname because he ran without a jockstrap. A star runner, he moved through the pain by remembering that it was nothing compared to Christ's suffering on the cross. I have a number of *Sky of Heads* stories plotted which I hope to draw up as backup stories in *Concrete*.

"Fitful Sleep" was a framing device for the first *DHP* annual. The cover was a parody of a silver-age DC giant, and the central image was Concrete being hit by lightning; he is consequently waking up from a dream of that, as real thunder rumbles outside. I'm told that Chris Warner, using whiteout and Xerox, created an amended version of the second page that suggested the dog is reacting to an extreme case of flatulence on Concrete's part, to the great amusement of the Dark Horse office gang. I'll get him for that.

"Goodwill Ambassador" is a type of story which I'd like to do more aften. Rather than a further examination of Concrete's psyche or predicament, it's a look at another aspect of the world with Concrete being a visiting catalyst. One notion in the story quite struck me when some literacy workers pointed it out to me during my Nepal trek; people need training to understand pictures. They were having trouble teaching people to read because their workbook's line drawings, even of familiar things like water buffalo, were themselves unreadable to these villagers, deprived of printed matter as they were. "Stay Tuned for Pearl Harbor" germinated for years. I think I originally conceived it during a driving trip in the late seventies. We live, we judge, we feel by what we see; if only we could collectively see more, and understand consequences better.

"Visible Breath" has elicited bafflement from some people, to which I reply that I'm allowed a mood piece now and then. In part I was trying to capture the mystery that remote motels have — containing as they do, the unknown stories of your fellow travellers. Who can resist speculating about their lives, based on the scanty evidence of their cars and appearance, and their noises through the wall?

There's one *DHP* story by me from the period this collection covers that's not in this volume: a non-Concrete story entitled "Brighter!" I commend the collection, *The Best of Dark Horse Presents, Vol. 1*, to true completists; it's in there. From the first issue of the magazine, it is a whimsical afterthought about my stint on *Dazzler*.

I hope you enjoy this collection.

Paul Chadwick
Warren, CT
August 1990

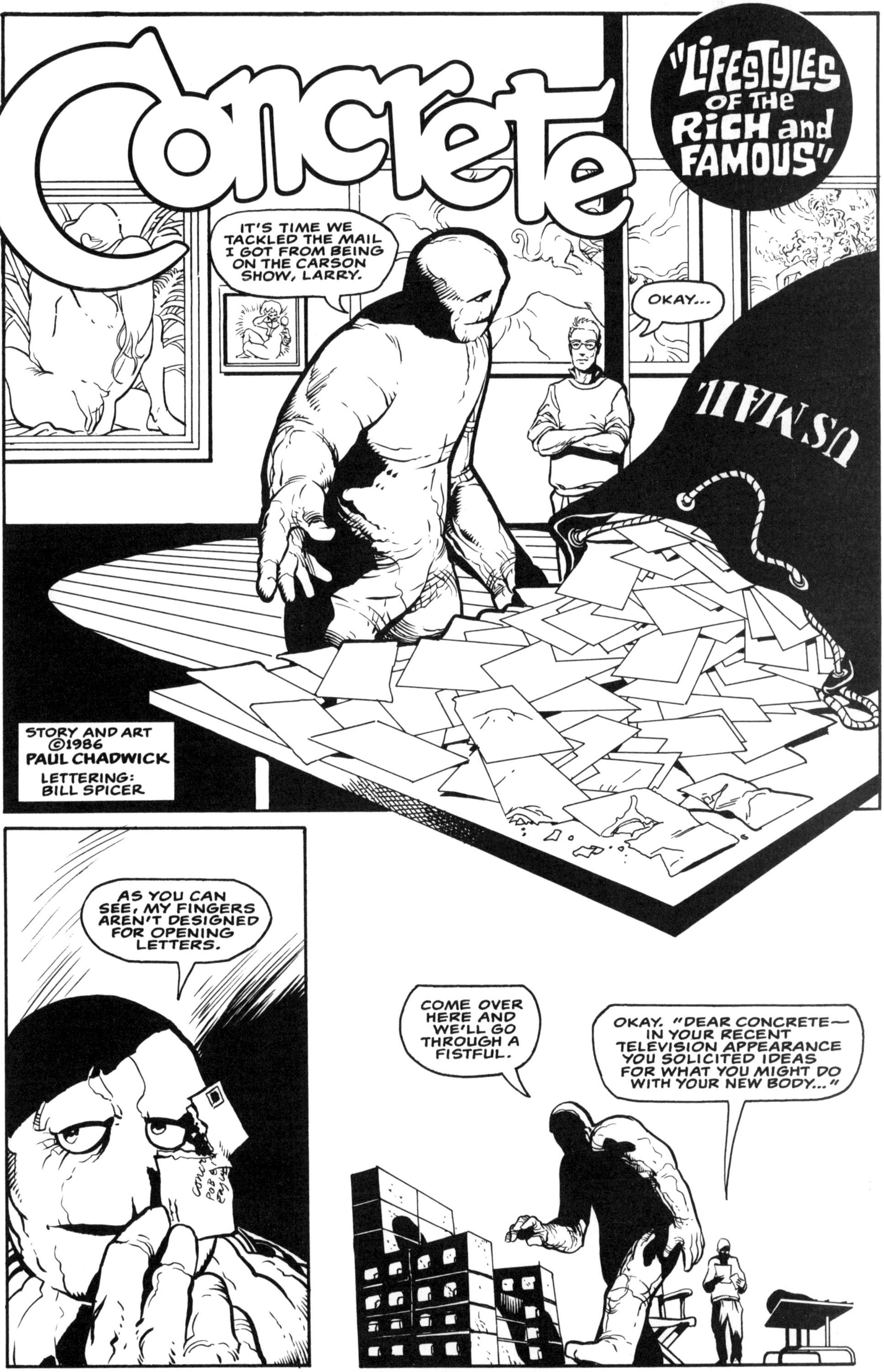
Concrete
"Lifestyles of the Rich and Famous"
IT'S TIME WE TACKLED THE MAIL I GOT FROM BEING ON THE CARSON SHOW, LARRY.
OKAY...
STORY AND ART ©1986 PAUL CHADWICK
LETTERING: BILL SPICER
AS YOU CAN SEE, MY FINGERS AREN'T DESIGNED FOR OPENING LETTERS.
COME OVER HERE AND WE'LL GO THROUGH A FISTFUL.
OKAY. "DEAR CONCRETE— IN YOUR RECENT TELEVISION APPEARANCE YOU SOLICITED IDEAS FOR WHAT YOU MIGHT DO WITH YOUR NEW BODY..."

"I APPLAUD THIS OPENNESS AND AM ELECTRIFIED BY THE POSSIBILITIES BEFORE YOU. WHY? BECAUSE YOU ARE A MAN IN A SINGULAR POSITION TO *MAKE A DIFFERENCE* IN THIS WORLD."

"FOR ONE THING, YOU ARE ALMOST PERFECTLY SUITED FOR *PASSIVE RESISTANCE.* IMAGINE YOURSELF IN A NONVIOLENT RALLY IN SOUTH AFRICA...OR POLAND...LEADING THOSE ASSEMBLED IN A ROUSING CHORUS OF 'WE SHALL NOT BE MOVED'. CONSIDER: YOU REALLY *COULDN'T* BE!"

"YOU SEEM UN-KILLABLE EXCEPT BY THE MOST EXTRAORDINARY MEANS. I URGE YOU, THEREFORE, TO THROW YOUR WEIGHT BEHIND THE CAUSE OF SOCIAL JUSTICE..."

"...NOT WITH FISTS FLYING, BUT WITH A CLEAR, UNAFRAID VOICE AND ROCK-LIKE STEADFASTNESS. SINCERELY, CHESTER DOMINGUEZ"

INTERESTING.

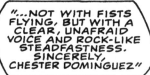

I'M NOT READY TO SAVE THE WORLD THIS MORNING, BUT LET'S DO THIS...

START A FILE CALLED "HAS POSSIBILITIES", AND PUT MR. DOMINGUEZ IN IT.

NEXT?

"DEAR CONCRETE: I AM SO HOT FOR YOU... I WANT YOUR HOT..."

UH...SHE ENCLOSES A PHOTO...

SHALL I THROW IT AWAY?

WHAT?! HOW CAN SHE...?

OH, EXCUSE ME. NO, I'LL TAKE CARE OF IT. NEXT?

"DEAR CONCRETE: PLEASE HELP. MY HUSBAND BEATS ME AND WHEN I GO TO MY FOLKS TO GET AWAY HE GETS MAD AND HITS MY FATHER AND BEATS ME WORSE."

"HE SAYS I LOVE MY LITTLE GIRL BY MY FIRST HUSBAND MORE THAN OUR CHILD TOGETHER BUT IT'S NOT TRUE. HE WON'T LISTEN."

"HE DRINKS AND HITS AND MY WRIST IS BROKE AND MY LITTLE GIRL IS SO SCARED SHE HAS A RASH AND NOW HE'S DEALING COKE. PLEASE *PLEASE HELP!!*"

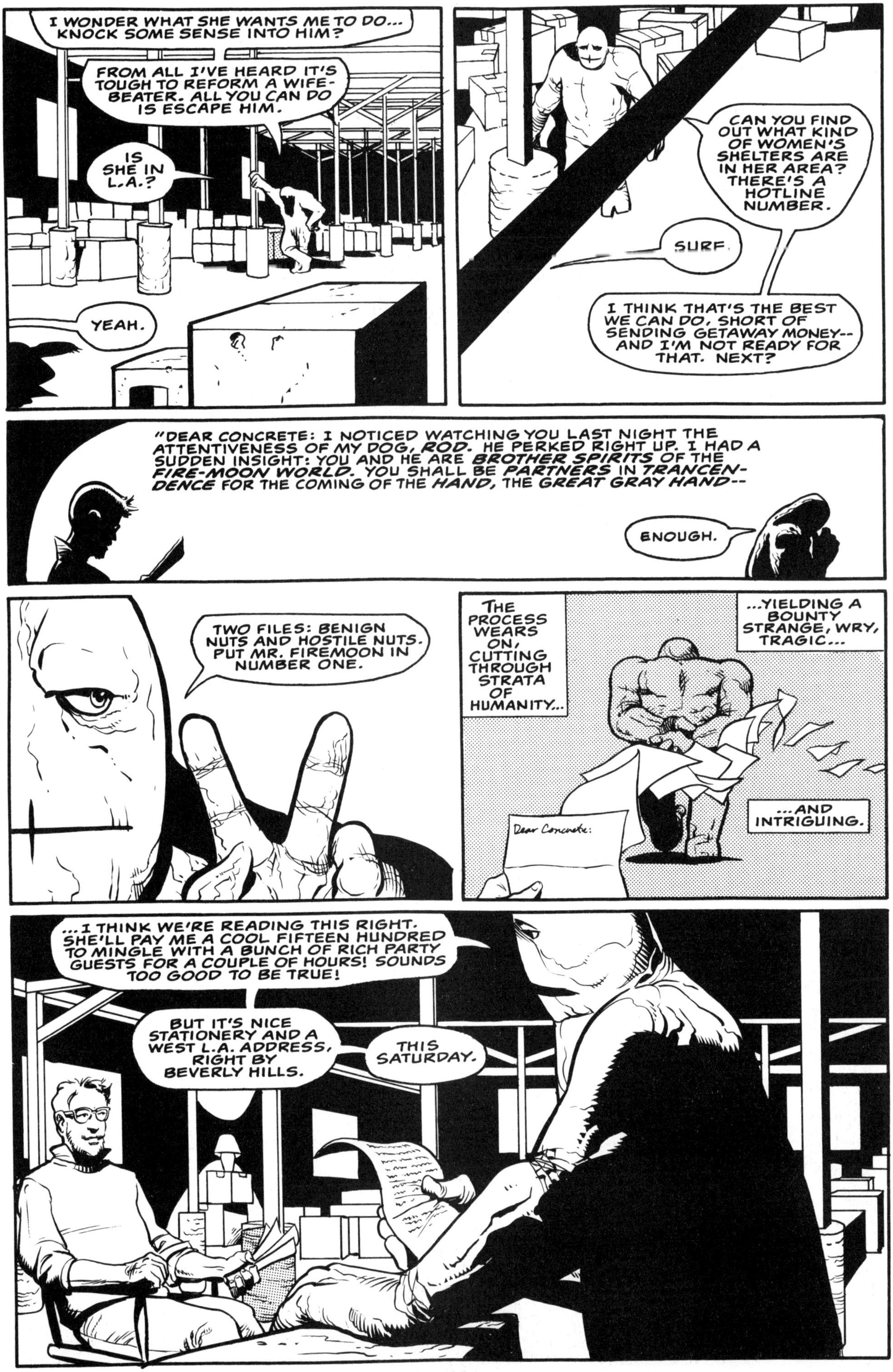
I WONDER WHAT SHE WANTS ME TO DO... KNOCK SOME SENSE INTO HIM?
FROM ALL I'VE HEARD IT'S TOUGH TO REFORM A WIFE-BEATER. ALL YOU CAN DO IS ESCAPE HIM.
IS SHE IN L.A.?
YEAH.
CAN YOU FIND OUT WHAT KIND OF WOMEN'S SHELTERS ARE IN HER AREA? THERE'S A HOTLINE NUMBER.
SURE.
I THINK THAT'S THE BEST WE CAN DO, SHORT OF SENDING GETAWAY MONEY-- AND I'M NOT READY FOR THAT. NEXT?
"DEAR CONCRETE: I NOTICED WATCHING YOU LAST NIGHT THE ATTENTIVENESS OF MY DOG, ROD. HE PERKED RIGHT UP. I HAD A SUDDEN INSIGHT: YOU AND HE ARE BROTHER SPIRITS OF THE FIRE-MOON WORLD. YOU SHALL BE PARTNERS IN TRANCENDENCE FOR THE COMING OF THE HAND, THE GREAT GRAY HAND--
ENOUGH.
TWO FILES: BENIGN NUTS AND HOSTILE NUTS. PUT MR. FIREMOON IN NUMBER ONE.
THE PROCESS WEARS ON, CUTTING THROUGH STRATA OF HUMANITY...
...YIELDING A BOUNTY STRANGE, WRY, TRAGIC...
...AND INTRIGUING.
Dear Concrete:
...I THINK WE'RE READING THIS RIGHT. SHE'LL PAY ME A COOL FIFTEEN HUNDRED TO MINGLE WITH A BUNCH OF RICH PARTY GUESTS FOR A COUPLE OF HOURS! SOUNDS TOO GOOD TO BE TRUE!
BUT IT'S NICE STATIONERY AND A WEST L.A. ADDRESS, RIGHT BY BEVERLY HILLS.
THIS SATURDAY.

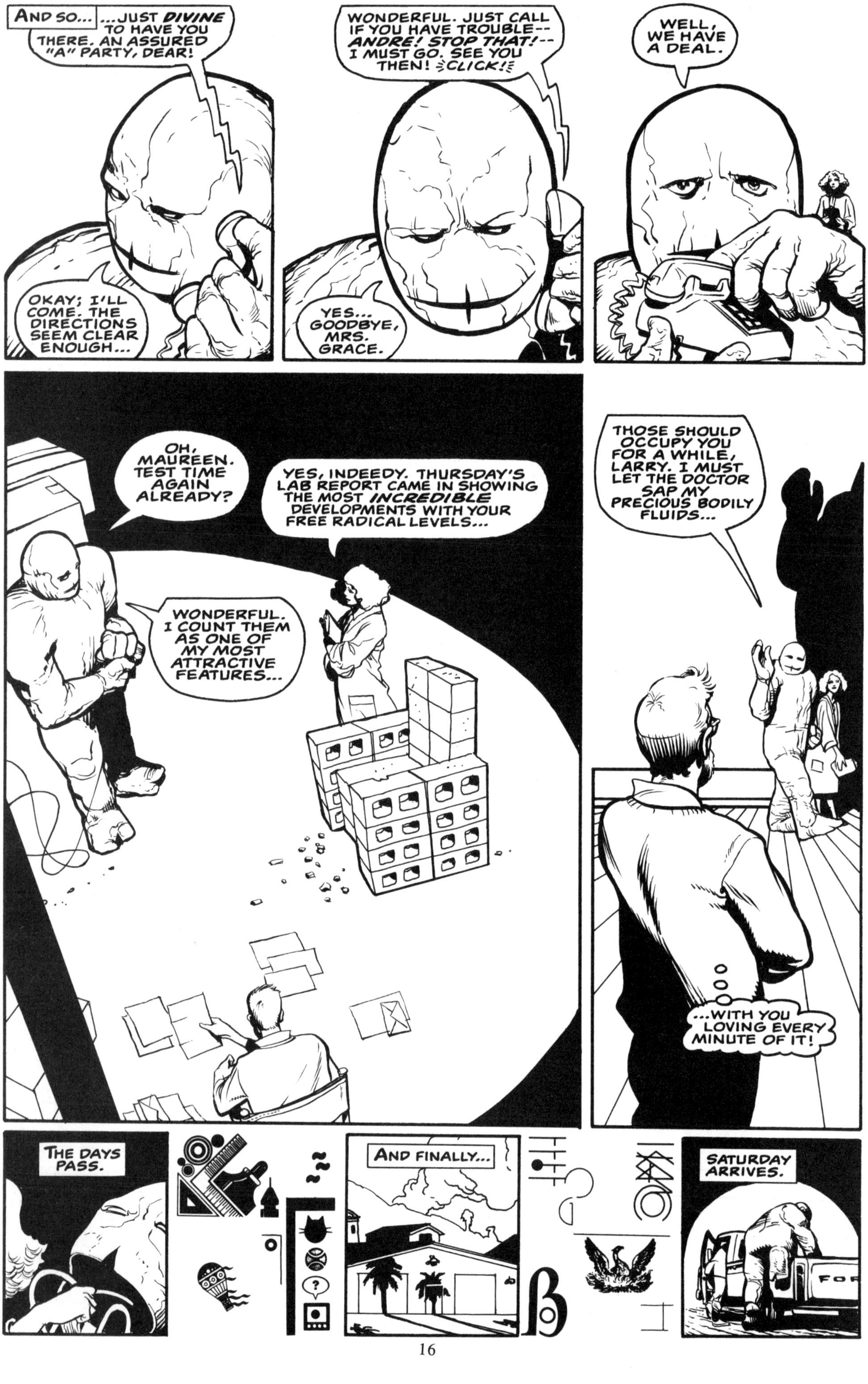
AND SO...
...JUST DIVINE TO HAVE YOU THERE. AN ASSURED "A" PARTY, DEAR!
OKAY; I'LL COME. THE DIRECTIONS SEEM CLEAR ENOUGH...
WONDERFUL. JUST CALL IF YOU HAVE TROUBLE-- ANDRE! STOP THAT!-- I MUST GO. SEE YOU THEN! CLICK!
YES... GOODBYE, MRS. GRACE.
WELL, WE HAVE A DEAL.
OH, MAUREEN. TEST TIME AGAIN ALREADY?
YES, INDEEDY. THURSDAY'S LAB REPORT CAME IN SHOWING THE MOST INCREDIBLE DEVELOPMENTS WITH YOUR FREE RADICAL LEVELS...
WONDERFUL. I COUNT THEM AS ONE OF MY MOST ATTRACTIVE FEATURES...
THOSE SHOULD OCCUPY YOU FOR A WHILE, LARRY. I MUST LET THE DOCTOR SAP MY PRECIOUS BODILY FLUIDS...
...WITH YOU LOVING EVERY MINUTE OF IT!
THE DAYS PASS.
AND FINALLY...
SATURDAY ARRIVES.
FOR

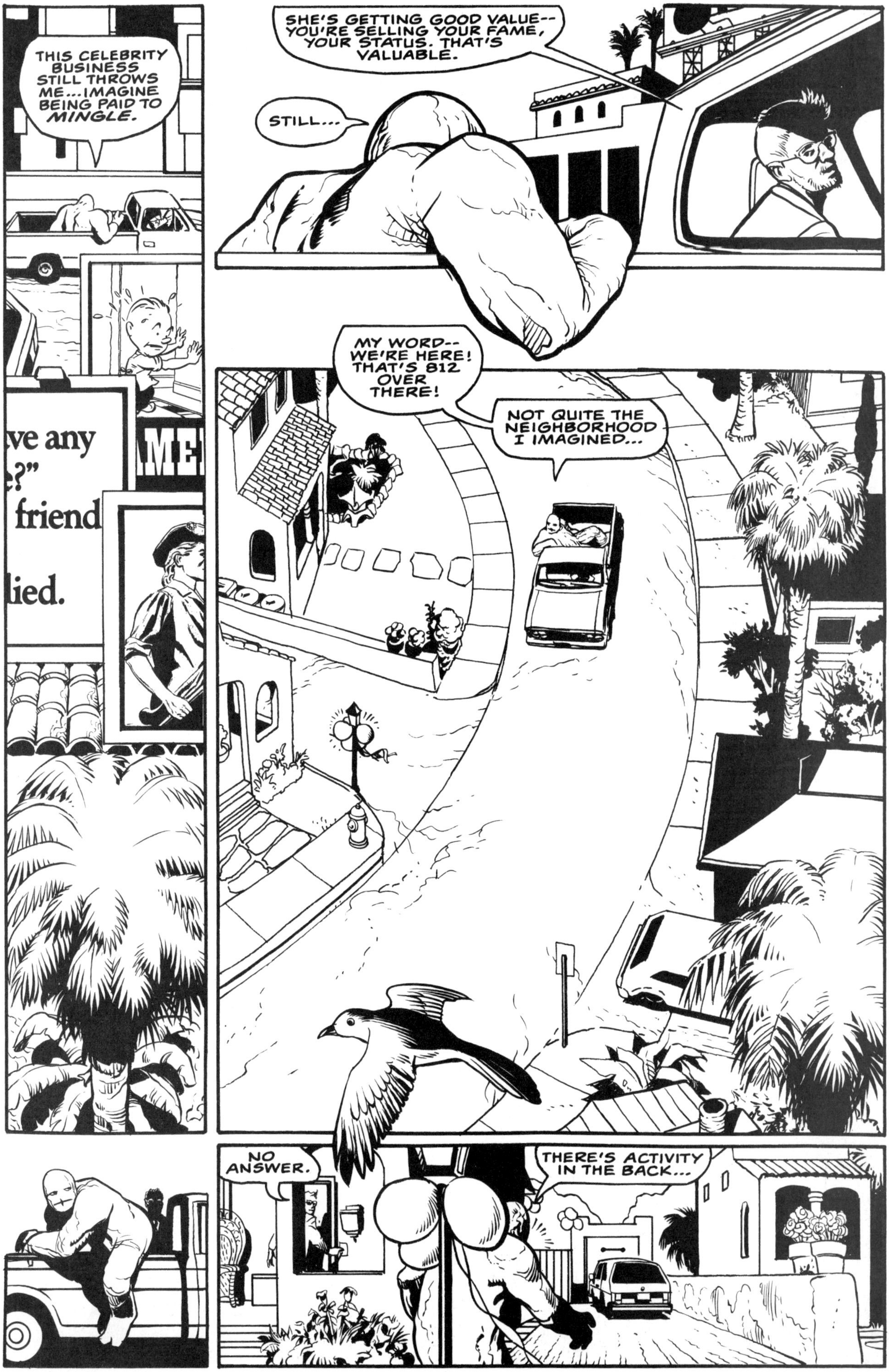
THIS CELEBRITY BUSINESS STILL THROWS ME...IMAGINE BEING PAID TO MINGLE.
SHE'S GETTING GOOD VALUE-- YOU'RE SELLING YOUR FAME, YOUR STATUS. THAT'S VALUABLE.
STILL...
MY WORD-- WE'RE HERE! THAT'S 812 OVER THERE!
NOT QUITE THE NEIGHBORHOOD I IMAGINED...
NO ANSWER.
THERE'S ACTIVITY IN THE BACK...

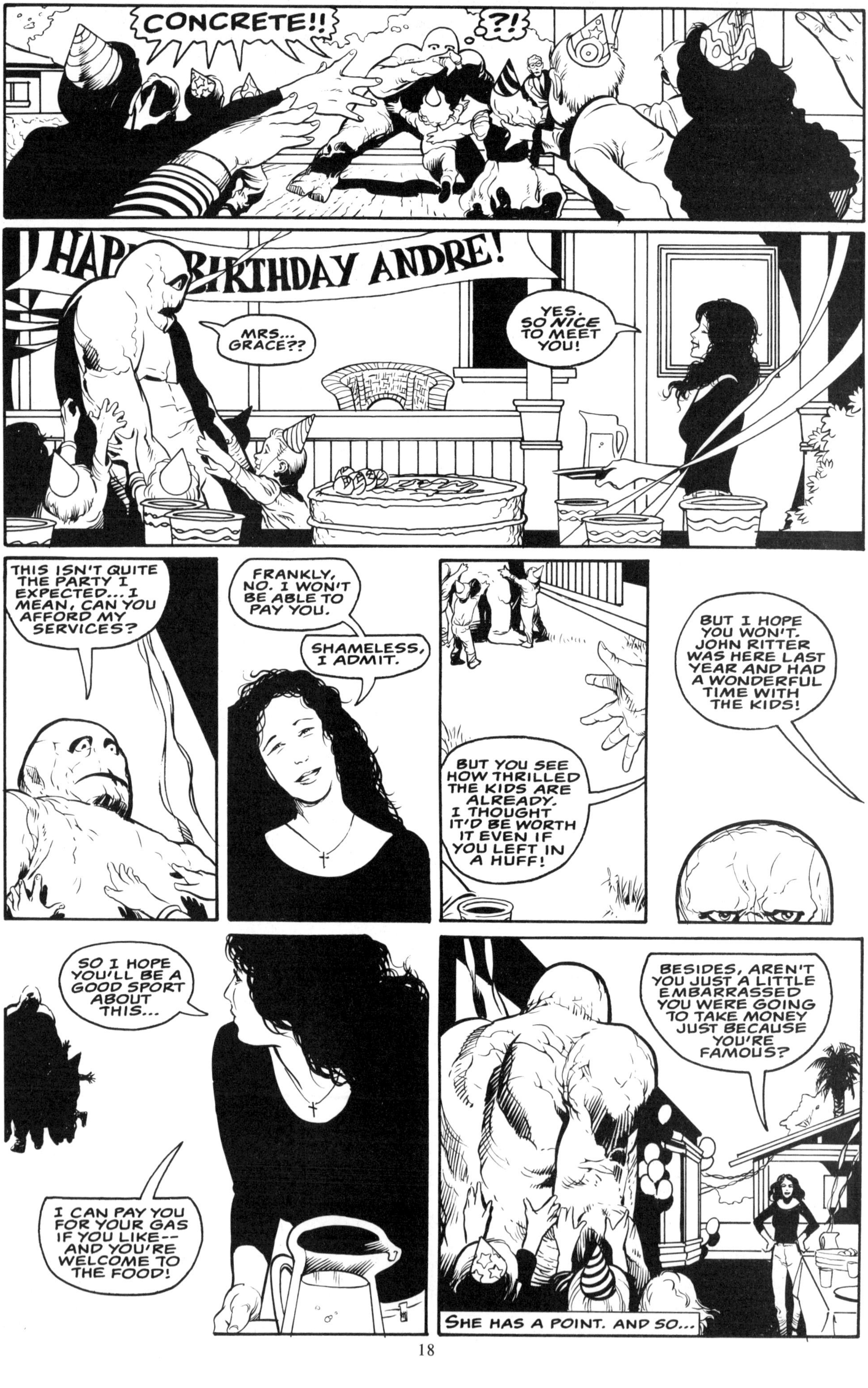
CONCRETE!!
?!
HAPPY BIRTHDAY ANDRE!
MRS... GRACE??
YES. SO NICE TO MEET YOU!
THIS ISN'T QUITE THE PARTY I EXPECTED... I MEAN, CAN YOU AFFORD MY SERVICES?
FRANKLY, NO. I WON'T BE ABLE TO PAY YOU.
SHAMELESS, I ADMIT.
BUT YOU SEE HOW THRILLED THE KIDS ARE ALREADY. I THOUGHT IT'D BE WORTH IT EVEN IF YOU LEFT IN A HUFF!
BUT I HOPE YOU WON'T. JOHN RITTER WAS HERE LAST YEAR AND HAD A WONDERFUL TIME WITH THE KIDS!
SO I HOPE YOU'LL BE A GOOD SPORT ABOUT THIS...
I CAN PAY YOU FOR YOUR GAS IF YOU LIKE-- AND YOU'RE WELCOME TO THE FOOD!
BESIDES, AREN'T YOU JUST A LITTLE EMBARRASSED YOU WERE GOING TO TAKE MONEY JUST BECAUSE YOU'RE FAMOUS?
SHE HAS A POINT. AND SO...

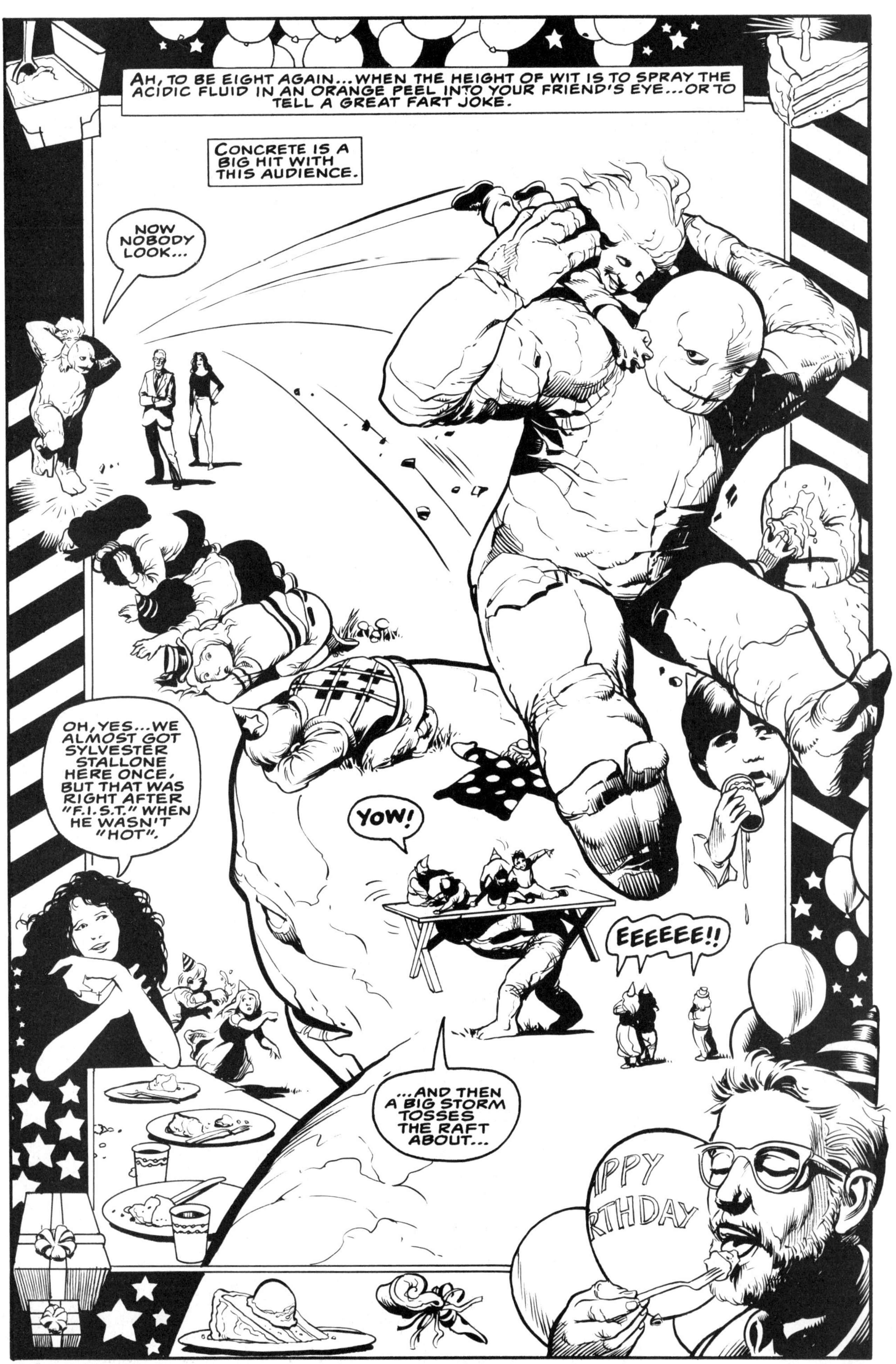
AH, TO BE EIGHT AGAIN...WHEN THE HEIGHT OF WIT IS TO SPRAY THE ACIDIC FLUID IN AN ORANGE PEEL INTO YOUR FRIEND'S EYE...OR TO TELL A GREAT FART JOKE.
CONCRETE IS A BIG HIT WITH THIS AUDIENCE.
NOW NOBODY LOOK...
OH, YES...WE ALMOST GOT SYLVESTER STALLONE HERE ONCE, BUT THAT WAS RIGHT AFTER "F.I.S.T." WHEN HE WASN'T "HOT".
YOW!
EEEEEE!!
...AND THEN A BIG STORM TOSSES THE RAFT ABOUT...
APPY
RTHDAY

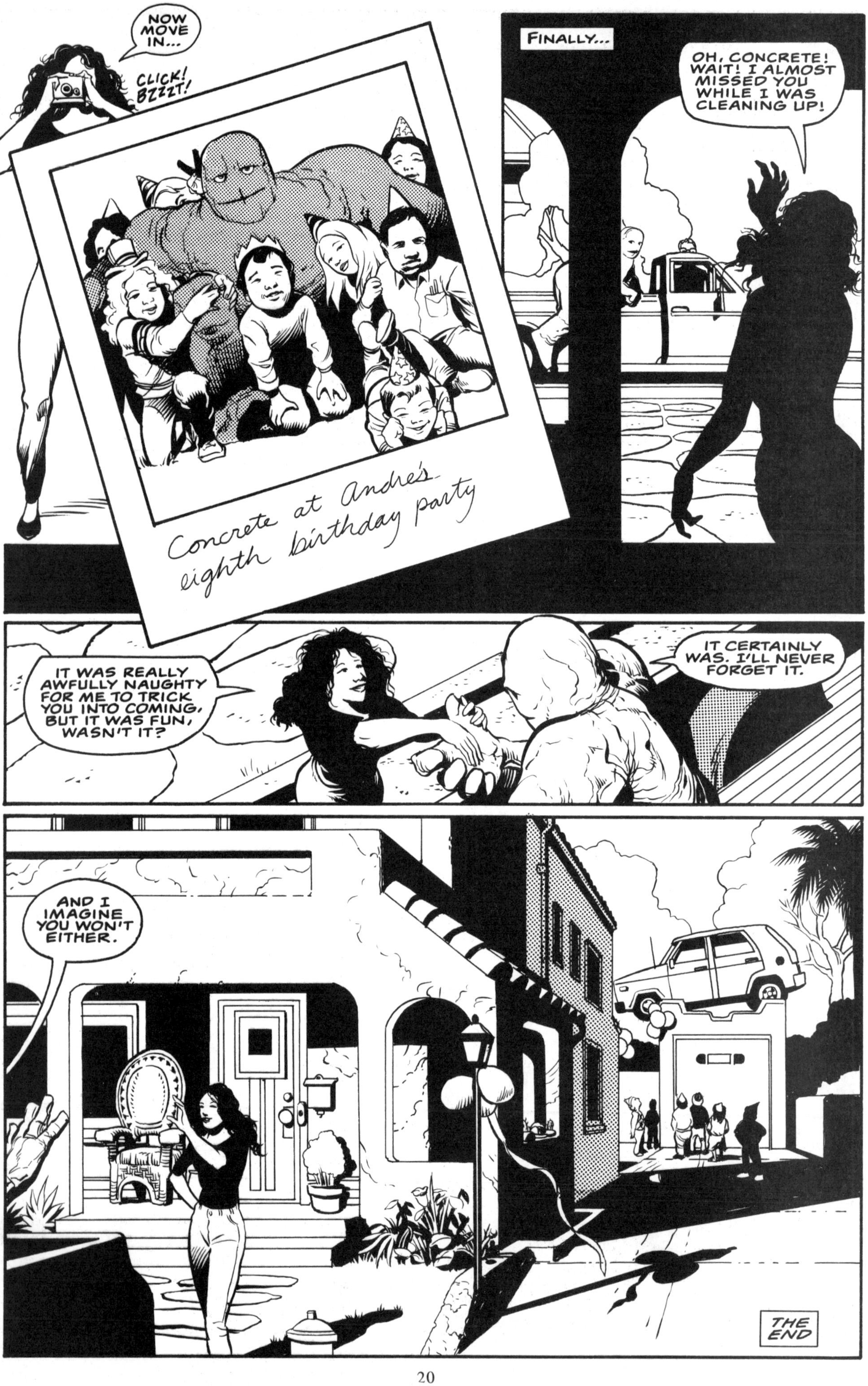
NOW MOVE IN...
CLICK! BZZZT!
Concrete at Andre's eighth birthday party
FINALLY...
OH, CONCRETE! WAIT! I ALMOST MISSED YOU WHILE I WAS CLEANING UP!
IT WAS REALLY AWFULLY NAUGHTY FOR ME TO TRICK YOU INTO COMING, BUT IT WAS FUN, WASN'T IT?
IT CERTAINLY WAS. I'LL NEVER FORGET IT.
AND I IMAGINE YOU WON'T EITHER.
THE END

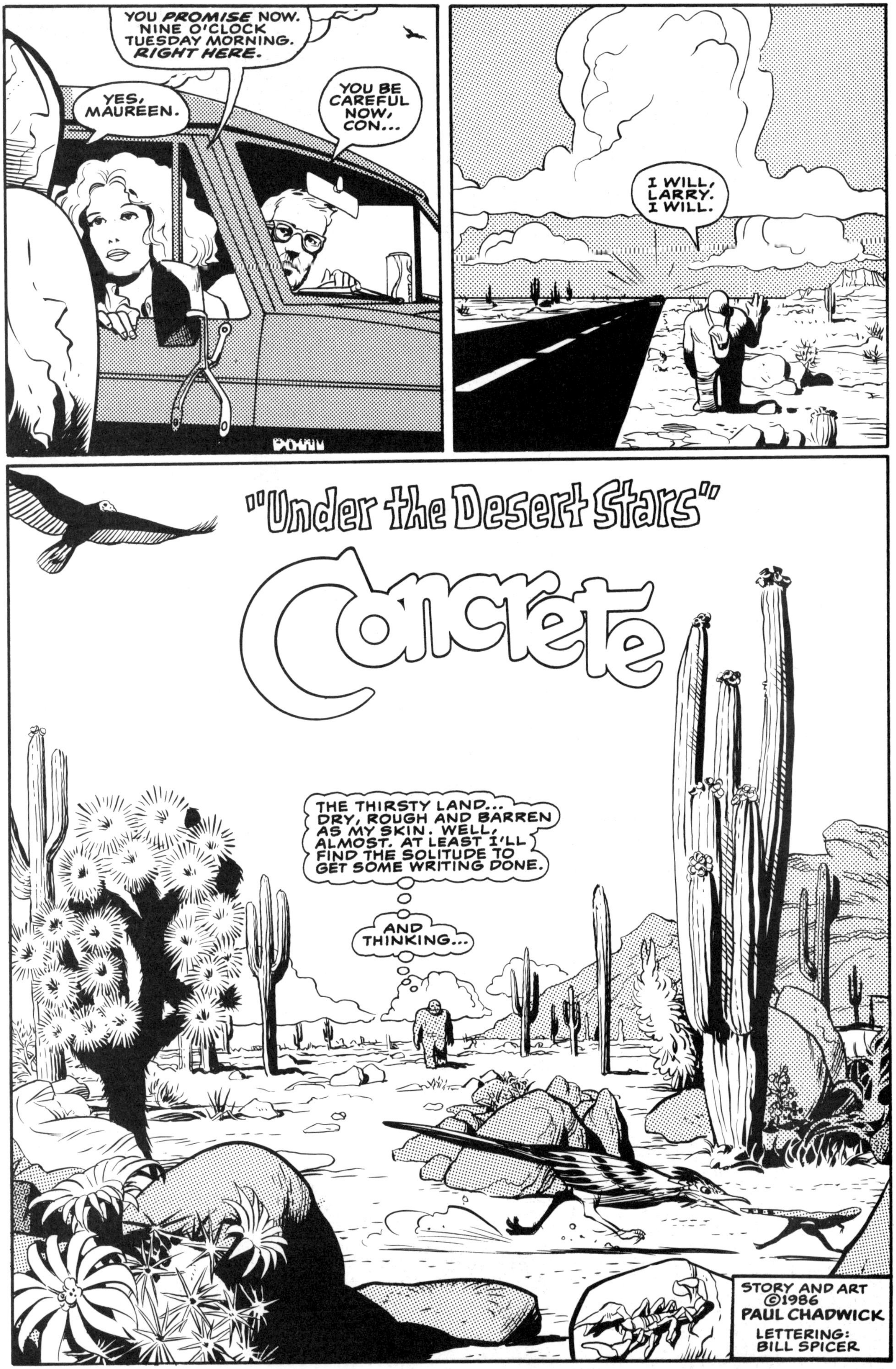
YOU *PROMISE* NOW. NINE O'CLOCK TUESDAY MORNING. *RIGHT HERE.*
YES, MAUREEN.
YOU BE CAREFUL NOW, CON...
I WILL, LARRY. I WILL.
"Under the Desert Stars"
Concrete
THE THIRSTY LAND... DRY, ROUGH AND BARREN AS MY SKIN. WELL, ALMOST. AT LEAST I'LL FIND THE SOLITUDE TO GET SOME WRITING DONE.
AND THINKING...
STORY AND ART ©1986 PAUL CHADWICK
LETTERING: BILL SPICER

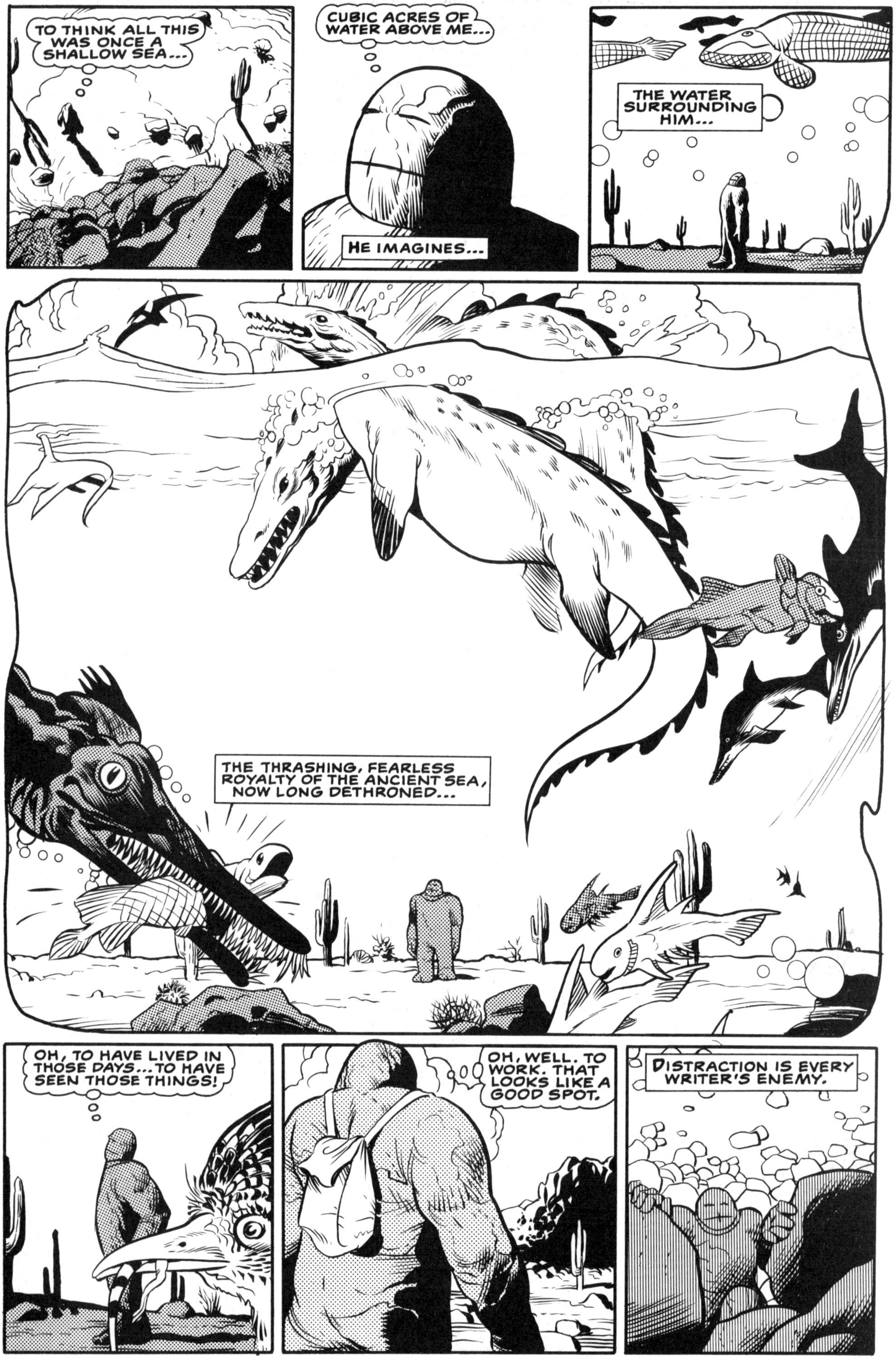
TO THINK ALL THIS WAS ONCE A SHALLOW SEA...
CUBIC ACRES OF WATER ABOVE ME...
HE IMAGINES...
THE WATER SURROUNDING HIM...
THE THRASHING, FEARLESS ROYALTY OF THE ANCIENT SEA, NOW LONG DETHRONED...
OH, TO HAVE LIVED IN THOSE DAYS... TO HAVE SEEN THOSE THINGS!
OH, WELL. TO WORK. THAT LOOKS LIKE A GOOD SPOT.
DISTRACTION IS EVERY WRITER'S ENEMY.

WHEN TOO ACUTE, SOMETIMES RADICAL SURGERY IS REQUIRED...

TOTAL EXCISION OF WRITER FROM HIS DAILY LIFE...

TRANSPLANTATION TO NOWHERE.

CONCRETE'S PEN BEGINS ITS LONG DANCE... THROUGH DAY...

SUNSET...

AND INTO THE NIGHT. FOR CONCRETE'S EYES ARE SPECIAL; THEY ARE THE ONE GREAT GIFT TO COME WITH HIS CLUMSY, ENCRUSTED BODY.

THEY DILATE ENORMOUSLY, ADDING LIGHT-GATHERING POWER TO THEIR HIGH RESOLUTION...

ENABLING HIM TO READ AND WRITE... BY STARLIGHT.

TIME FOR A BREAK!

23

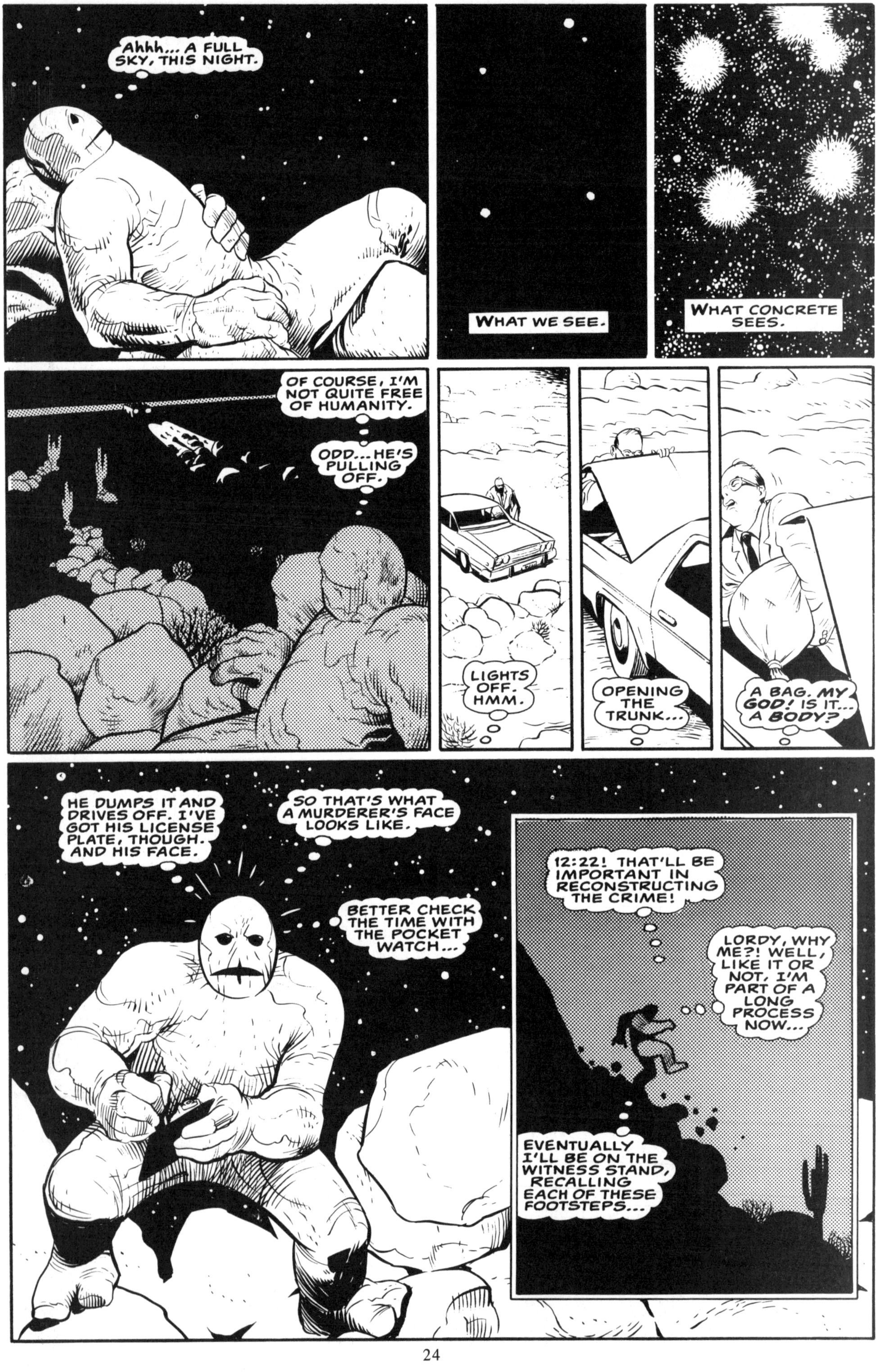
Ahhh... A FULL SKY, THIS NIGHT.
WHAT WE SEE.
WHAT CONCRETE SEES.
OF COURSE, I'M NOT QUITE FREE OF HUMANITY.
ODD... HE'S PULLING OFF.
LIGHTS OFF. HMM.
OPENING THE TRUNK...
A BAG. MY GOD! IS IT... A BODY?
HE DUMPS IT AND DRIVES OFF. I'VE GOT HIS LICENSE PLATE, THOUGH. AND HIS FACE.
SO THAT'S WHAT A MURDERER'S FACE LOOKS LIKE.
BETTER CHECK THE TIME WITH THE POCKET WATCH...
12:22! THAT'LL BE IMPORTANT IN RECONSTRUCTING THE CRIME!
LORDY, WHY ME?! WELL, LIKE IT OR NOT, I'M PART OF A LONG PROCESS NOW...
EVENTUALLY I'LL BE ON THE WITNESS STAND, RECALLING EACH OF THESE FOOTSTEPS...

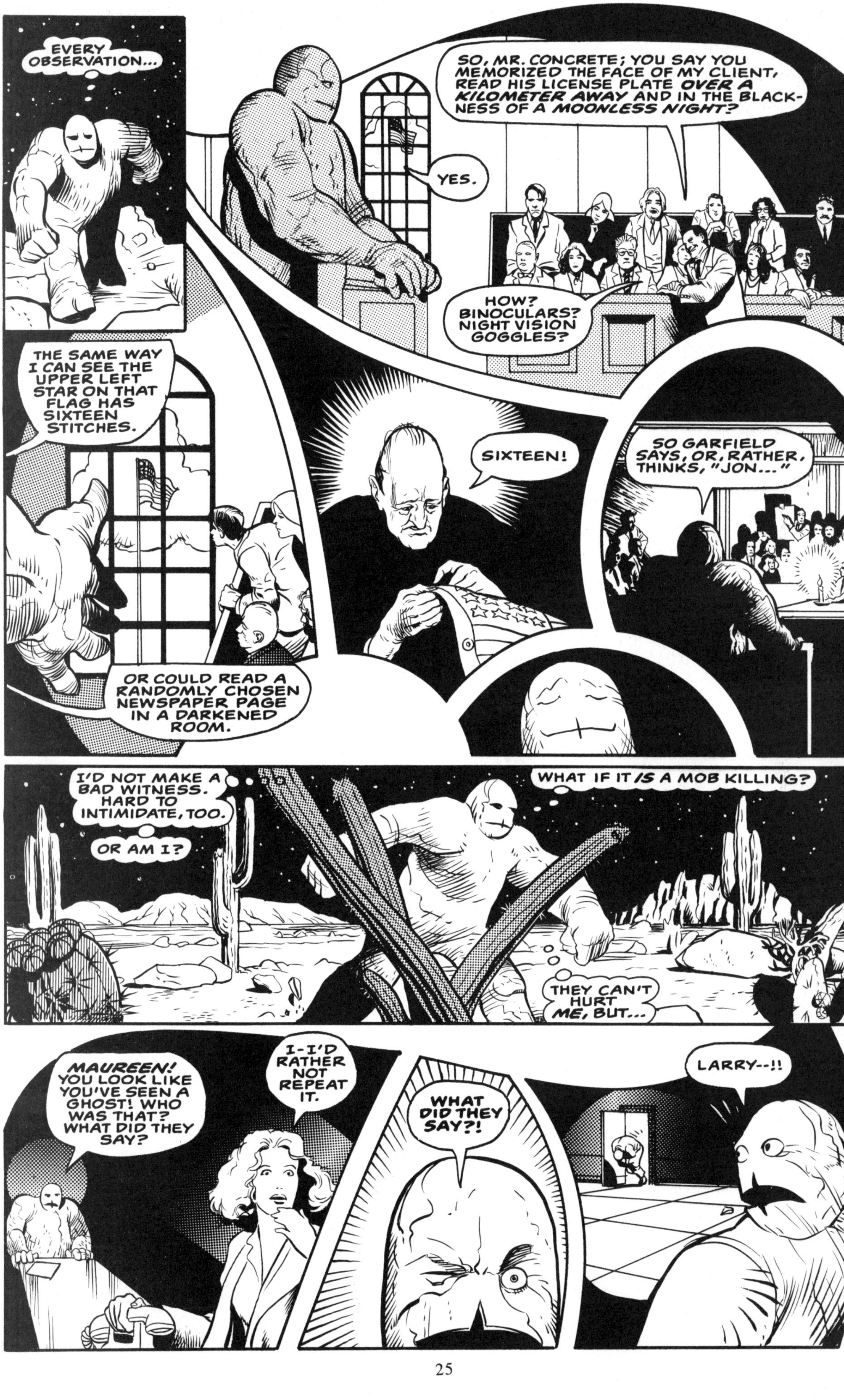

EVERY OBSERVATION...
SO, MR. CONCRETE; YOU SAY YOU MEMORIZED THE FACE OF MY CLIENT, READ HIS LICENSE PLATE OVER A KILOMETER AWAY AND IN THE BLACKNESS OF A MOONLESS NIGHT?
YES.
HOW? BINOCULARS? NIGHT VISION GOGGLES?
THE SAME WAY I CAN SEE THE UPPER LEFT STAR ON THAT FLAG HAS SIXTEEN STITCHES.
SIXTEEN!
OR COULD READ A RANDOMLY CHOSEN NEWSPAPER PAGE IN A DARKENED ROOM.
SO GARFIELD SAYS, OR, RATHER, THINKS, "JON..."
I'D NOT MAKE A BAD WITNESS. HARD TO INTIMIDATE, TOO.
OR AM I?
WHAT IF IT IS A MOB KILLING?
THEY CAN'T HURT ME, BUT...
MAUREEN! YOU LOOK LIKE YOU'VE SEEN A GHOST! WHO WAS THAT? WHAT DID THEY SAY?
I-I'D RATHER NOT REPEAT IT.
WHAT DID THEY SAY?!
LARRY--!!

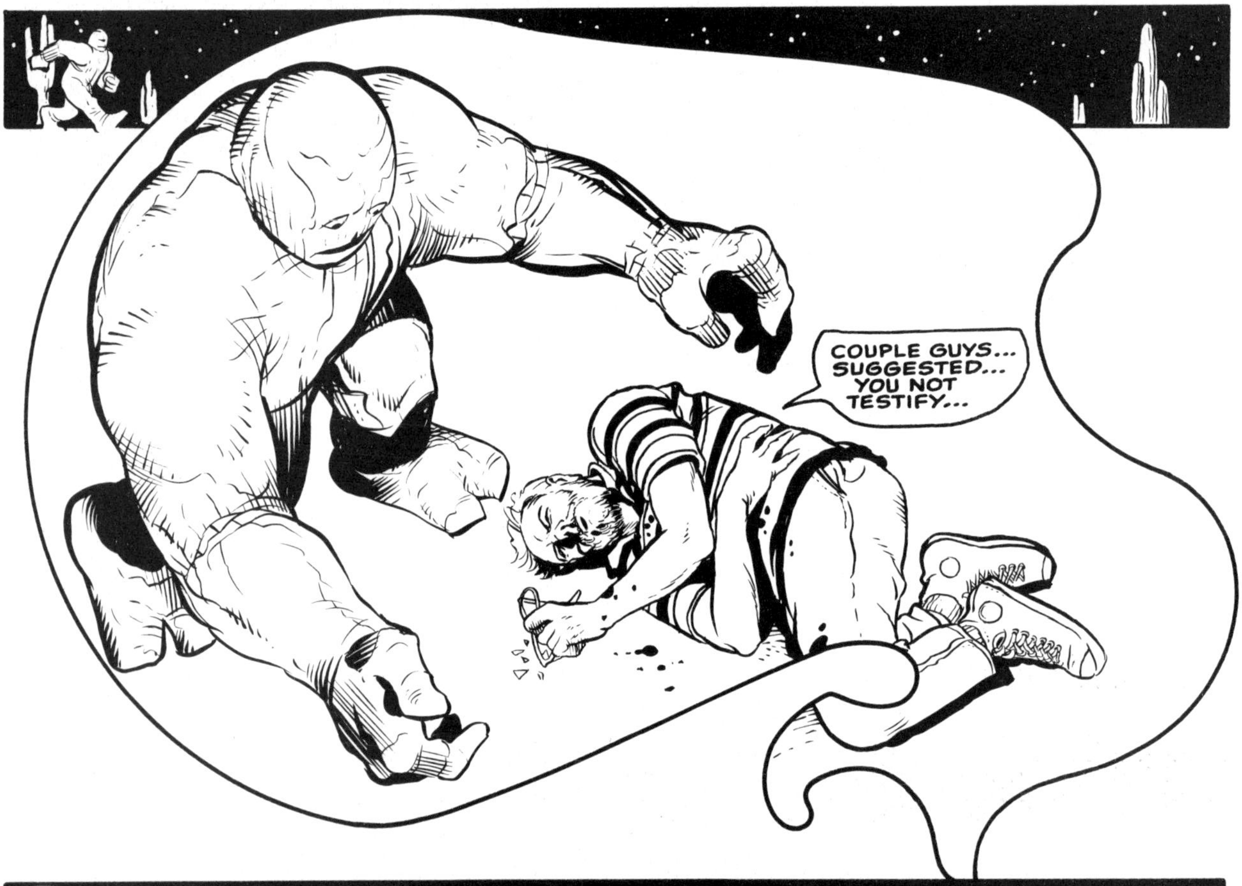
COUPLE GUYS... SUGGESTED... YOU NOT TESTIFY...

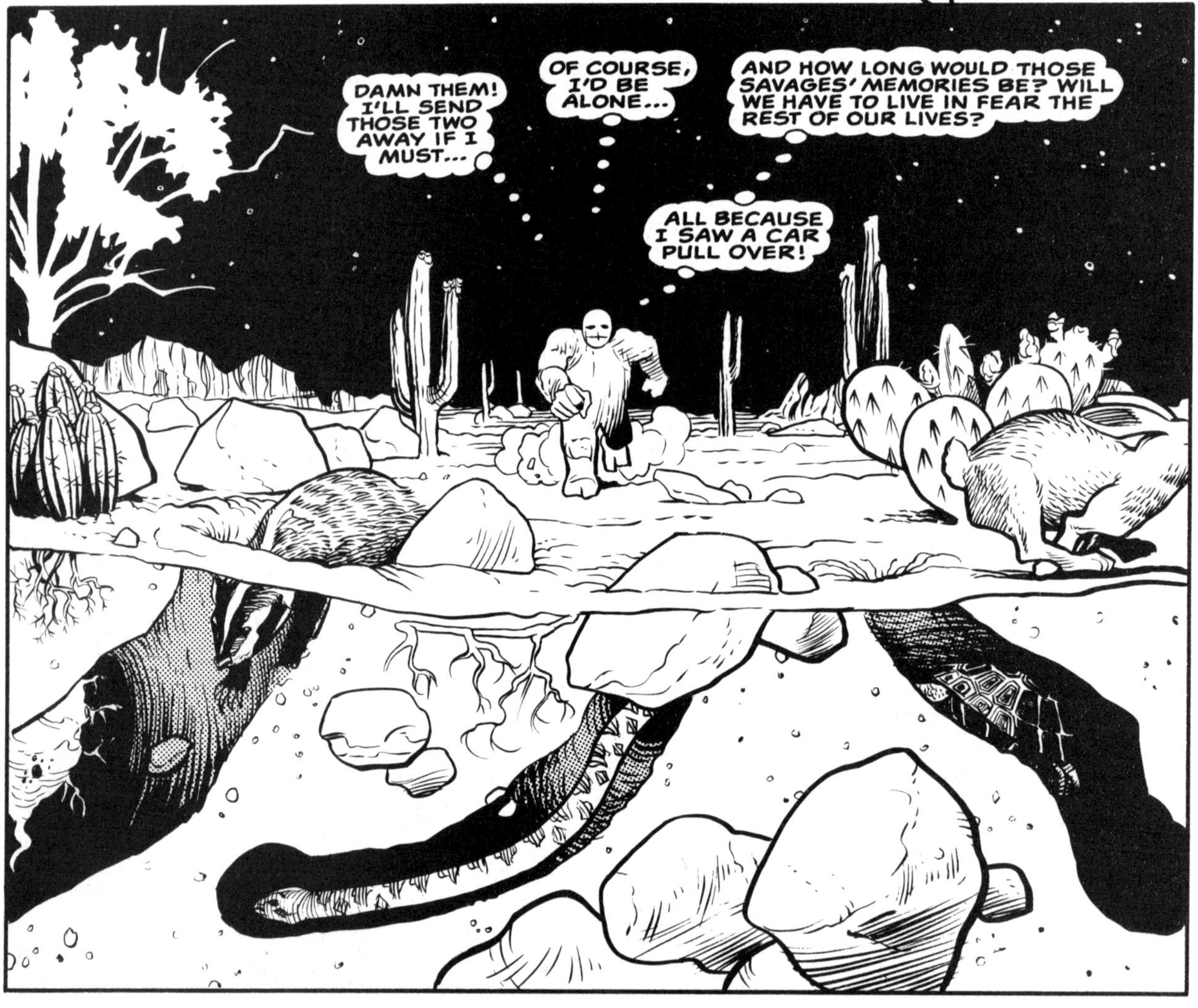
DAMN THEM! I'LL SEND THOSE TWO AWAY IF I MUST...
OF COURSE, I'D BE ALONE...
AND HOW LONG WOULD THOSE SAVAGES' MEMORIES BE? WILL WE HAVE TO LIVE IN FEAR THE REST OF OUR LIVES?
ALL BECAUSE I SAW A CAR PULL OVER!

TRUE, I COULD TURN AROUND RIGHT NOW AND FORGET ALL THIS.
LET EVIL PASS BY, UNMOLESTED...
YEAH, SURE!
I'D BE SEEING THAT BODY BAG BEHIND ME EVERY TIME I LOOKED IN A MIRROR!
MAYBE HE...OR SHE...WAS A WITNESS WHO REFUSED TO CLAM UP...A WHISTLE BLOWER...
SORRY, QUIGLEY, BUT YOU HAD YOUR CHANCE TO COOPERATE.
BOB, STRAIGHTEN THE TARP. WE DON'T WANT THE RUG SPLATTERED.
HELLO, FRIEND. AM I AS BRAVE AS YOU WERE?
MY HANDS ARE SHAKING!

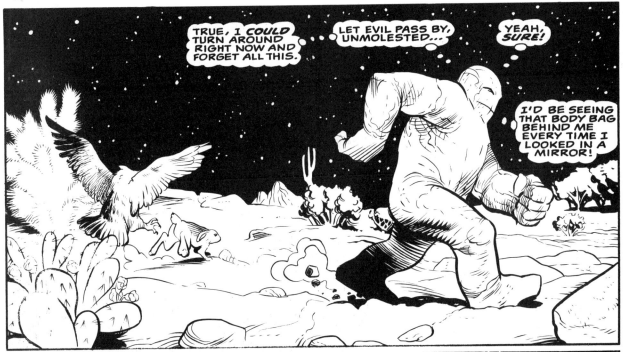

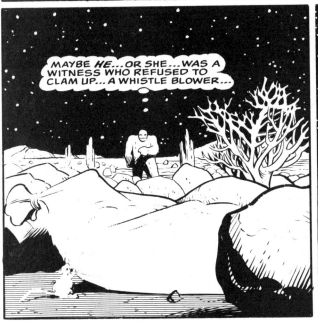

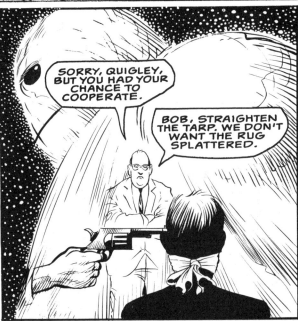

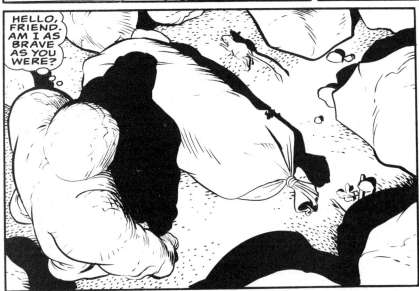

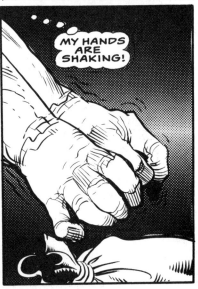

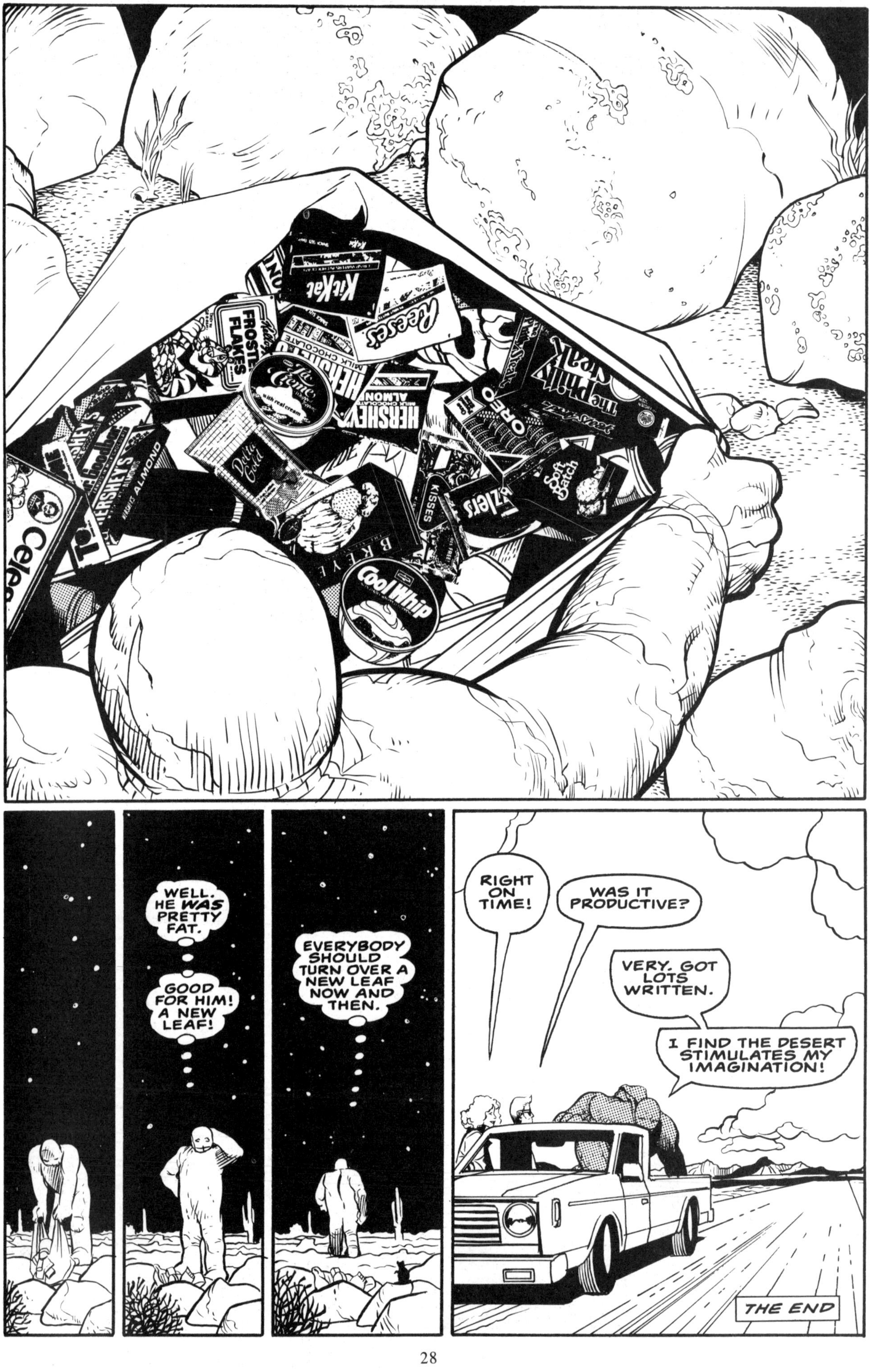

WELL. HE *WAS* PRETTY FAT.
GOOD FOR HIM! A NEW LEAF!
EVERYBODY SHOULD TURN OVER A NEW LEAF NOW AND THEN.
RIGHT ON TIME!
WAS IT PRODUCTIVE?
VERY. GOT LOTS WRITTEN.
I FIND THE DESERT STIMULATES MY IMAGINATION!
THE END

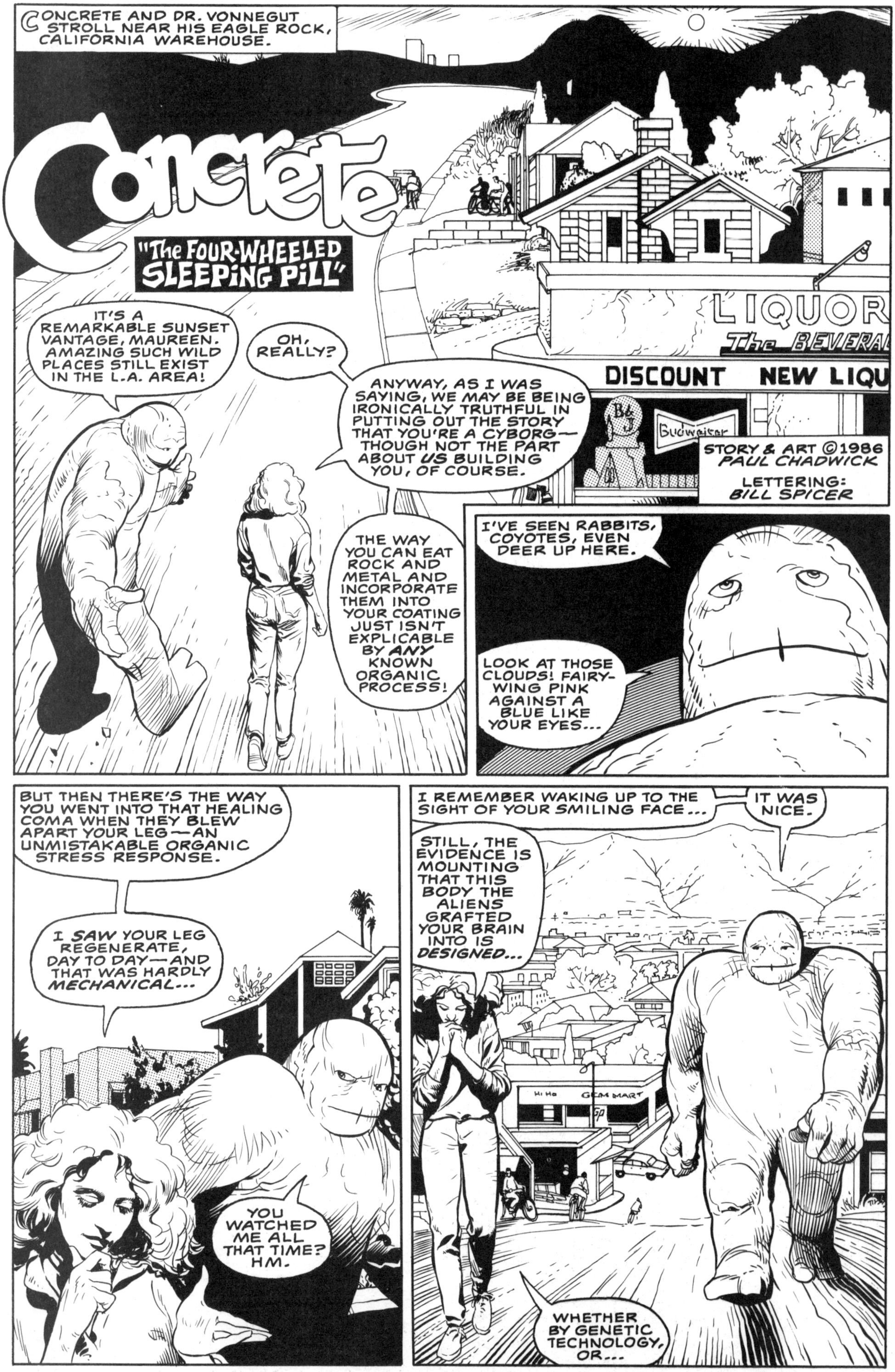

CONCRETE AND DR. VONNEGUT STROLL NEAR HIS EAGLE ROCK, CALIFORNIA WAREHOUSE.
Concrete
"The FOUR-WHEELED SLEEPING PILL"
LIQUOR
DISCOUNT NEW LIQU
Budweiser
IT'S A REMARKABLE SUNSET VANTAGE, MAUREEN. AMAZING SUCH WILD PLACES STILL EXIST IN THE L.A. AREA!
OH, REALLY?
ANYWAY, AS I WAS SAYING, WE MAY BE BEING IRONICALLY TRUTHFUL IN PUTTING OUT THE STORY THAT YOU'RE A CYBORG— THOUGH NOT THE PART ABOUT US BUILDING YOU, OF COURSE.
THE WAY YOU CAN EAT ROCK AND METAL AND INCORPORATE THEM INTO YOUR COATING JUST ISN'T EXPLICABLE BY ANY KNOWN ORGANIC PROCESS!
STORY & ART ©1986 PAUL CHADWICK
LETTERING: BILL SPICER
I'VE SEEN RABBITS, COYOTES, EVEN DEER UP HERE.
LOOK AT THOSE CLOUDS! FAIRY-WING PINK AGAINST A BLUE LIKE YOUR EYES...
BUT THEN THERE'S THE WAY YOU WENT INTO THAT HEALING COMA WHEN THEY BLEW APART YOUR LEG—AN UNMISTAKABLE ORGANIC STRESS RESPONSE.
I SAW YOUR LEG REGENERATE, DAY TO DAY—AND THAT WAS HARDLY MECHANICAL...
YOU WATCHED ME ALL THAT TIME? HM.
I REMEMBER WAKING UP TO THE SIGHT OF YOUR SMILING FACE...
IT WAS NICE.
STILL, THE EVIDENCE IS MOUNTING THAT THIS BODY THE ALIENS GRAFTED YOUR BRAIN INTO IS DESIGNED...
HI HO GEM MART
WHETHER BY GENETIC TECHNOLOGY, OR...

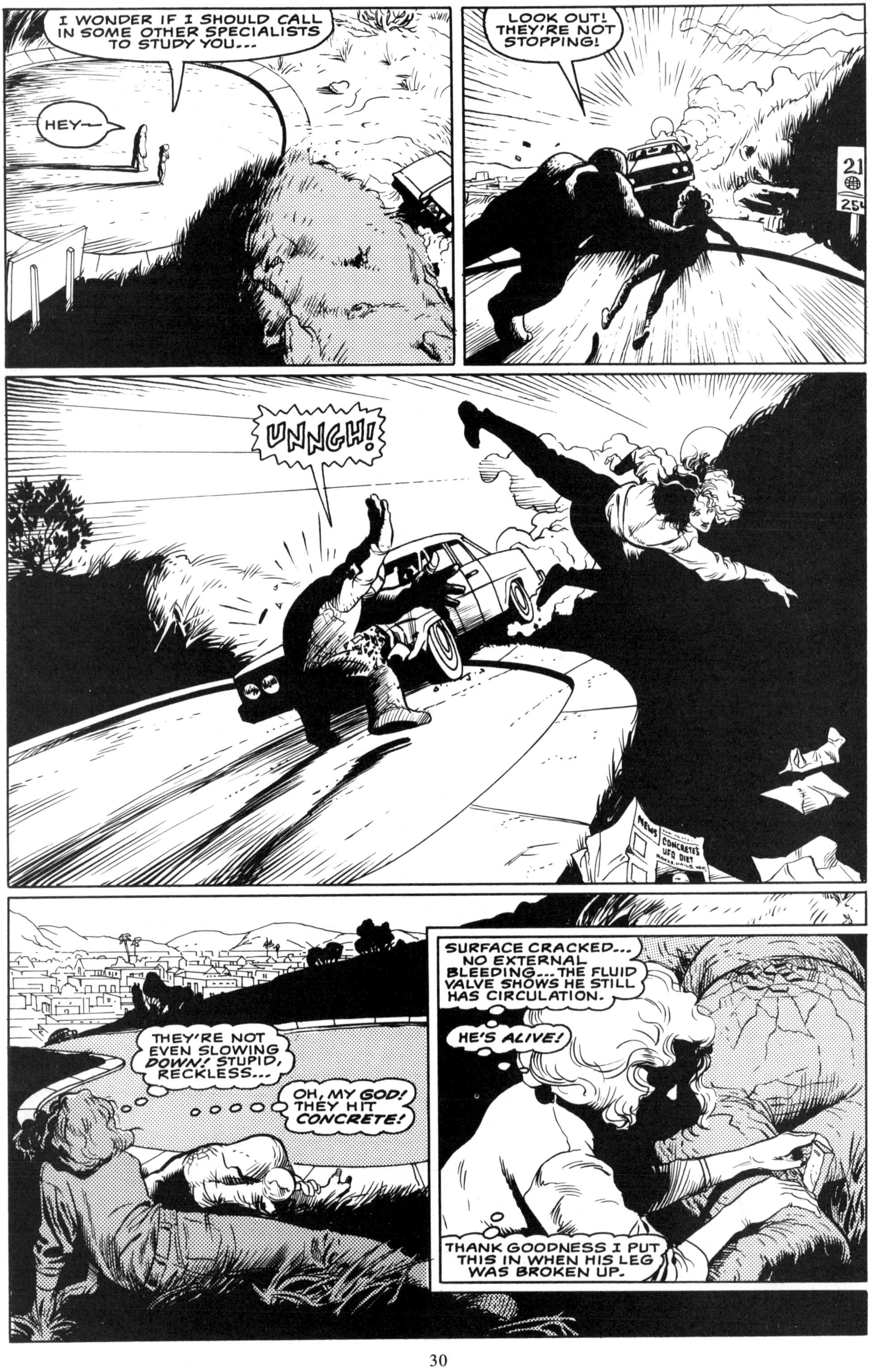
I WONDER IF I SHOULD CALL IN SOME OTHER SPECIALISTS TO STUDY YOU...
HEY—
LOOK OUT! THEY'RE NOT STOPPING!
21
254
UNNGH!
NEWS
CONCRETE'S UFO DIET
THEY'RE NOT EVEN SLOWING DOWN! STUPID, RECKLESS...
OH, MY GOD! THEY HIT CONCRETE!
SURFACE CRACKED... NO EXTERNAL BLEEDING... THE FLUID VALVE SHOWS HE STILL HAS CIRCULATION.
HE'S ALIVE!
THANK GOODNESS I PUT THIS IN WHEN HIS LEG WAS BROKEN UP.

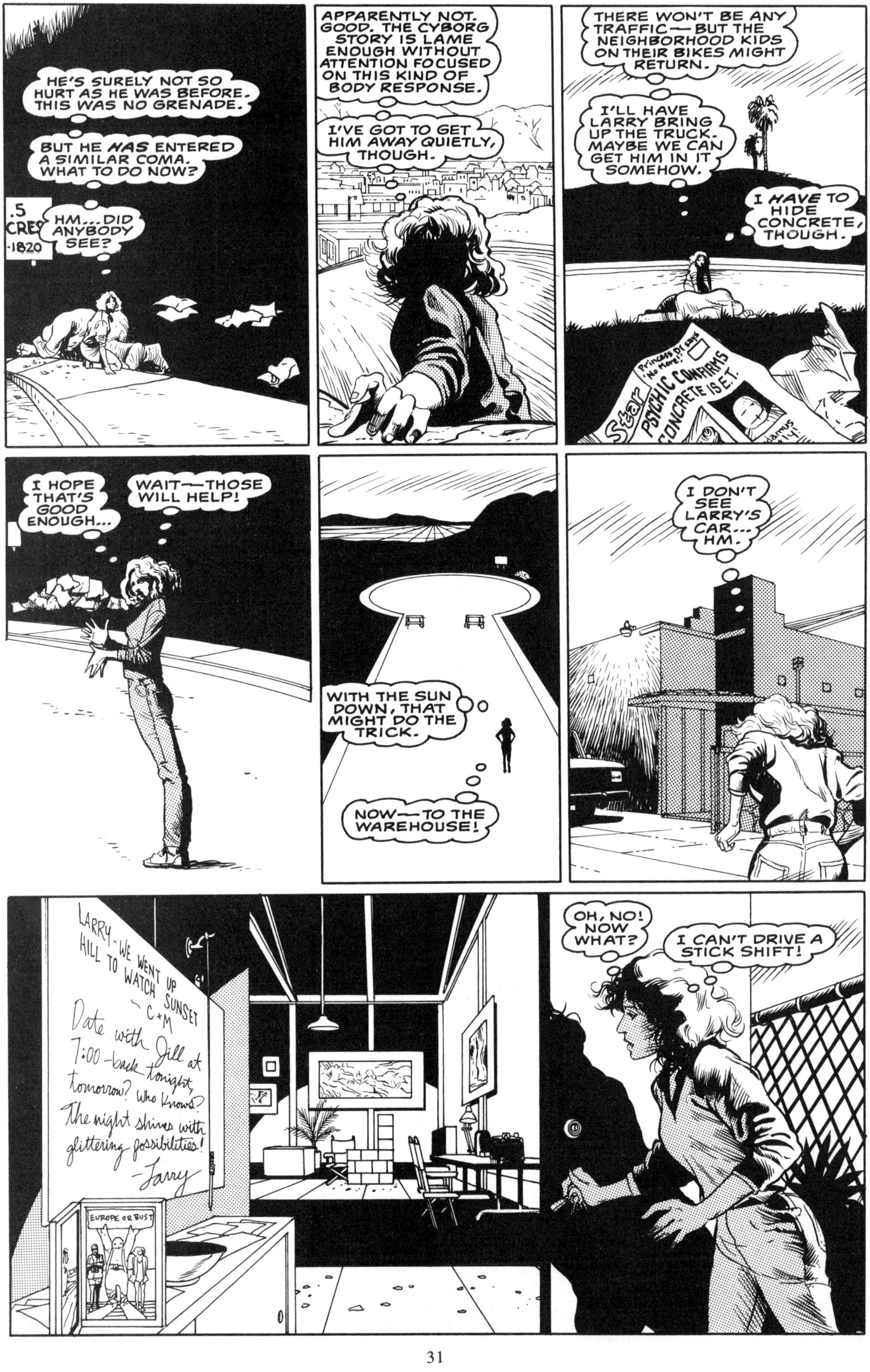
HE'S SURELY NOT SO HURT AS HE WAS BEFORE. THIS WAS NO GRENADE.
BUT HE *HAS* ENTERED A SIMILAR COMA. WHAT TO DO NOW?
HM... DID ANYBODY SEE?
APPARENTLY NOT. GOOD. THE CYBORG STORY IS LAME ENOUGH WITHOUT ATTENTION FOCUSED ON THIS KIND OF BODY RESPONSE.
I'VE GOT TO GET HIM AWAY QUIETLY, THOUGH.
THERE WON'T BE ANY TRAFFIC—BUT THE NEIGHBORHOOD KIDS ON THEIR BIKES MIGHT RETURN.
I'LL HAVE LARRY BRING UP THE TRUCK. MAYBE WE CAN GET HIM IN IT SOMEHOW.
I *HAVE* TO HIDE CONCRETE, THOUGH.
Star
Princess Di says "No More!"
PSYCHIC CONFIRMS CONCRETE IS E.T.
I HOPE THAT'S GOOD ENOUGH...
WAIT—THOSE WILL HELP!
WITH THE SUN DOWN, THAT MIGHT DO THE TRICK.
NOW—TO THE WAREHOUSE!
I DON'T SEE LARRY'S CAR... HM.
LARRY- WE WENT UP HILL TO WATCH SUNSET ~ C+M
Date with Jill at 7:00 - back tonight, tomorrow? Who Knows? The night shines with glittering possibilities! -Larry
EUROPE OR BUST
OH, NO! NOW WHAT?
I CAN'T DRIVE A STICK SHIFT!

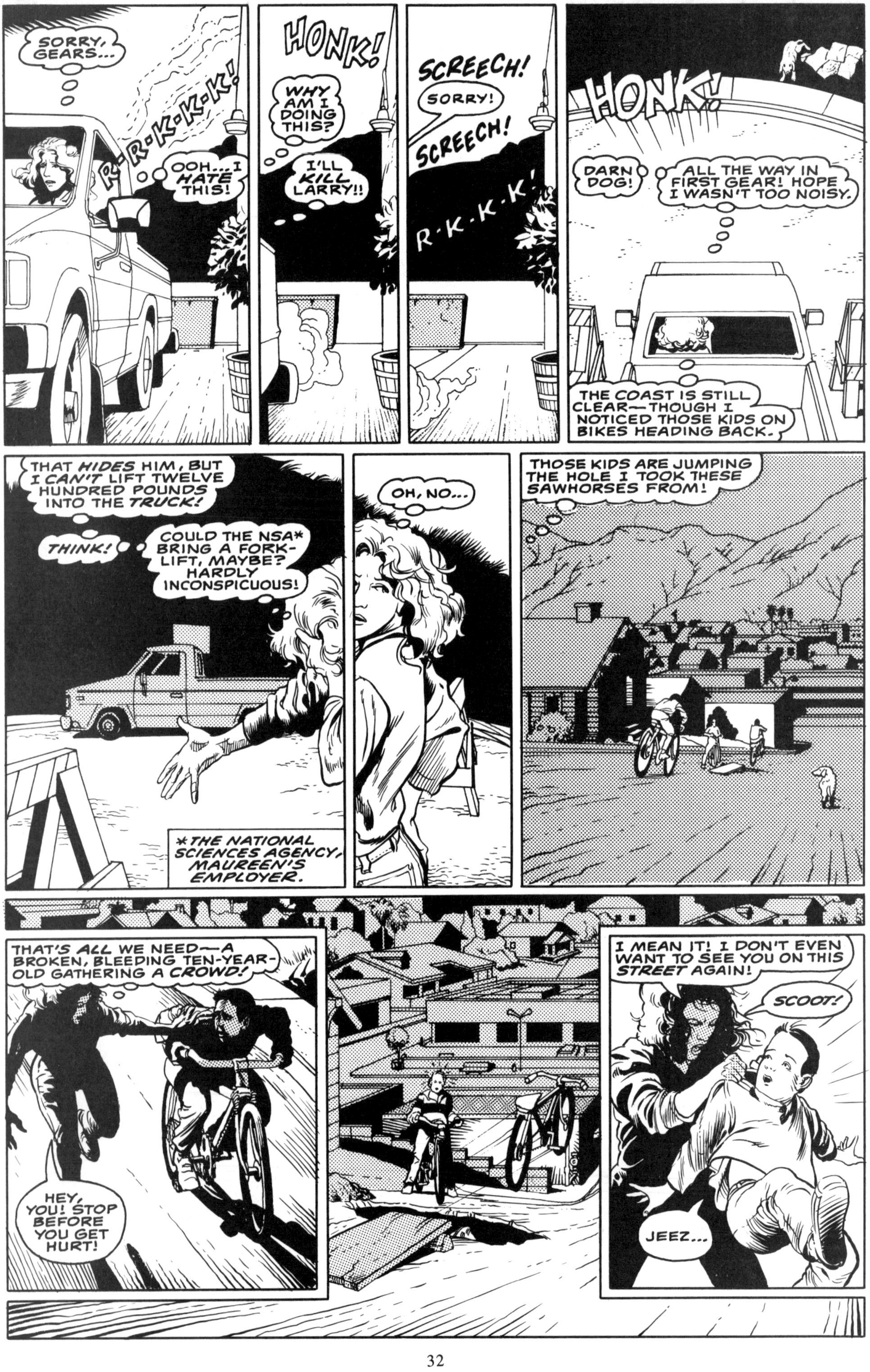
SORRY, GEARS...
R-R-K-K-K-K!
OOH... I HATE THIS!
HONK!
WHY AM I DOING THIS?
I'LL KILL LARRY!!
SCREECH!
SORRY!
SCREECH!
R-K-K-K!
HONK!
DARN DOG!
ALL THE WAY IN FIRST GEAR! HOPE I WASN'T TOO NOISY.
THE COAST IS STILL CLEAR— THOUGH I NOTICED THOSE KIDS ON BIKES HEADING BACK.
THAT HIDES HIM, BUT I CAN'T LIFT TWELVE HUNDRED POUNDS INTO THE TRUCK!
THINK!
COULD THE NSA* BRING A FORK-LIFT, MAYBE? HARDLY INCONSPICUOUS!
*THE NATIONAL SCIENCES AGENCY, MAUREEN'S EMPLOYER.
OH, NO...
THOSE KIDS ARE JUMPING THE HOLE I TOOK THESE SAWHORSES FROM!
THAT'S ALL WE NEED— A BROKEN, BLEEDING TEN-YEAR-OLD GATHERING A CROWD!
HEY, YOU! STOP BEFORE YOU GET HURT!
I MEAN IT! I DON'T EVEN WANT TO SEE YOU ON THIS STREET AGAIN!
SCOOT!
JEEZ...

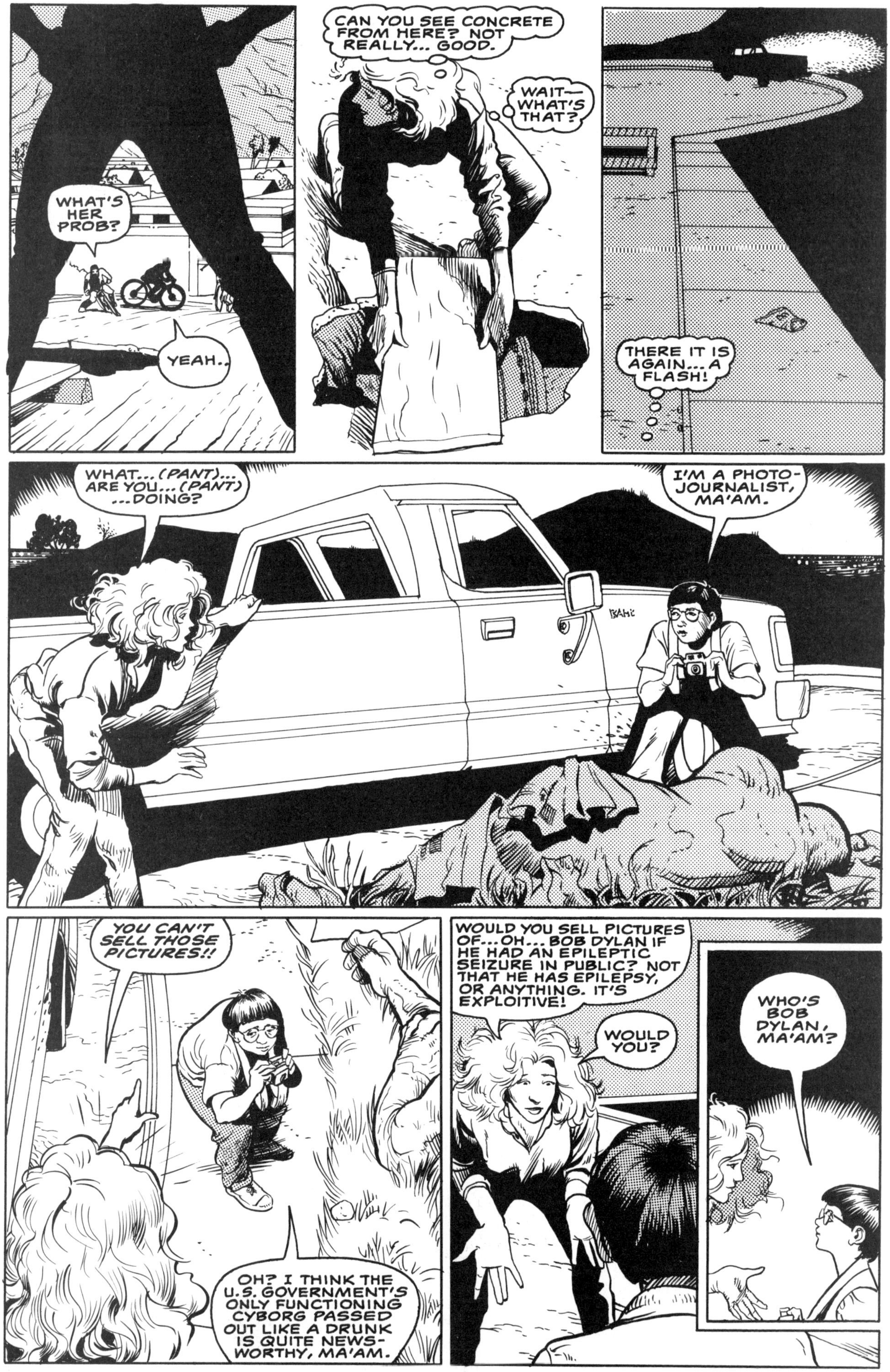
WHAT'S HER PROB?
YEAH..
CAN YOU SEE CONCRETE FROM HERE? NOT REALLY... GOOD.
WAIT— WHAT'S THAT?
THERE IT IS AGAIN... A FLASH!
WHAT... (PANT)... ARE YOU... (PANT) ...DOING?
I'M A PHOTO-JOURNALIST, MA'AM.
YOU CAN'T SELL THOSE PICTURES!!
OH? I THINK THE U.S. GOVERNMENT'S ONLY FUNCTIONING CYBORG PASSED OUT LIKE A DRUNK IS QUITE NEWS-WORTHY, MA'AM.
WOULD YOU SELL PICTURES OF... OH... BOB DYLAN IF HE HAD AN EPILEPTIC SEIZURE IN PUBLIC? NOT THAT HE HAS EPILEPSY, OR ANYTHING. IT'S EXPLOITIVE!
WOULD YOU?
WHO'S BOB DYLAN, MA'AM?

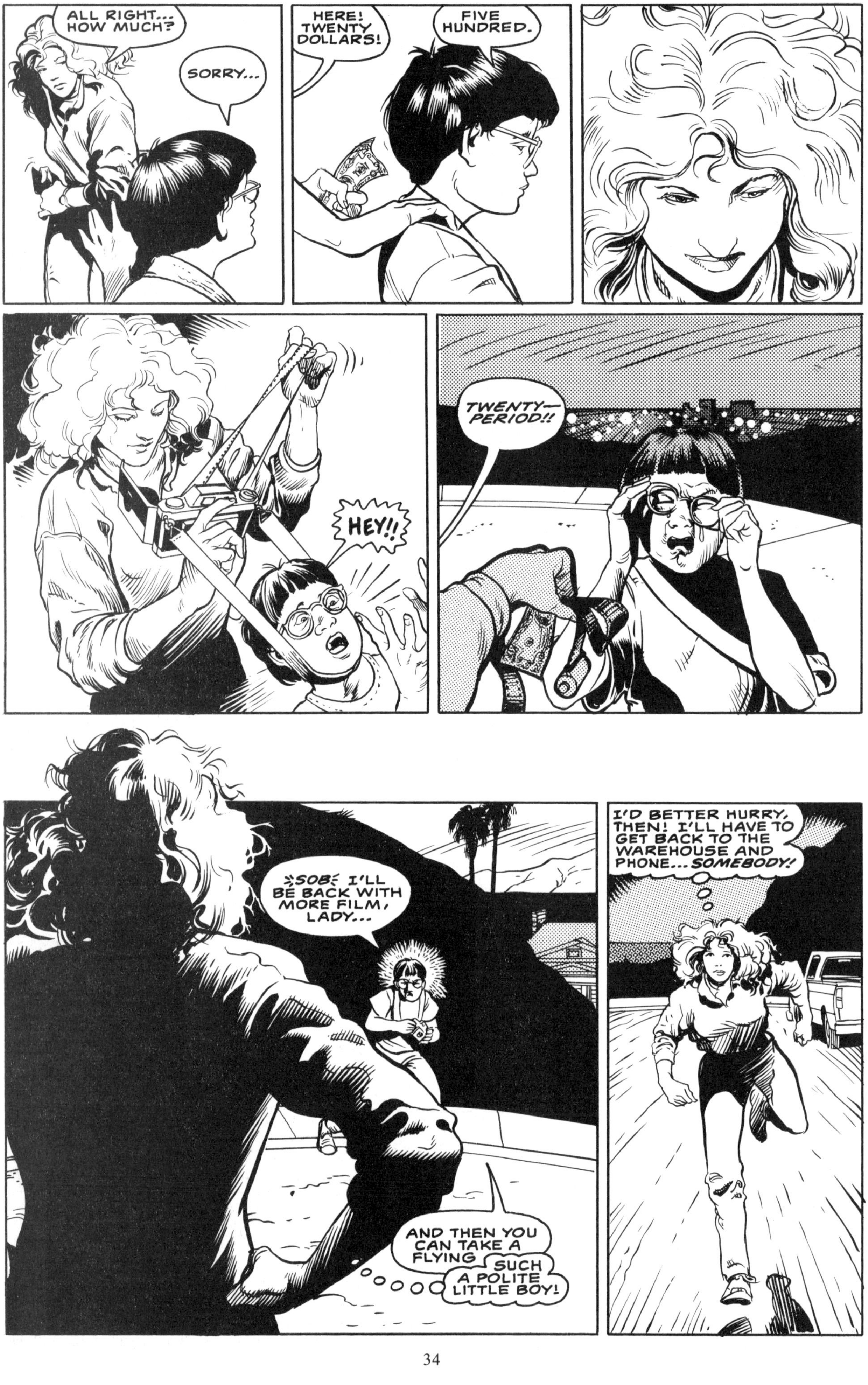
ALL RIGHT... HOW MUCH?
SORRY...
HERE! TWENTY DOLLARS!
FIVE HUNDRED.
TWENTY— PERIOD!!
HEY!!
SOB I'LL BE BACK WITH MORE FILM, LADY...
AND THEN YOU CAN TAKE A FLYING
SUCH A POLITE LITTLE BOY!
I'D BETTER HURRY, THEN! I'LL HAVE TO GET BACK TO THE WAREHOUSE AND PHONE... SOMEBODY!

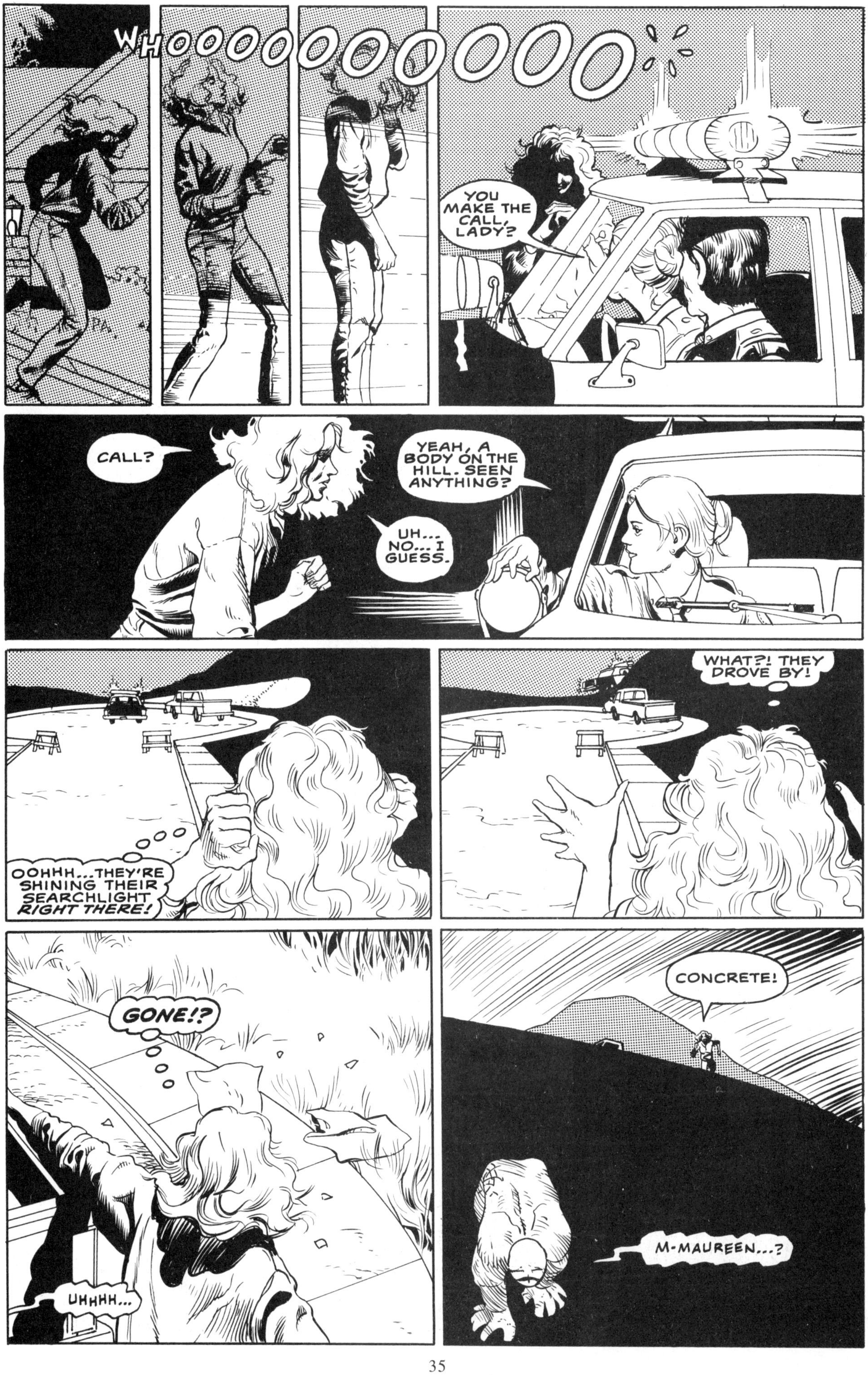
WHOOOOOOOOOOO
YOU MAKE THE CALL, LADY?
CALL?
YEAH, A BODY ON THE HILL. SEEN ANYTHING?
UH... NO... I GUESS.
OOHHH...THEY'RE SHINING THEIR SEARCHLIGHT RIGHT THERE!
WHAT?! THEY DROVE BY!
GONE!?
UHHHH...
CONCRETE!
M-MAUREEN...?

THEY'RE STILL UP ON THE HILL.... ODD.

THANK GOODNESS YOU'RE ALL RIGHT!

Y-YOU OKAY?

YES, FINE. YOU SAVED MY LIFE BACK THERE, PROBABLY.

THANK YOU, BY THE WAY.

STAY DOWN, NOW.

HI, FOLKS. GOT SOMEBODY WHO'D LIKE TO MEET...

SHUSH, LARRY!

VICTOR "LOCOBOY" FUENTE WAS FOUND SHOT TO DEATH ON AN EAGLE ROCK HILLSIDE THIS EVENING. POLICE SAY THAT FUENTE, WHO HAD A HISTORY OF DRUG ARRESTS, MAY HAVE RUN AFOUL OF SOME OTHER DEALERS.

POLICE WERE TIPPED ABOUT THE BODY BY AN ANONYMOUS CALLER.

...THE GUY WHO SHOT HIM, I BET.

THERE'S NO FILM, BUT HERE ARE SOME STILL PHOTOS OF THE CRIME SCENE TAKEN BY ONE OF THE NEIGHBORHOOD BOYS, TEN-YEAR-OLD MICHAEL FLORES...

MICHAEL SAYS HE WANTS TO BE A PHOTO-JOURNALIST...

DID HE TALK? DID THEY BELIEVE HIM?

...AND I'D SAY HE'S OFF TO A GOOD START, WOULDN'T YOU, CHRISTINE?

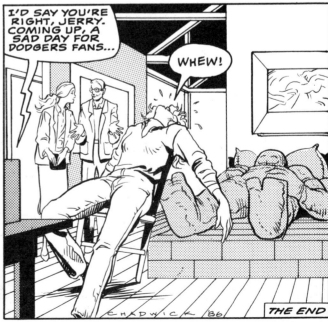

I'D SAY YOU'RE RIGHT, JERRY. COMING UP, A SAD DAY FOR DODGERS FANS...

WHEW!

THE END

36

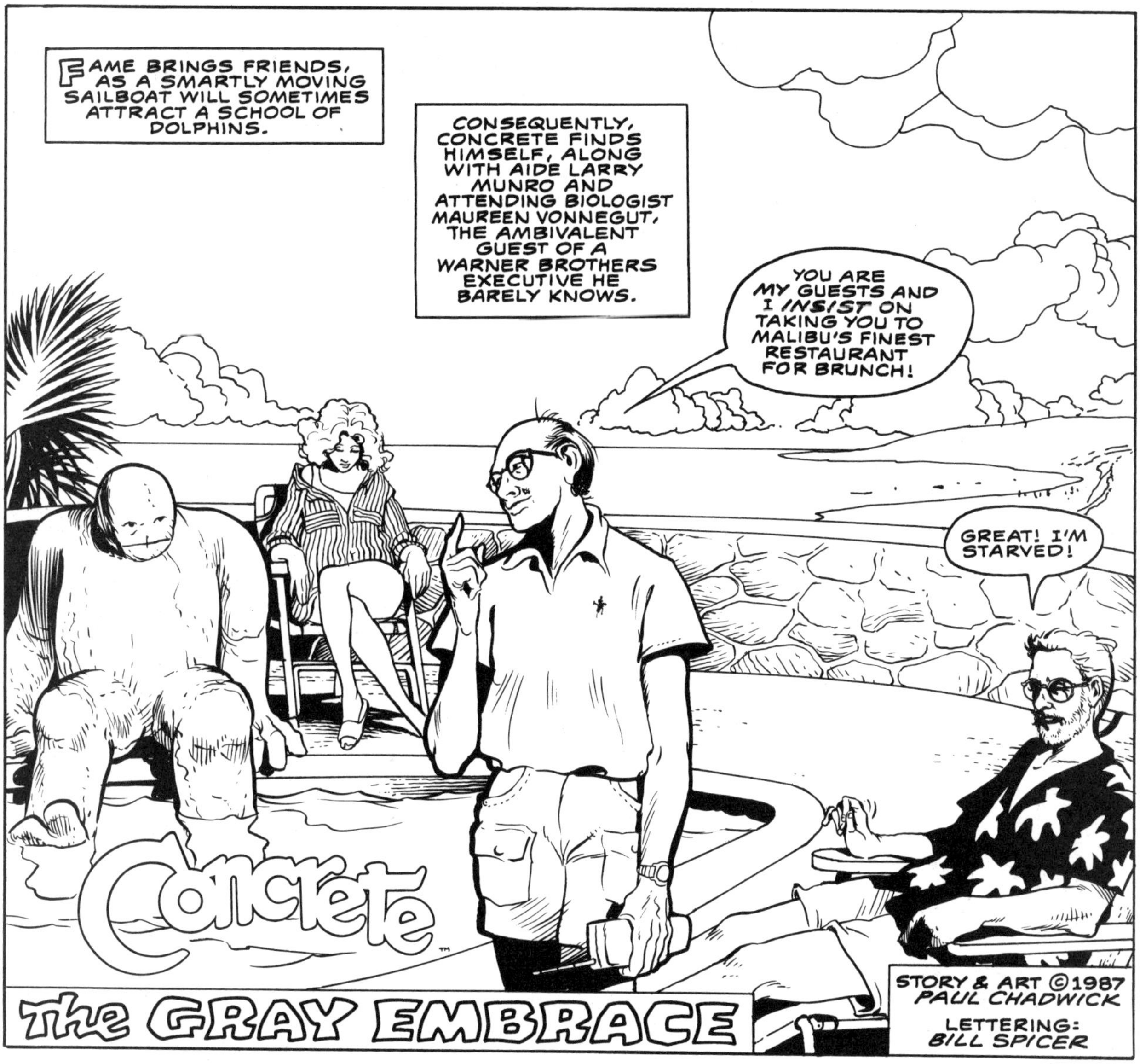
FAME BRINGS FRIENDS, AS A SMARTLY MOVING SAILBOAT WILL SOMETIMES ATTRACT A SCHOOL OF DOLPHINS.
CONSEQUENTLY, CONCRETE FINDS HIMSELF, ALONG WITH AIDE LARRY MUNRO AND ATTENDING BIOLOGIST MAUREEN VONNEGUT, THE AMBIVALENT GUEST OF A WARNER BROTHERS EXECUTIVE HE BARELY KNOWS.
YOU ARE MY GUESTS AND I *INSIST* ON TAKING YOU TO MALIBU'S FINEST RESTAURANT FOR BRUNCH!
GREAT! I'M STARVED!
Concrete™
The GRAY EMBRACE
STORY & ART ©1987 PAUL CHADWICK
LETTERING: BILL SPICER

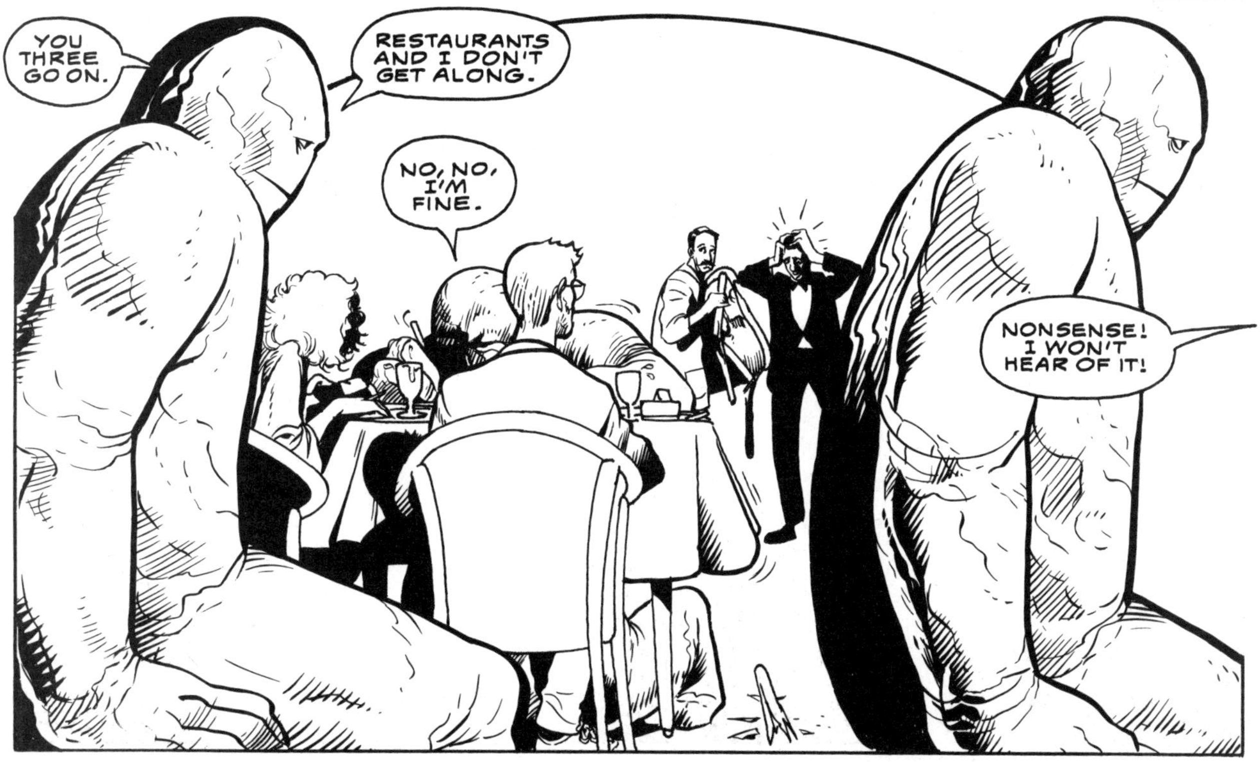
YOU THREE GO ON.
RESTAURANTS AND I DON'T GET ALONG.
NO, NO, I'M FINE.
NONSENSE! I WON'T HEAR OF IT!

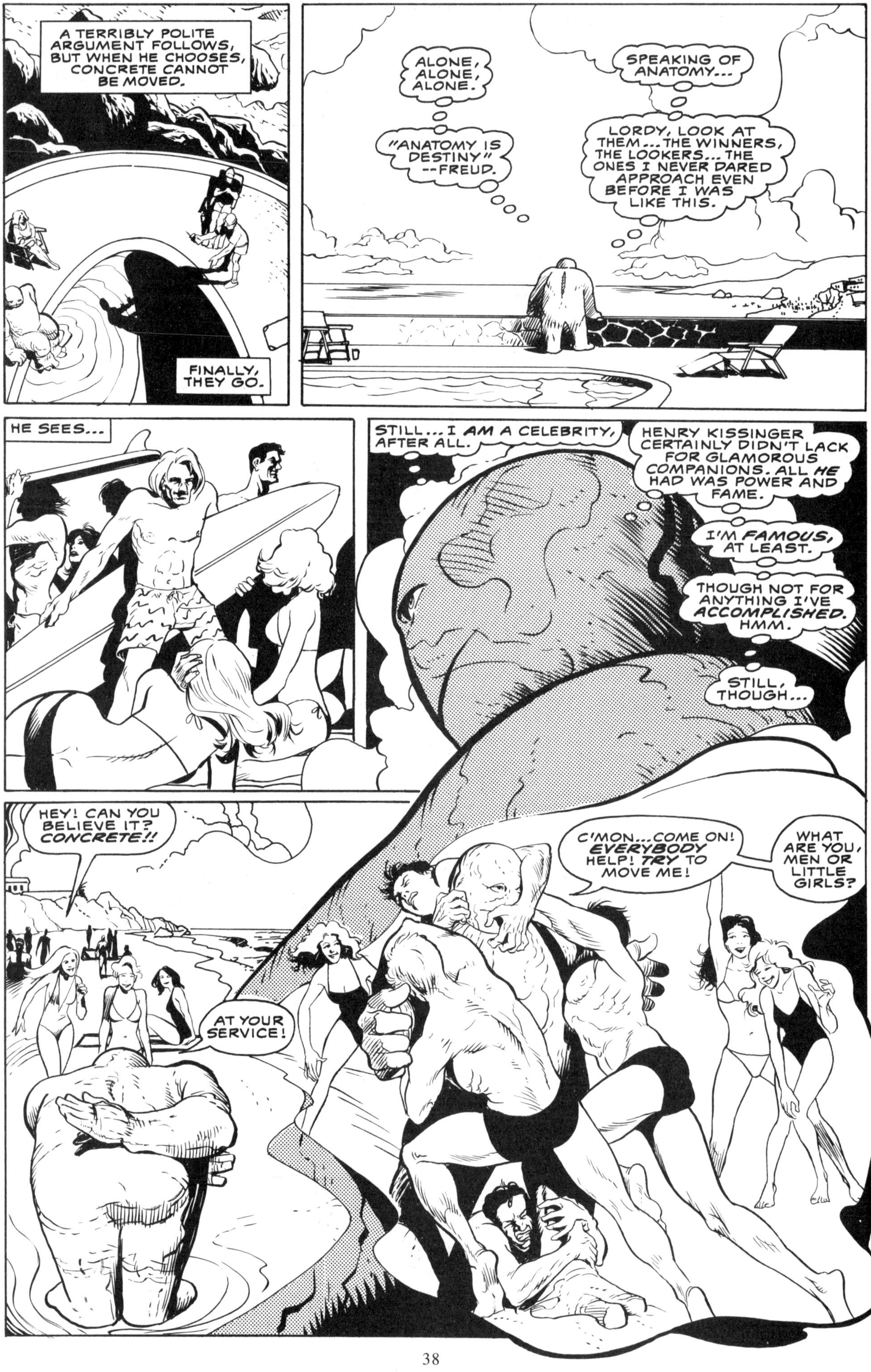
A TERRIBLY POLITE ARGUMENT FOLLOWS, BUT WHEN HE CHOOSES, CONCRETE CANNOT BE MOVED.
FINALLY, THEY GO.
ALONE, ALONE, ALONE.
"ANATOMY IS DESTINY" --FREUD.
SPEAKING OF ANATOMY...
LORDY, LOOK AT THEM... THE WINNERS, THE LOOKERS... THE ONES I NEVER DARED APPROACH EVEN BEFORE I WAS LIKE THIS.
HE SEES...
STILL... I AM A CELEBRITY, AFTER ALL.
HENRY KISSINGER CERTAINLY DIDN'T LACK FOR GLAMOROUS COMPANIONS. ALL HE HAD WAS POWER AND FAME.
I'M FAMOUS, AT LEAST.
THOUGH NOT FOR ANYTHING I'VE ACCOMPLISHED. HMM.
STILL, THOUGH...
HEY! CAN YOU BELIEVE IT? CONCRETE!!
AT YOUR SERVICE!
C'MON... COME ON! EVERYBODY HELP! TRY TO MOVE ME!
WHAT ARE YOU, MEN OR LITTLE GIRLS?

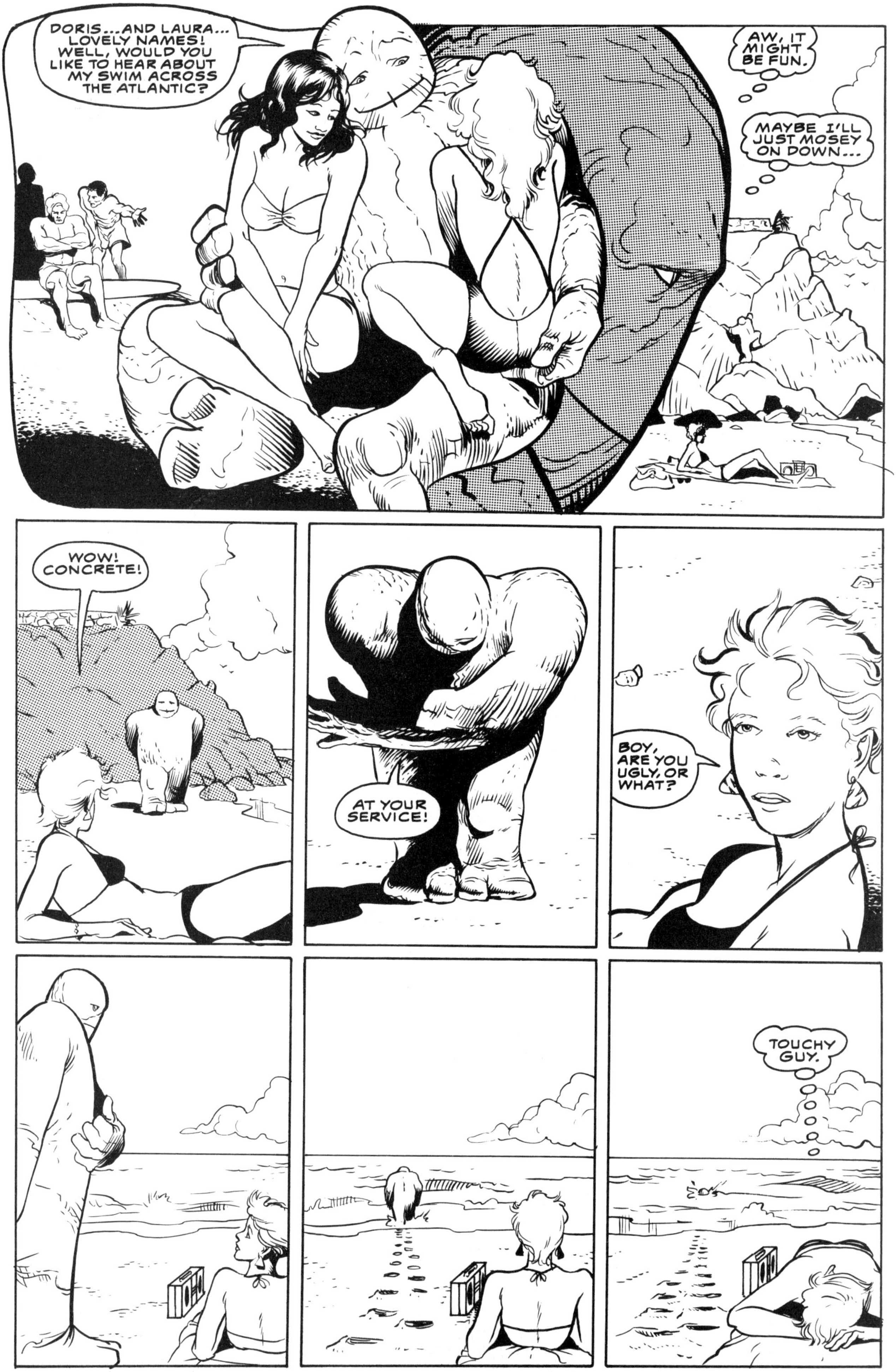
DORIS...AND LAURA... LOVELY NAMES! WELL, WOULD YOU LIKE TO HEAR ABOUT MY SWIM ACROSS THE ATLANTIC?
AW, IT MIGHT BE FUN.
MAYBE I'LL JUST MOSEY ON DOWN...
WOW! CONCRETE!
AT YOUR SERVICE!
BOY, ARE YOU UGLY, OR WHAT?
TOUCHY GUY.

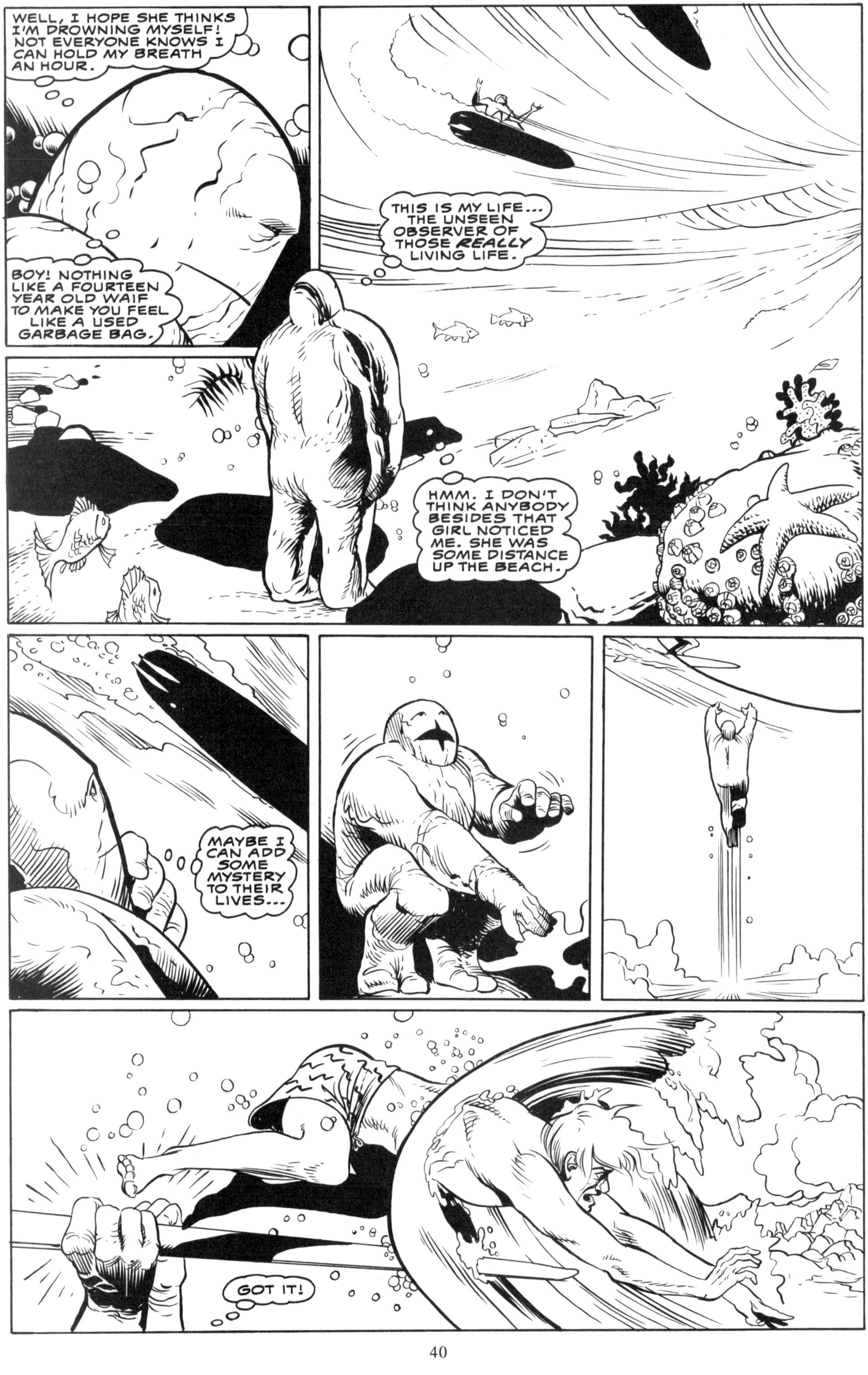
WELL, I HOPE SHE THINKS I'M DROWNING MYSELF! NOT EVERYONE KNOWS I CAN HOLD MY BREATH AN HOUR.
BOY! NOTHING LIKE A FOURTEEN YEAR OLD WAIF TO MAKE YOU FEEL LIKE A USED GARBAGE BAG.
THIS IS MY LIFE... THE UNSEEN OBSERVER OF THOSE REALLY LIVING LIFE.
HMM. I DON'T THINK ANYBODY BESIDES THAT GIRL NOTICED ME. SHE WAS SOME DISTANCE UP THE BEACH.
MAYBE I CAN ADD SOME MYSTERY TO THEIR LIVES...
GOT IT!

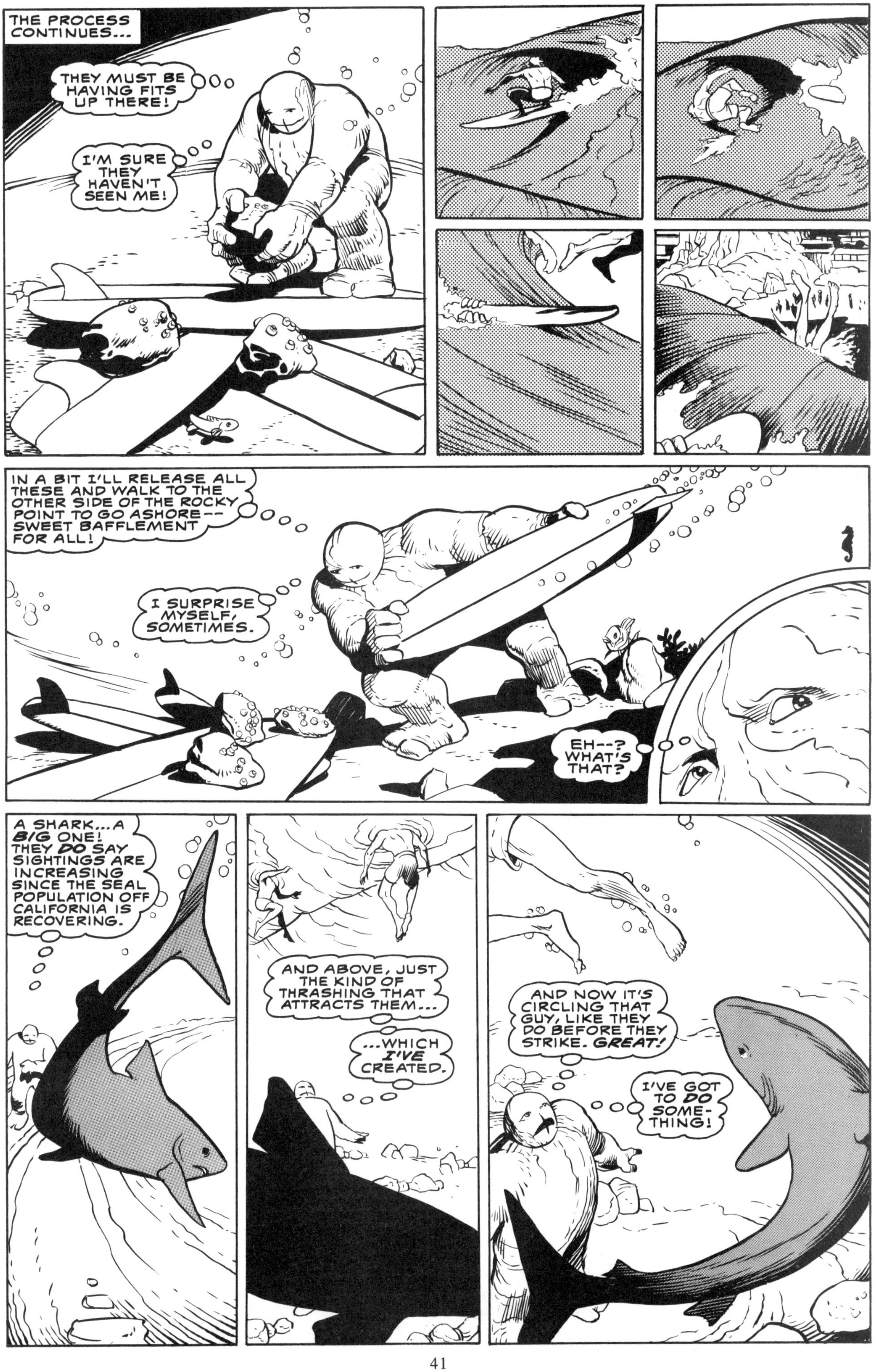
THE PROCESS CONTINUES...
THEY MUST BE HAVING FITS UP THERE!
I'M SURE THEY HAVEN'T SEEN ME!
IN A BIT I'LL RELEASE ALL THESE AND WALK TO THE OTHER SIDE OF THE ROCKY POINT TO GO ASHORE-- SWEET BAFFLEMENT FOR ALL!
I SURPRISE MYSELF, SOMETIMES.
EH--? WHAT'S THAT?
A SHARK...A BIG ONE! THEY DO SAY SIGHTINGS ARE INCREASING SINCE THE SEAL POPULATION OFF CALIFORNIA IS RECOVERING.
AND ABOVE, JUST THE KIND OF THRASHING THAT ATTRACTS THEM...
...WHICH I'VE CREATED.
AND NOW IT'S CIRCLING THAT GUY, LIKE THEY DO BEFORE THEY STRIKE. GREAT!
I'VE GOT TO DO SOME-THING!

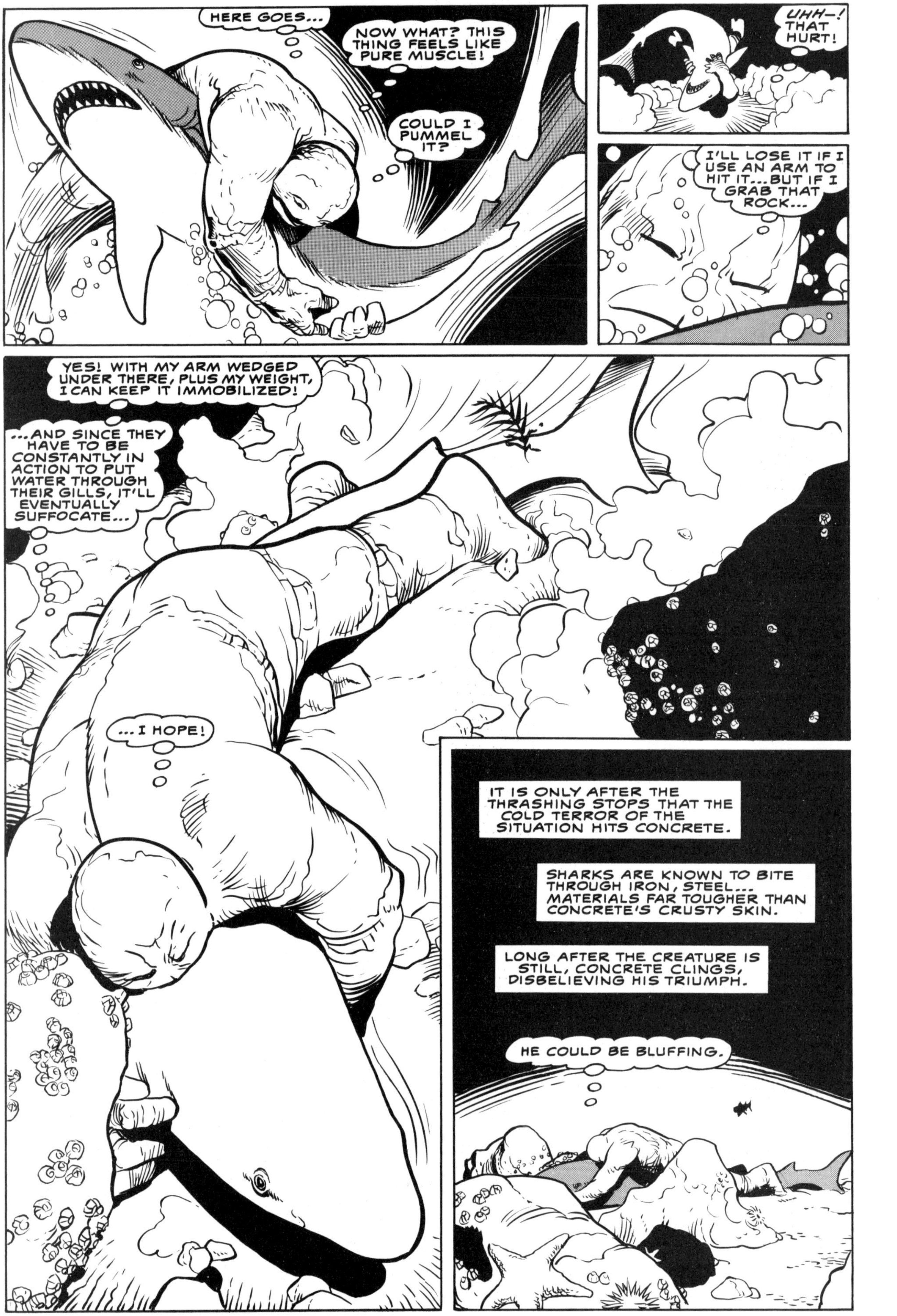
HERE GOES...
NOW WHAT? THIS THING FEELS LIKE PURE MUSCLE!
COULD I PUMMEL IT?
UHH-! THAT HURT!
I'LL LOSE IT IF I USE AN ARM TO HIT IT... BUT IF I GRAB THAT ROCK...
YES! WITH MY ARM WEDGED UNDER THERE, PLUS MY WEIGHT, I CAN KEEP IT IMMOBILIZED!
...AND SINCE THEY HAVE TO BE CONSTANTLY IN ACTION TO PUT WATER THROUGH THEIR GILLS, IT'LL EVENTUALLY SUFFOCATE...
...I HOPE!
IT IS ONLY AFTER THE THRASHING STOPS THAT THE COLD TERROR OF THE SITUATION HITS CONCRETE.
SHARKS ARE KNOWN TO BITE THROUGH IRON, STEEL... MATERIALS FAR TOUGHER THAN CONCRETE'S CRUSTY SKIN.
LONG AFTER THE CREATURE IS STILL, CONCRETE CLINGS, DISBELIEVING HIS TRIUMPH.
HE COULD BE BLUFFING.

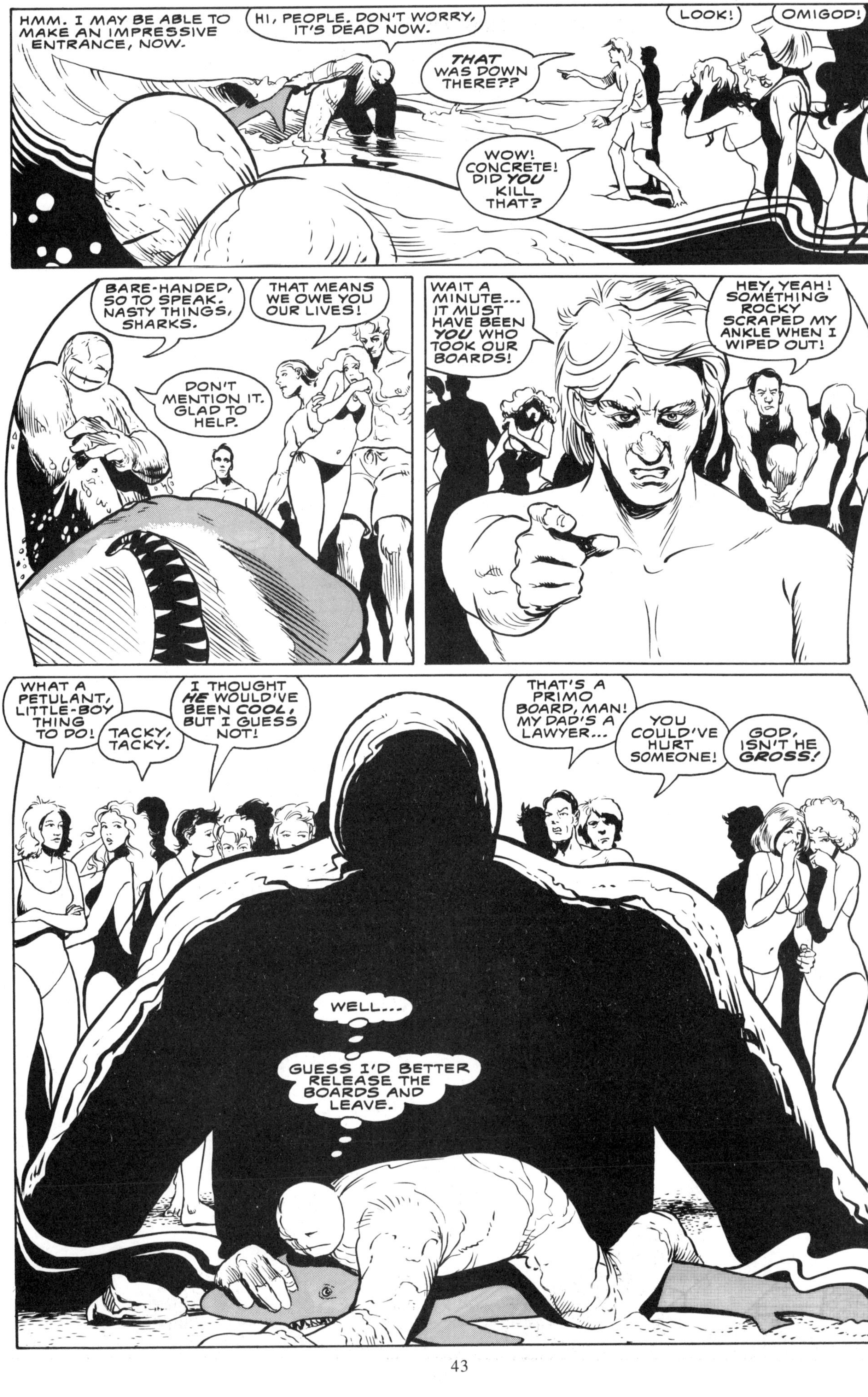

HMM. I MAY BE ABLE TO MAKE AN IMPRESSIVE ENTRANCE, NOW.
HI, PEOPLE. DON'T WORRY, IT'S DEAD NOW.
LOOK!
OMIGOD!
THAT WAS DOWN THERE??
WOW! CONCRETE! DID YOU KILL THAT?
BARE-HANDED, SO TO SPEAK. NASTY THINGS, SHARKS.
THAT MEANS WE OWE YOU OUR LIVES!
DON'T MENTION IT. GLAD TO HELP.
WAIT A MINUTE... IT MUST HAVE BEEN YOU WHO TOOK OUR BOARDS!
HEY, YEAH! SOMETHING ROCKY SCRAPED MY ANKLE WHEN I WIPED OUT!
WHAT A PETULANT, LITTLE-BOY THING TO DO!
TACKY, TACKY.
I THOUGHT HE WOULD'VE BEEN COOL, BUT I GUESS NOT!
THAT'S A PRIMO BOARD, MAN! MY DAD'S A LAWYER...
YOU COULD'VE HURT SOMEONE!
GOD, ISN'T HE GROSS!
WELL...
GUESS I'D BETTER RELEASE THE BOARDS AND LEAVE.

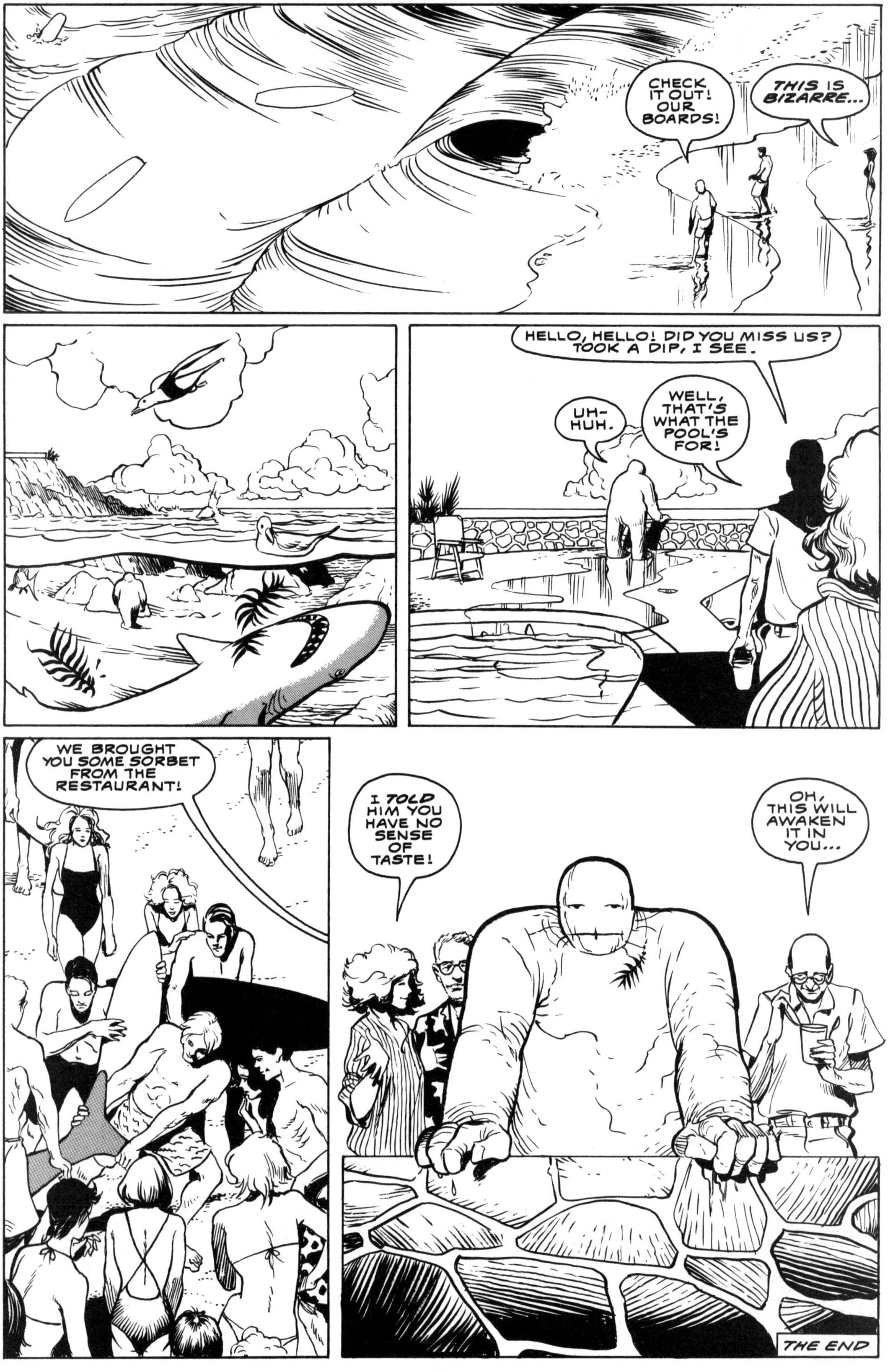
CHECK IT OUT! OUR BOARDS!
THIS IS BIZARRE...
HELLO, HELLO! DID YOU MISS US? TOOK A DIP, I SEE.
UH-HUH.
WELL, THAT'S WHAT THE POOL'S FOR!
WE BROUGHT YOU SOME SORBET FROM THE RESTAURANT!
I TOLD HIM YOU HAVE NO SENSE OF TASTE!
OH, THIS WILL AWAKEN IT IN YOU...
THE END

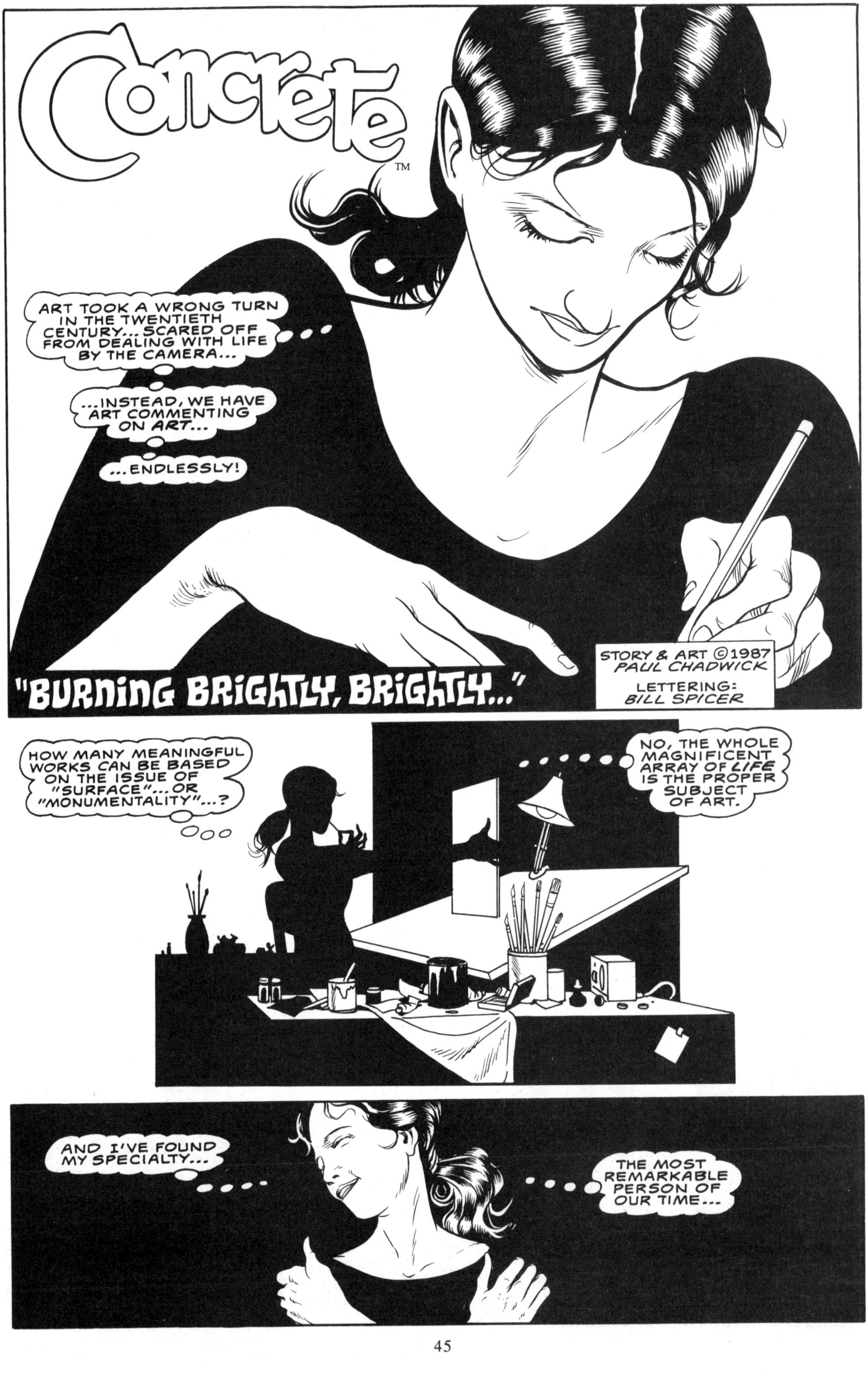
Concrete™
ART TOOK A WRONG TURN IN THE TWENTIETH CENTURY... SCARED OFF FROM DEALING WITH LIFE BY THE CAMERA...
...INSTEAD, WE HAVE ART COMMENTING ON ART...
...ENDLESSLY!
"BURNING BRIGHTLY, BRIGHTLY..."
STORY & ART ©1987 PAUL CHADWICK
LETTERING: BILL SPICER
HOW MANY MEANINGFUL WORKS CAN BE BASED ON THE ISSUE OF "SURFACE"... OR "MONUMENTALITY"...?
NO, THE WHOLE MAGNIFICENT ARRAY OF LIFE IS THE PROPER SUBJECT OF ART.
AND I'VE FOUND MY SPECIALTY...
THE MOST REMARKABLE PERSON OF OUR TIME...

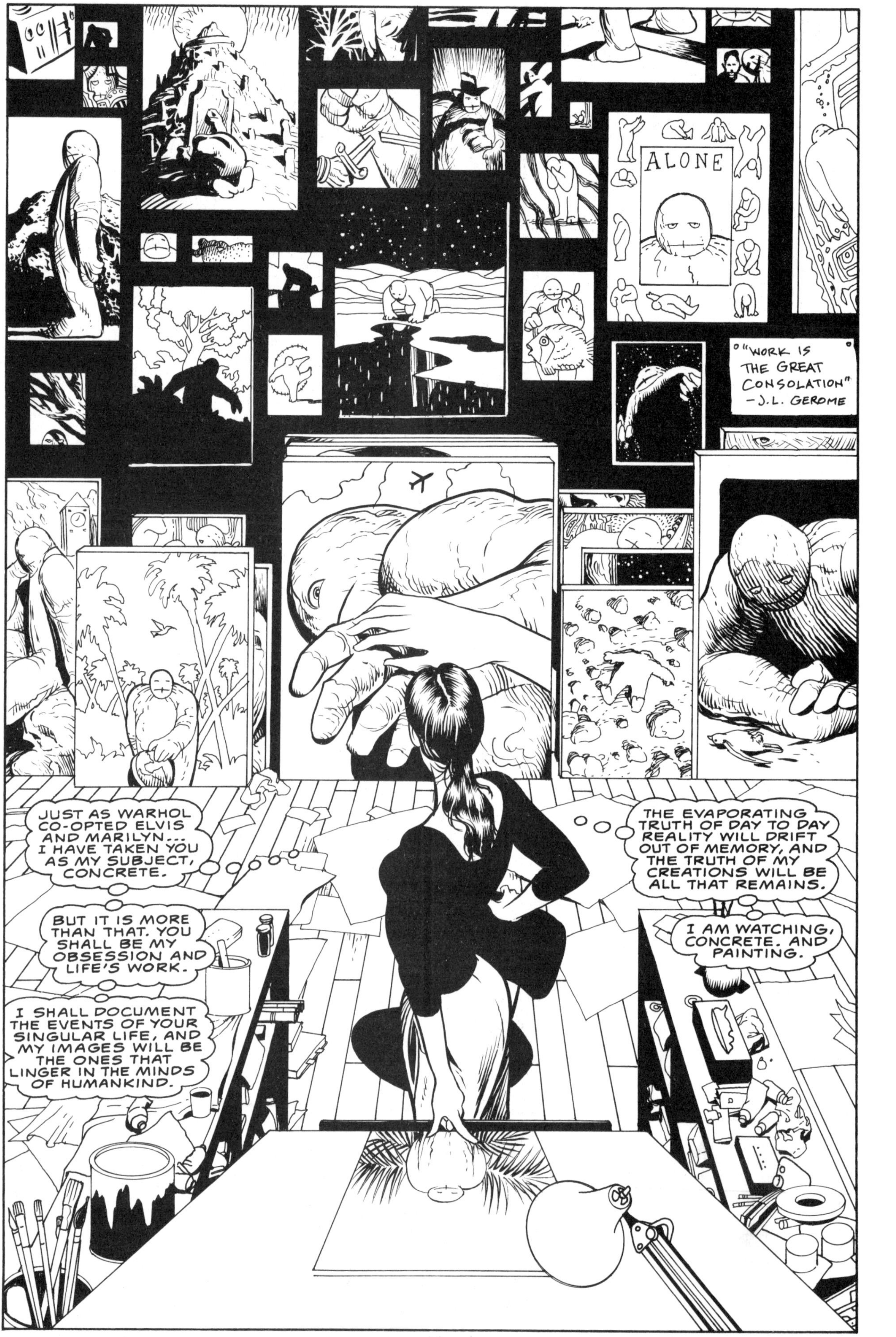
ALONE
"WORK IS THE GREAT CONSOLATION" —J.L. GEROME
JUST AS WARHOL CO-OPTED ELVIS AND MARILYN... I HAVE TAKEN YOU AS MY SUBJECT, CONCRETE.
BUT IT IS MORE THAN THAT. YOU SHALL BE MY OBSESSION AND LIFE'S WORK.
I SHALL DOCUMENT THE EVENTS OF YOUR SINGULAR LIFE, AND MY IMAGES WILL BE THE ONES THAT LINGER IN THE MINDS OF HUMANKIND.
THE EVAPORATING TRUTH OF DAY TO DAY REALITY WILL DRIFT OUT OF MEMORY, AND THE TRUTH OF MY CREATIONS WILL BE ALL THAT REMAINS.
I AM WATCHING, CONCRETE. AND PAINTING.

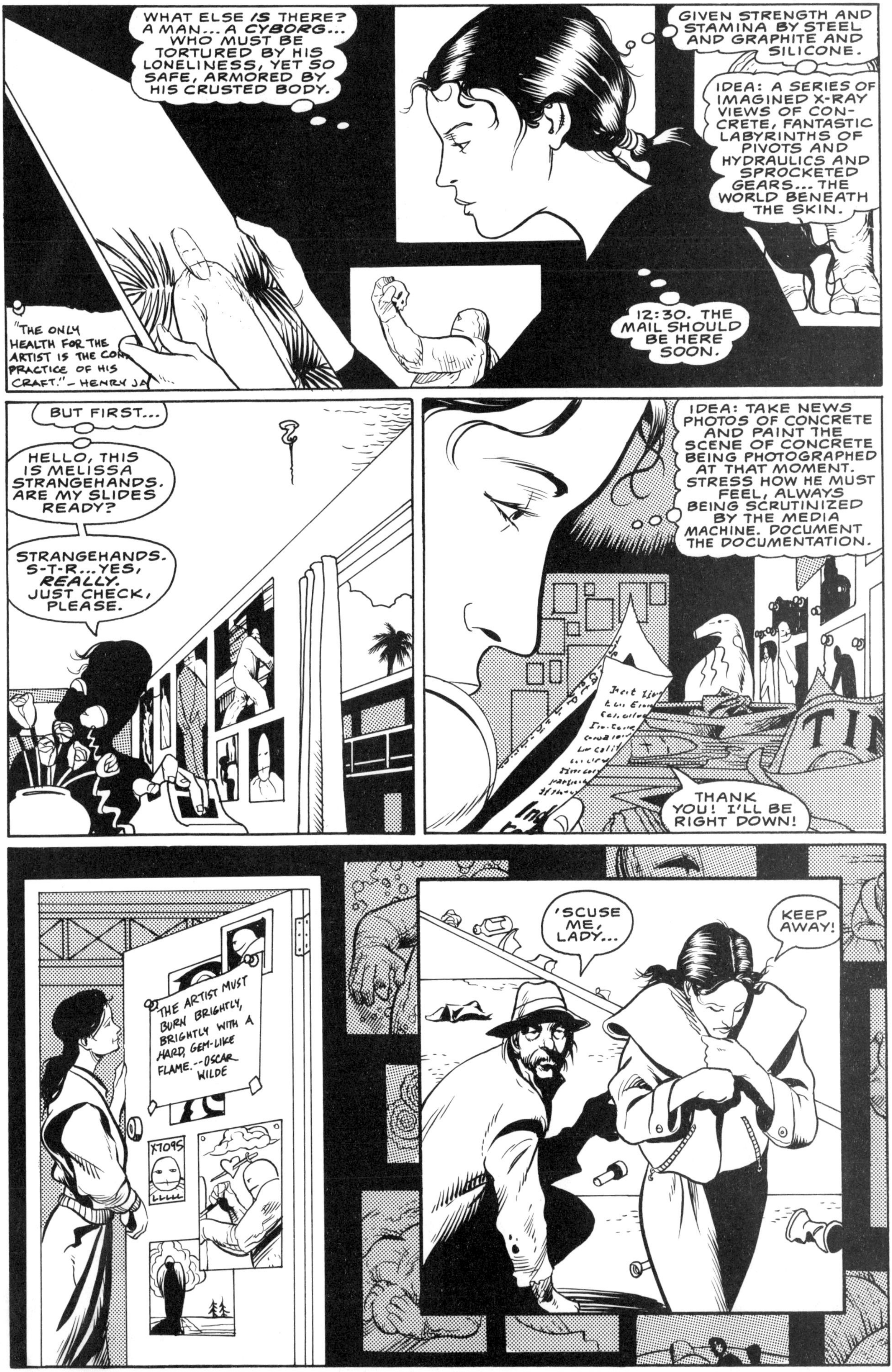
WHAT ELSE IS THERE? A MAN... A CYBORG... WHO MUST BE TORTURED BY HIS LONELINESS, YET SO SAFE, ARMORED BY HIS CRUSTED BODY.
GIVEN STRENGTH AND STAMINA BY STEEL AND GRAPHITE AND SILICONE.
IDEA: A SERIES OF IMAGINED X-RAY VIEWS OF CONCRETE, FANTASTIC LABYRINTHS OF PIVOTS AND HYDRAULICS AND SPROCKETED GEARS... THE WORLD BENEATH THE SKIN.
"THE ONLY HEALTH FOR THE ARTIST IS THE CON PRACTICE OF HIS CRAFT." - HENRY JA
12:30. THE MAIL SHOULD BE HERE SOON.
BUT FIRST...
HELLO, THIS IS MELISSA STRANGEHANDS. ARE MY SLIDES READY?
STRANGEHANDS. S-T-R... YES, REALLY. JUST CHECK, PLEASE.
IDEA: TAKE NEWS PHOTOS OF CONCRETE AND PAINT THE SCENE OF CONCRETE BEING PHOTOGRAPHED AT THAT MOMENT. STRESS HOW HE MUST FEEL, ALWAYS BEING SCRUTINIZED BY THE MEDIA MACHINE. DOCUMENT THE DOCUMENTATION.
THANK YOU! I'LL BE RIGHT DOWN!
THE ARTIST MUST BURN BRIGHTLY, BRIGHTLY WITH A HARD, GEM-LIKE FLAME. --OSCAR WILDE
XT095
'SCUSE ME, LADY...
KEEP AWAY!

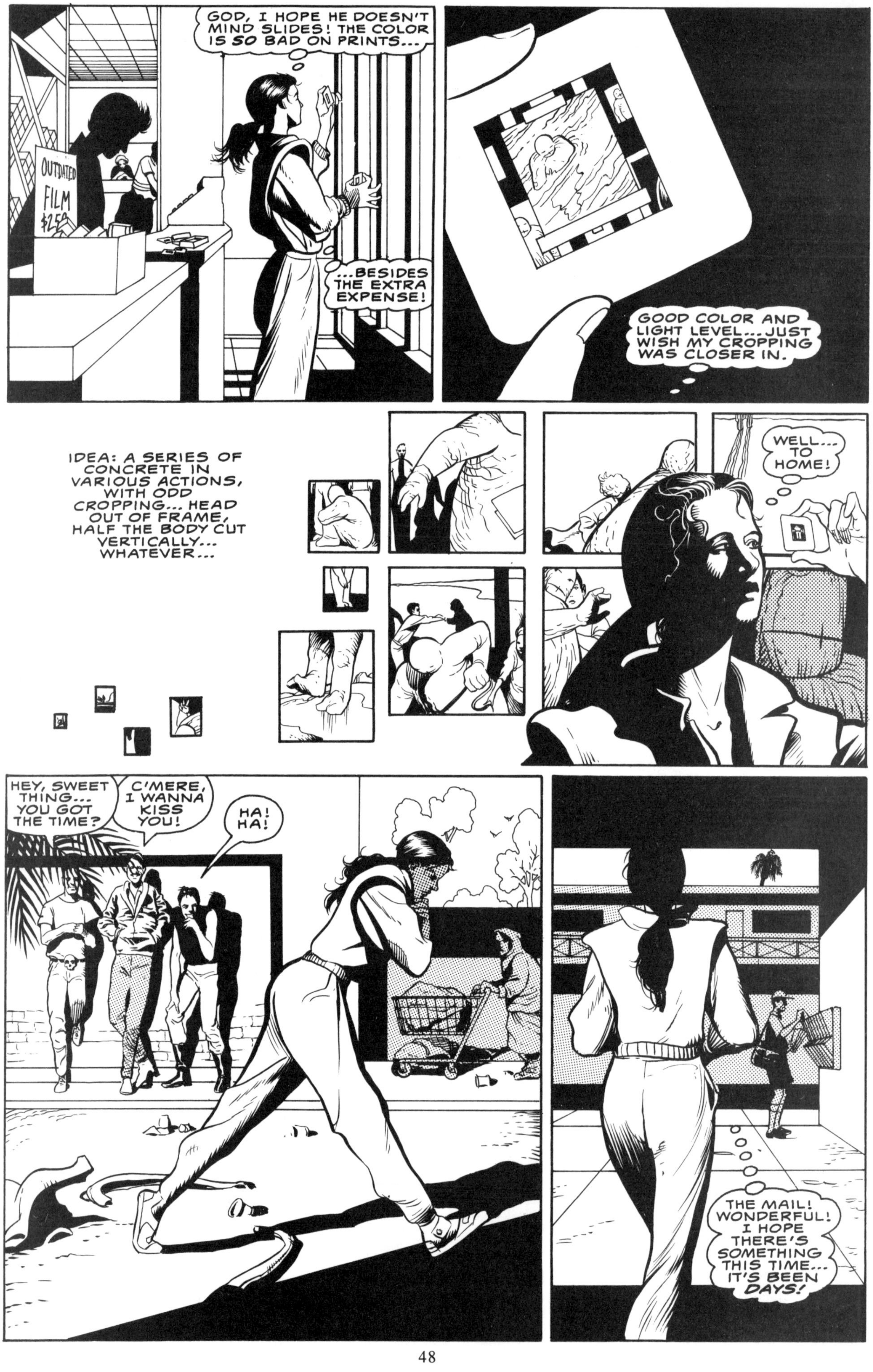
GOD, I HOPE HE DOESN'T MIND SLIDES! THE COLOR IS SO BAD ON PRINTS...
OUTDATED FILM $2.50
...BESIDES THE EXTRA EXPENSE!
GOOD COLOR AND LIGHT LEVEL... JUST WISH MY CROPPING WAS CLOSER IN.
IDEA: A SERIES OF CONCRETE IN VARIOUS ACTIONS, WITH ODD CROPPING... HEAD OUT OF FRAME, HALF THE BODY CUT VERTICALLY... WHATEVER...
WELL... TO HOME!
HEY, SWEET THING... YOU GOT THE TIME?
C'MERE, I WANNA KISS YOU!
HA! HA!
THE MAIL! WONDERFUL! I HOPE THERE'S SOMETHING THIS TIME... IT'S BEEN DAYS!

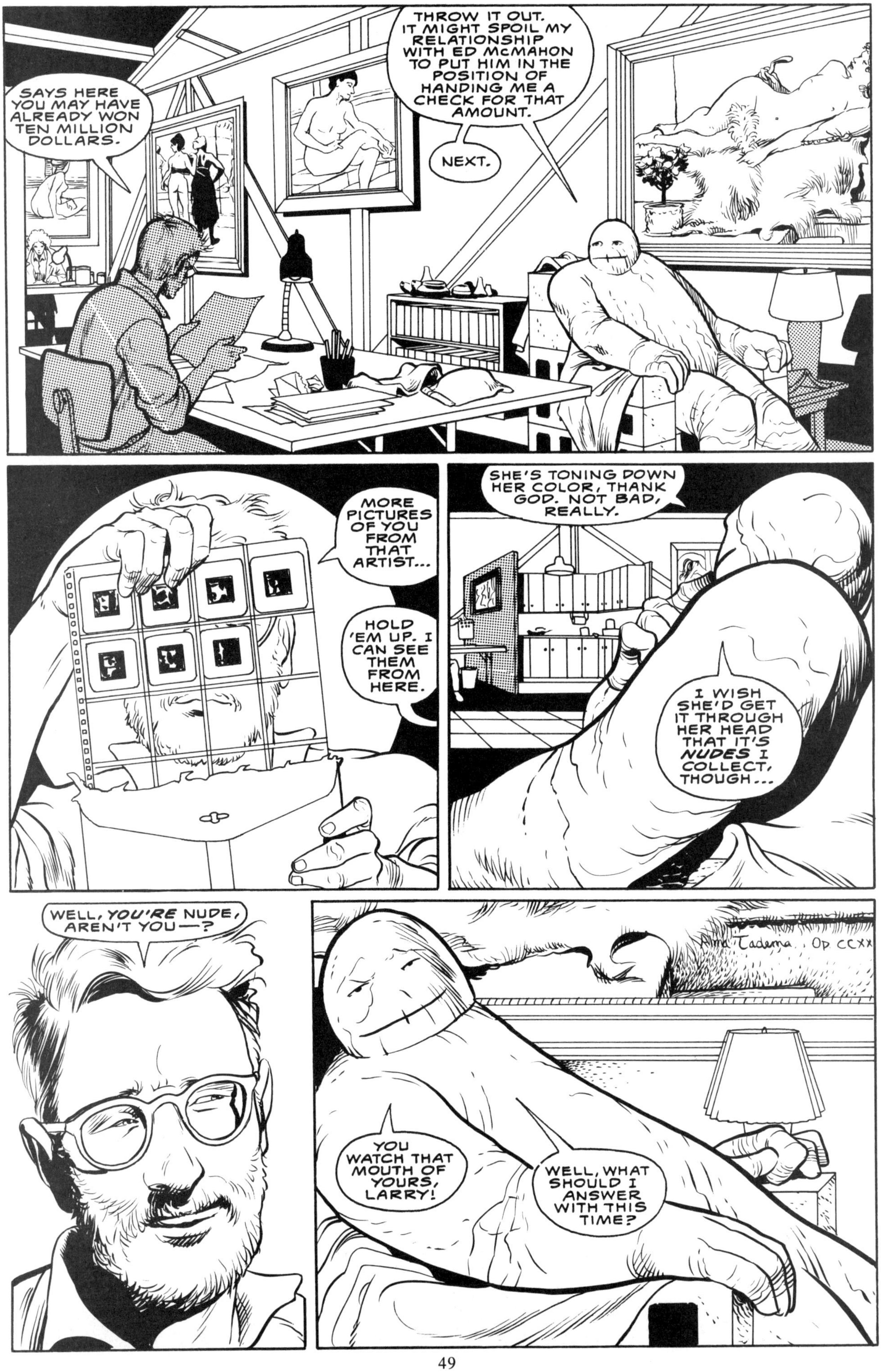

SAYS HERE YOU MAY HAVE ALREADY WON TEN MILLION DOLLARS.
THROW IT OUT. IT MIGHT SPOIL MY RELATIONSHIP WITH ED McMAHON TO PUT HIM IN THE POSITION OF HANDING ME A CHECK FOR THAT AMOUNT.
NEXT.
MORE PICTURES OF YOU FROM THAT ARTIST...
HOLD 'EM UP. I CAN SEE THEM FROM HERE.
SHE'S TONING DOWN HER COLOR, THANK GOD. NOT BAD, REALLY.
I WISH SHE'D GET IT THROUGH HER HEAD THAT IT'S *NUDES* I COLLECT, THOUGH...
WELL, *YOU'RE* NUDE, AREN'T YOU—?
Alma Tadema . Op CCXX
YOU WATCH THAT MOUTH OF YOURS, LARRY!
WELL, WHAT SHOULD I ANSWER WITH THIS TIME?

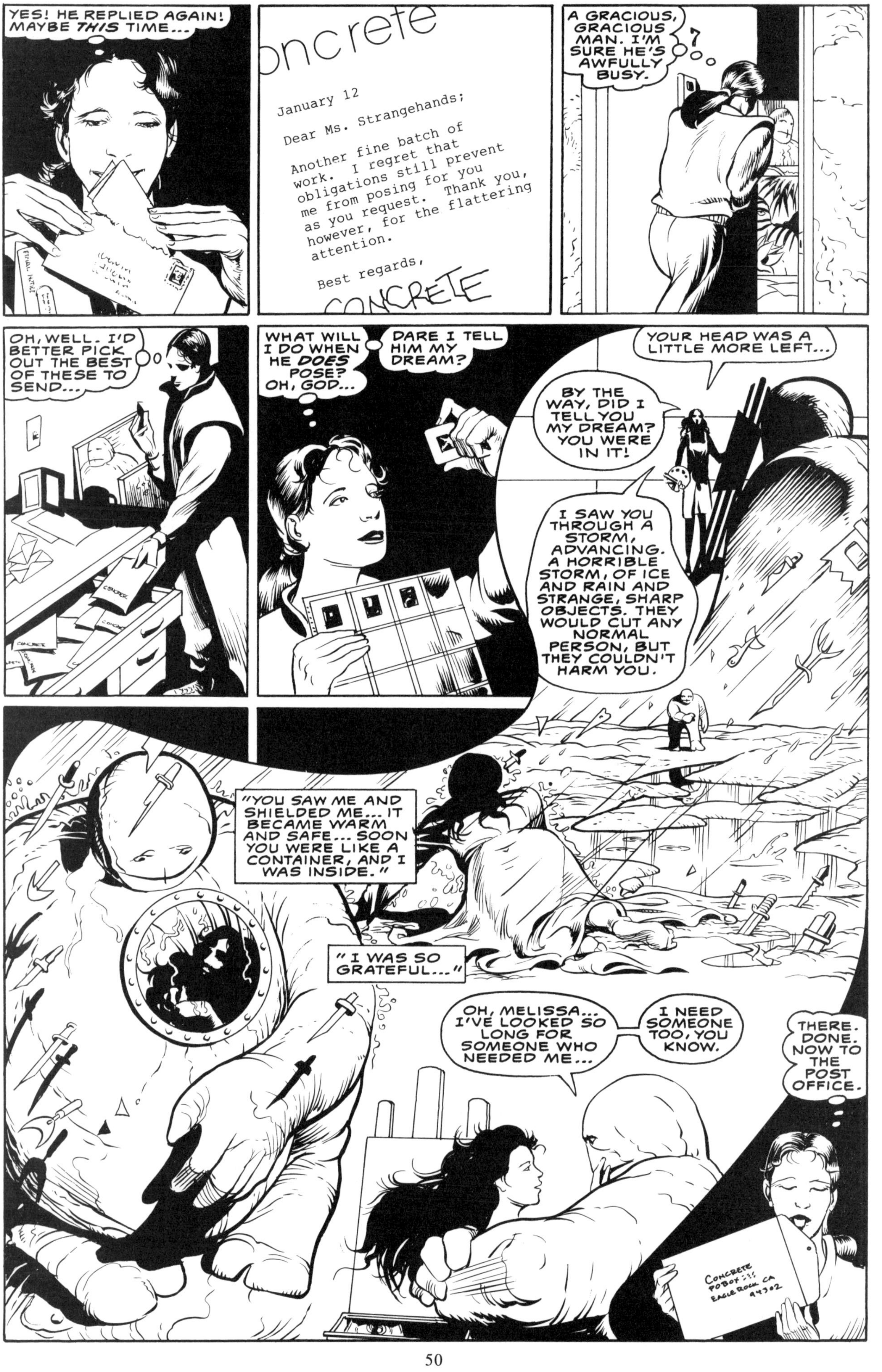
YES! HE REPLIED AGAIN! MAYBE THIS TIME...
oncrete
January 12
Dear Ms. Strangehands;
Another fine batch of work. I regret that obligations still prevent me from posing for you as you request. Thank you, however, for the flattering attention.
Best regards,
CONCRETE
A GRACIOUS, GRACIOUS MAN. I'M SURE HE'S AWFULLY BUSY.
OH, WELL. I'D BETTER PICK OUT THE BEST OF THESE TO SEND...
WHAT WILL I DO WHEN HE DOES POSE? OH, GOD...
DARE I TELL HIM MY DREAM?
YOUR HEAD WAS A LITTLE MORE LEFT...
BY THE WAY, DID I TELL YOU MY DREAM? YOU WERE IN IT!
I SAW YOU THROUGH A STORM, ADVANCING. A HORRIBLE STORM, OF ICE AND RAIN AND STRANGE, SHARP OBJECTS. THEY WOULD CUT ANY NORMAL PERSON, BUT THEY COULDN'T HARM YOU.
"YOU SAW ME AND SHIELDED ME... IT BECAME WARM AND SAFE... SOON YOU WERE LIKE A CONTAINER, AND I WAS INSIDE."
"I WAS SO GRATEFUL..."
OH, MELISSA... I'VE LOOKED SO LONG FOR SOMEONE WHO NEEDED ME...
I NEED SOMEONE TOO, YOU KNOW.
THERE. DONE. NOW TO THE POST OFFICE.
CONCRETE
EAGLE ROCK CA

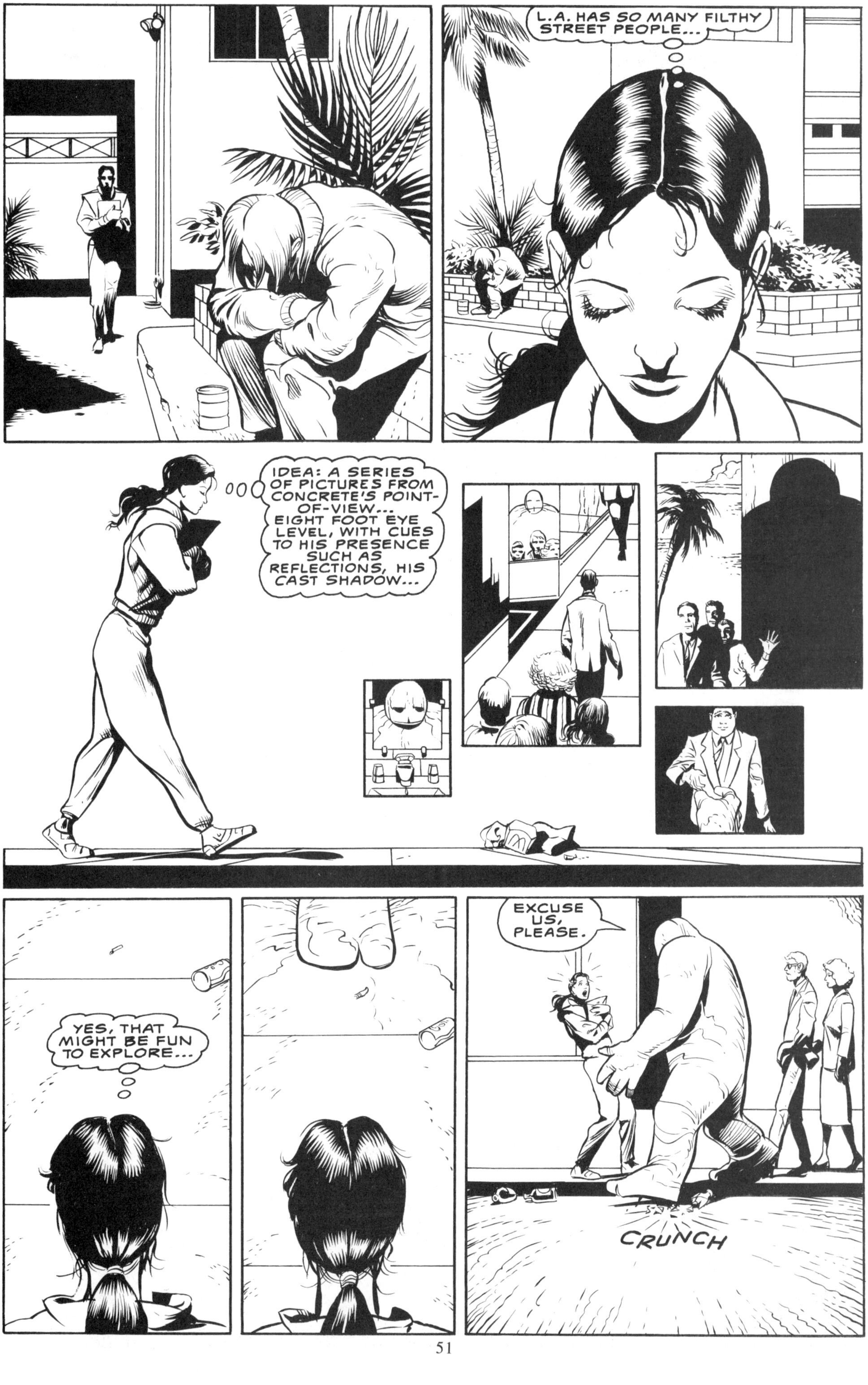
L.A. HAS SO MANY FILTHY STREET PEOPLE...
IDEA: A SERIES OF PICTURES FROM CONCRETE'S POINT-OF-VIEW... EIGHT FOOT EYE LEVEL, WITH CUES TO HIS PRESENCE SUCH AS REFLECTIONS, HIS CAST SHADOW...
YES, THAT MIGHT BE FUN TO EXPLORE...
EXCUSE US, PLEASE.
CRUNCH

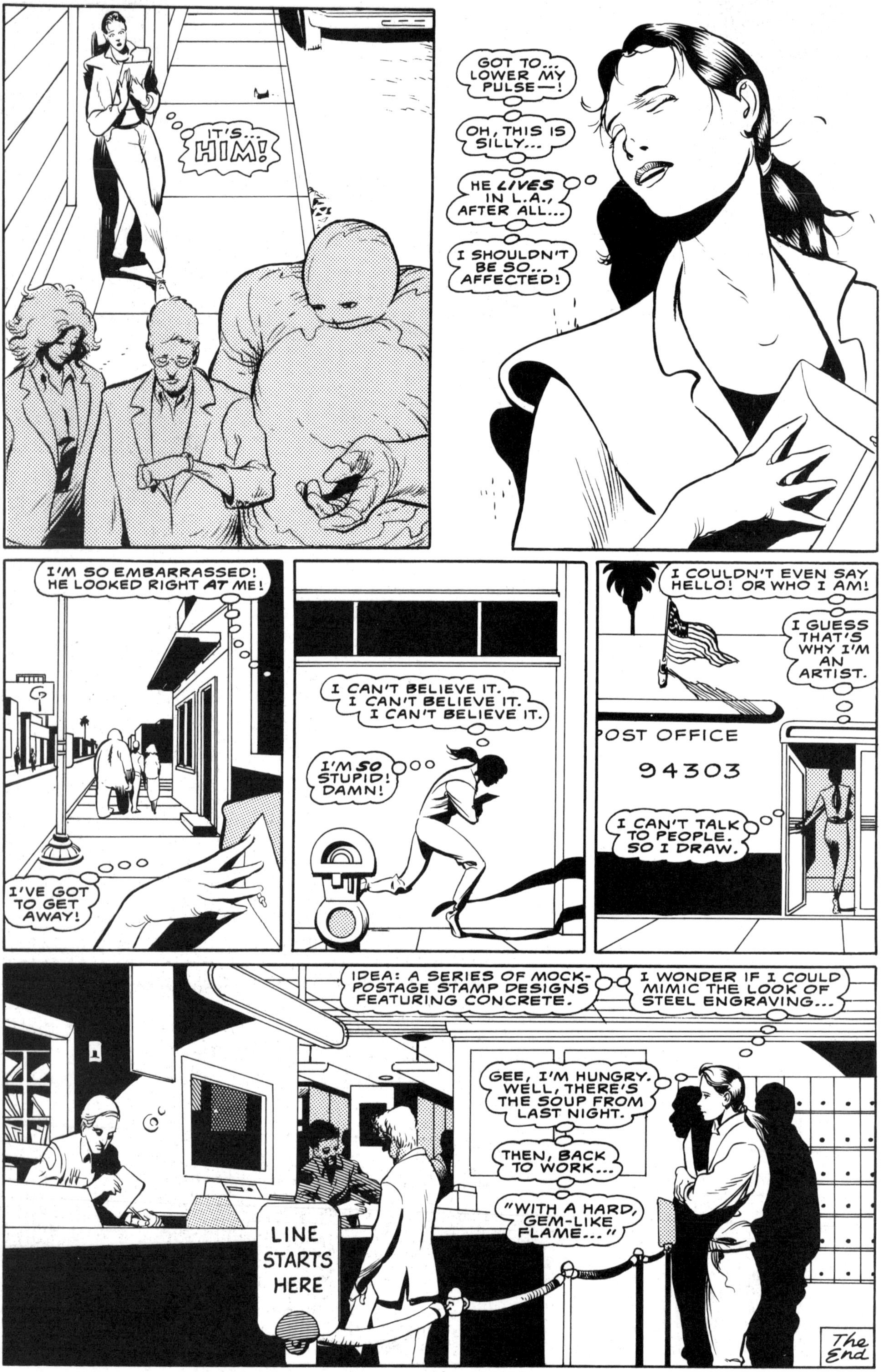
IT'S... HIM!
GOT TO... LOWER MY PULSE—!
OH, THIS IS SILLY...
HE LIVES IN L.A., AFTER ALL...
I SHOULDN'T BE SO... AFFECTED!
I'M SO EMBARRASSED! HE LOOKED RIGHT AT ME!
I'VE GOT TO GET AWAY!
I CAN'T BELIEVE IT. I CAN'T BELIEVE IT. I CAN'T BELIEVE IT.
I'M SO STUPID! DAMN!
I COULDN'T EVEN SAY HELLO! OR WHO I AM!
I GUESS THAT'S WHY I'M AN ARTIST.
POST OFFICE
94303
I CAN'T TALK TO PEOPLE. SO I DRAW.
IDEA: A SERIES OF MOCK-POSTAGE STAMP DESIGNS FEATURING CONCRETE.
I WONDER IF I COULD MIMIC THE LOOK OF STEEL ENGRAVING...
GEE, I'M HUNGRY. WELL, THERE'S THE SOUP FROM LAST NIGHT.
THEN, BACK TO WORK...
"WITH A HARD, GEM-LIKE FLAME..."
LINE STARTS HERE
The End

Little Pushes

RONALD LITHGOW ONCE WROTE IN HIS JOURNAL:

"THIS CAMPING TRIP WAS A GOOD IDEA. WITH EACH NEW STEP AND DROP OF SWEAT, I WORK A LITTLE MORE OF LISA OUT OF MY SYSTEM.

"I FELL ASLEEP LAST NIGHT MUSING HOW LIKE PLANETS WE ARE. LONELY, SPINNING STONES, SELF-CONTAINED AND ESSENTIALLY APART. BUT LIKE PLANETS, WE'RE IRRESISTABLY ATTRACTED TO EACH OTHER, AND WE OUR-SELVES REACH OUT WITH GRAVITIC TENDRILS TO PULL ANOTHER TO US.

"YET, IF PLANETS SHOULD EVER TOUCH, OR EVEN COME CLOSE, THOSE GRAVITIC FORCES IMMEDIATELY TEAR THEM TO PIECES.

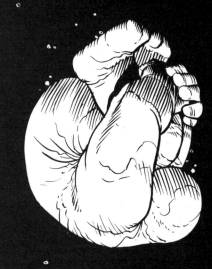

"THAT'S THE WAY A NEWLY-DIVORCED MAN CRIES IN HIS BEEF STEW, I GUESS.

"ACTUALLY, I'M QUITE EXCITED THIS MORNING. ONCE MICHAEL AWAKENS, WE'LL INVESTIGATE THAT LIGHT WE SAW ON THE BLUFF LAST NIGHT. I LOVE A MYSTERY."

THAT WAS A YEAR AGO.

STORY & ART ©1987
PAUL CHADWICK
LETTERING:
BILL SPICER

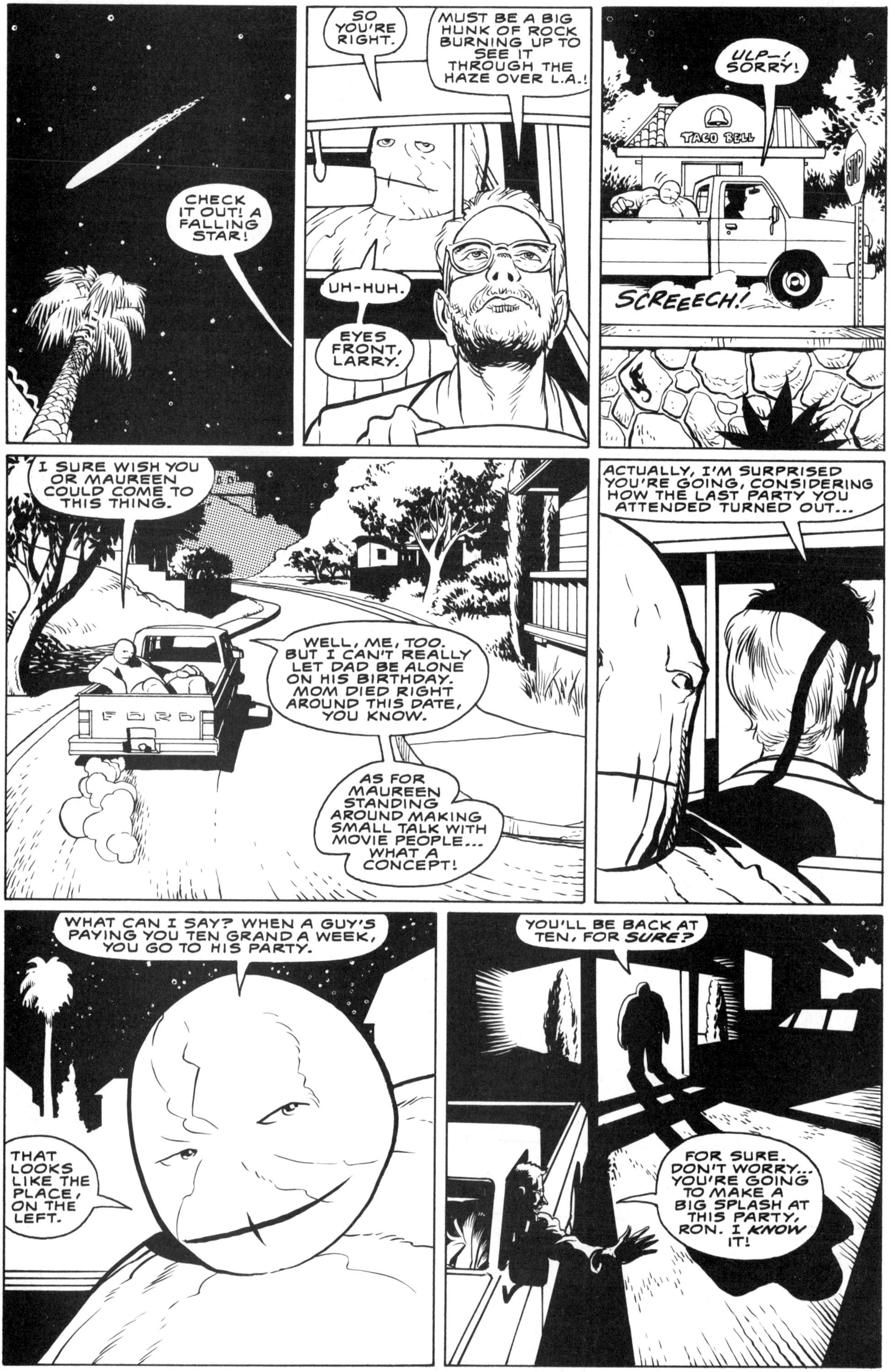
CHECK IT OUT! A FALLING STAR!
SO YOU'RE RIGHT.
MUST BE A BIG HUNK OF ROCK BURNING UP TO SEE IT THROUGH THE HAZE OVER L.A.!
UH-HUH.
EYES FRONT, LARRY.
ULP—! SORRY!
TACO BELL
STOP
SCREEECH!
I SURE WISH YOU OR MAUREEN COULD COME TO THIS THING.
WELL, ME, TOO. BUT I CAN'T REALLY LET DAD BE ALONE ON HIS BIRTHDAY. MOM DIED RIGHT AROUND THIS DATE, YOU KNOW.
AS FOR MAUREEN STANDING AROUND MAKING SMALL TALK WITH MOVIE PEOPLE... WHAT A CONCEPT!
FORD
ACTUALLY, I'M SURPRISED YOU'RE GOING, CONSIDERING HOW THE LAST PARTY YOU ATTENDED TURNED OUT...
WHAT CAN I SAY? WHEN A GUY'S PAYING YOU TEN GRAND A WEEK, YOU GO TO HIS PARTY.
THAT LOOKS LIKE THE PLACE, ON THE LEFT.
YOU'LL BE BACK AT TEN, FOR SURE?
FOR SURE. DON'T WORRY... YOU'RE GOING TO MAKE A BIG SPLASH AT THIS PARTY, RON. I KNOW IT!

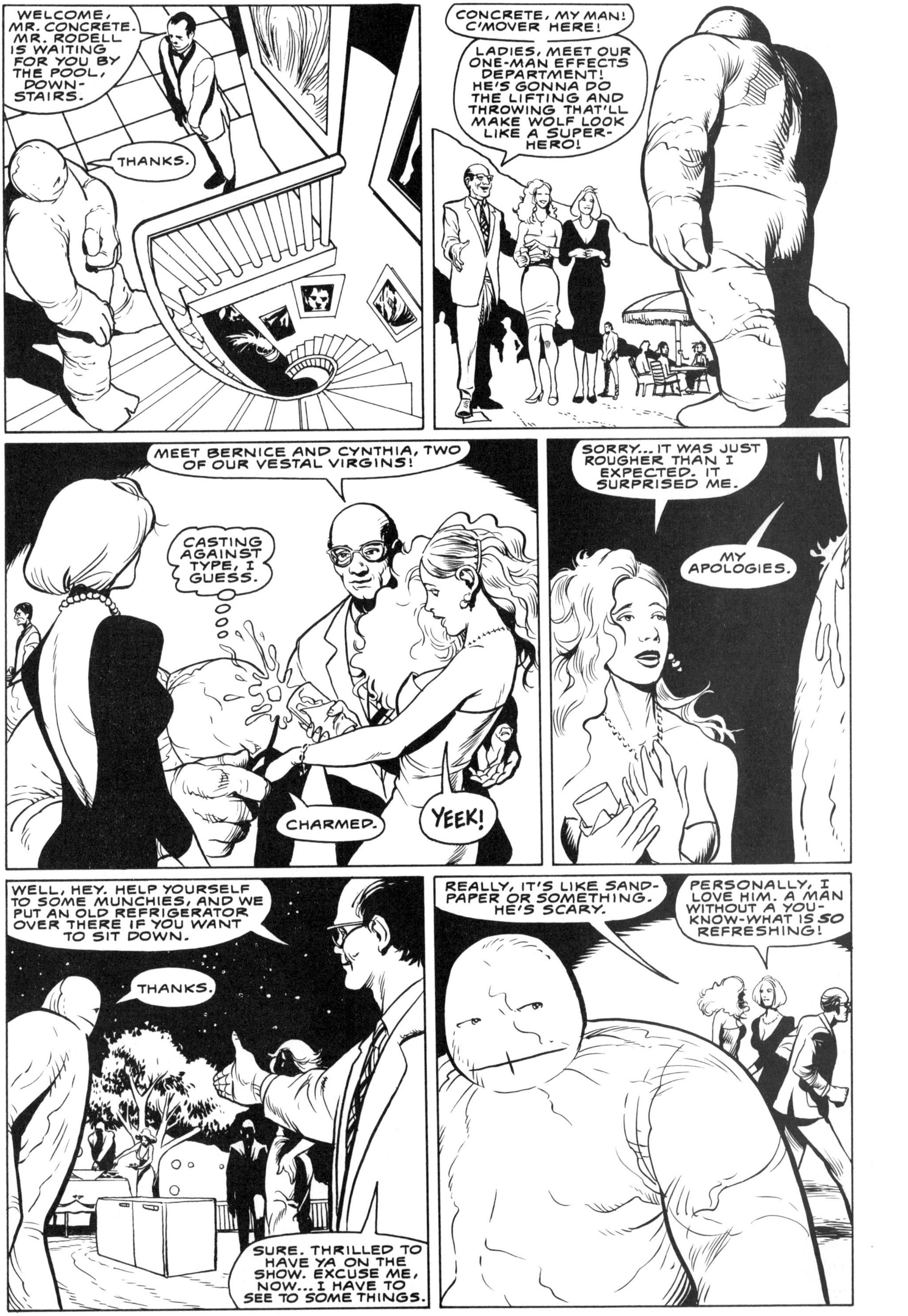
WELCOME, MR. CONCRETE. MR. RODELL IS WAITING FOR YOU BY THE POOL, DOWN-STAIRS.
THANKS.
CONCRETE, MY MAN! C'MOVER HERE!
LADIES, MEET OUR ONE-MAN EFFECTS DEPARTMENT! HE'S GONNA DO THE LIFTING AND THROWING THAT'LL MAKE WOLF LOOK LIKE A SUPER-HERO!
MEET BERNICE AND CYNTHIA, TWO OF OUR VESTAL VIRGINS!
CASTING AGAINST TYPE, I GUESS.
CHARMED.
YEEK!
SORRY... IT WAS JUST ROUGHER THAN I EXPECTED. IT SURPRISED ME.
MY APOLOGIES.
WELL, HEY. HELP YOURSELF TO SOME MUNCHIES, AND WE PUT AN OLD REFRIGERATOR OVER THERE IF YOU WANT TO SIT DOWN.
THANKS.
SURE. THRILLED TO HAVE YA ON THE SHOW. EXCUSE ME, NOW... I HAVE TO SEE TO SOME THINGS.
REALLY, IT'S LIKE SAND-PAPER OR SOMETHING. HE'S SCARY.
PERSONALLY, I LOVE HIM. A MAN WITHOUT A YOU-KNOW-WHAT IS *SO* REFRESHING!

A HUSH FALLS OVER THE PARTY AS PEOPLE NOTICE WOLF HULTGREN, STAR OF *RULERS OF THE OMNIVERSE*, CLIMBING THE HIGH DIVE.

A SPOTLIGHT SETS HIM AFIRE AS HE RISES ABOVE A POOL FILLED WITH PINK AND WHITE CARNATIONS.

FROM SOMEWHERE, COPLAND'S "FANFARE FOR THE COMMON MAN" BOOMS OUT...

AS THE FANFARE PLAYS OUT, WOLF POSES IN NAUTILUS-SCULPTED MAGNIFICENCE...

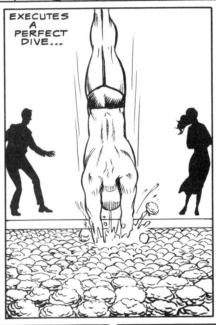

EXECUTES A PERFECT DIVE...

AND STAYS UNDER THE FLORAL ARRAY FOR A MOST ALARMING TIME...

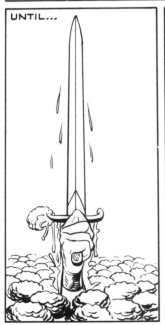

UNTIL...

HE EMERGES IN FULL COSTUME AS MANN, STAR-LORD SUPREME!

CLAP
CLAP
CLAP
CLAP
CLAP
CLA

THE TREASURE BAG IS TAKEN BY ATTENDANTS, WHO DISTRIBUTE *RULERS OF THE OMNIVERSE* DIGITAL ALARM CLOCKS TO THE GUESTS.

HAVING NO POCKETS TO DEPOSIT IT IN, CONCRETE EATS HIS.

HOW PATHETIC.

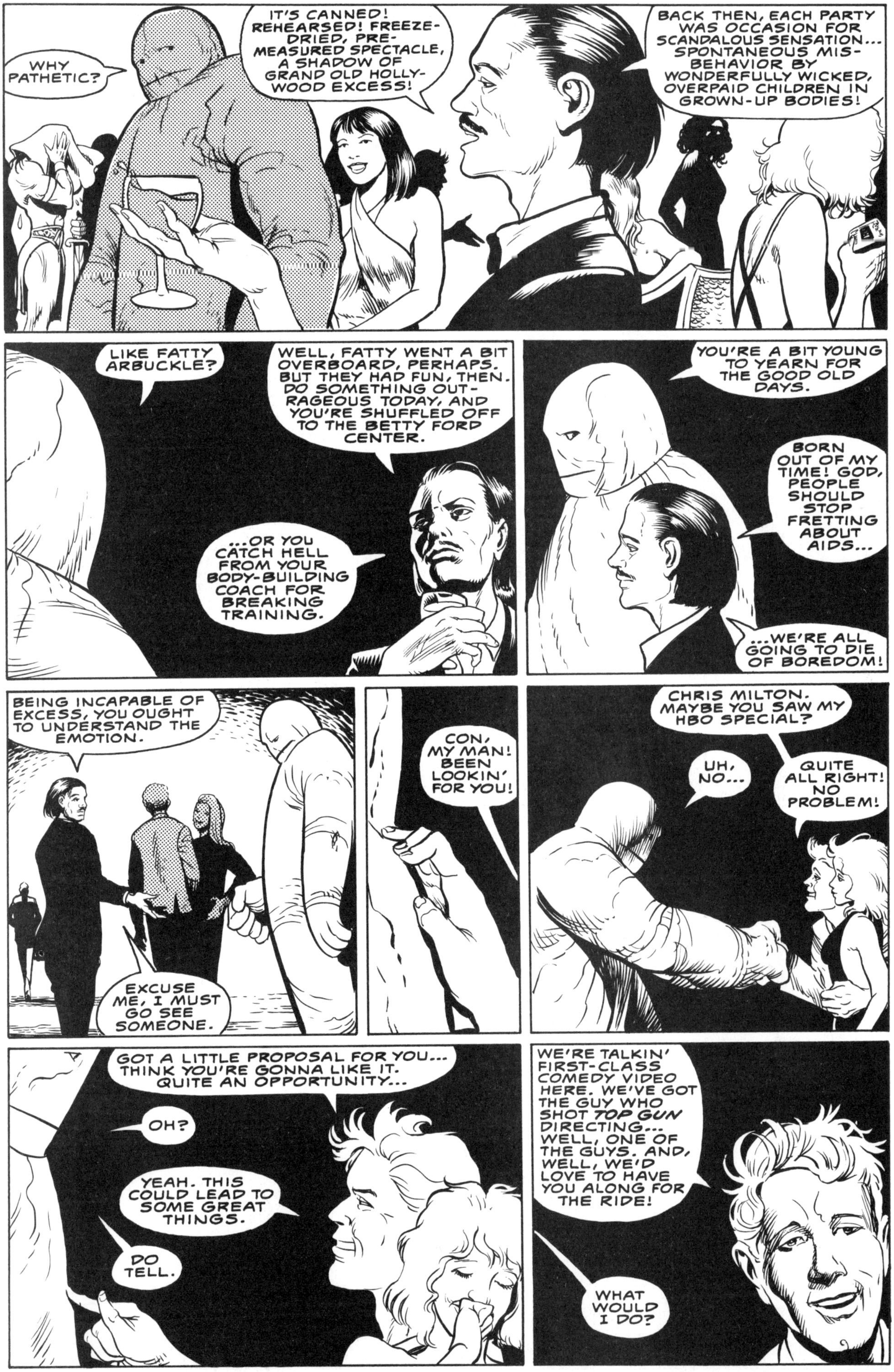
WHY PATHETIC?
IT'S CANNED! REHEARSED! FREEZE-DRIED, PRE-MEASURED SPECTACLE, A SHADOW OF GRAND OLD HOLLY-WOOD EXCESS!
BACK THEN, EACH PARTY WAS OCCASION FOR SCANDALOUS SENSATION... SPONTANEOUS MIS-BEHAVIOR BY WONDERFULLY WICKED, OVERPAID CHILDREN IN GROWN-UP BODIES!
LIKE FATTY ARBUCKLE?
WELL, FATTY WENT A BIT OVERBOARD, PERHAPS. BUT THEY HAD FUN, THEN. DO SOMETHING OUT-RAGEOUS TODAY, AND YOU'RE SHUFFLED OFF TO THE BETTY FORD CENTER.
...OR YOU CATCH HELL FROM YOUR BODY-BUILDING COACH FOR BREAKING TRAINING.
YOU'RE A BIT YOUNG TO YEARN FOR THE GOOD OLD DAYS.
BORN OUT OF MY TIME! GOD, PEOPLE SHOULD STOP FRETTING ABOUT AIDS...
...WE'RE ALL GOING TO DIE OF BOREDOM!
BEING INCAPABLE OF EXCESS, YOU OUGHT TO UNDERSTAND THE EMOTION.
EXCUSE ME, I MUST GO SEE SOMEONE.
CON, MY MAN! BEEN LOOKIN' FOR YOU!
CHRIS MILTON. MAYBE YOU SAW MY HBO SPECIAL?
UH, NO...
QUITE ALL RIGHT! NO PROBLEM!
GOT A LITTLE PROPOSAL FOR YOU... THINK YOU'RE GONNA LIKE IT. QUITE AN OPPORTUNITY...
OH?
YEAH. THIS COULD LEAD TO SOME GREAT THINGS.
DO TELL.
WE'RE TALKIN' FIRST-CLASS COMEDY VIDEO HERE. WE'VE GOT THE GUY WHO SHOT TOP GUN DIRECTING... WELL, ONE OF THE GUYS. AND, WELL, WE'D LOVE TO HAVE YOU ALONG FOR THE RIDE!
WHAT WOULD I DO?

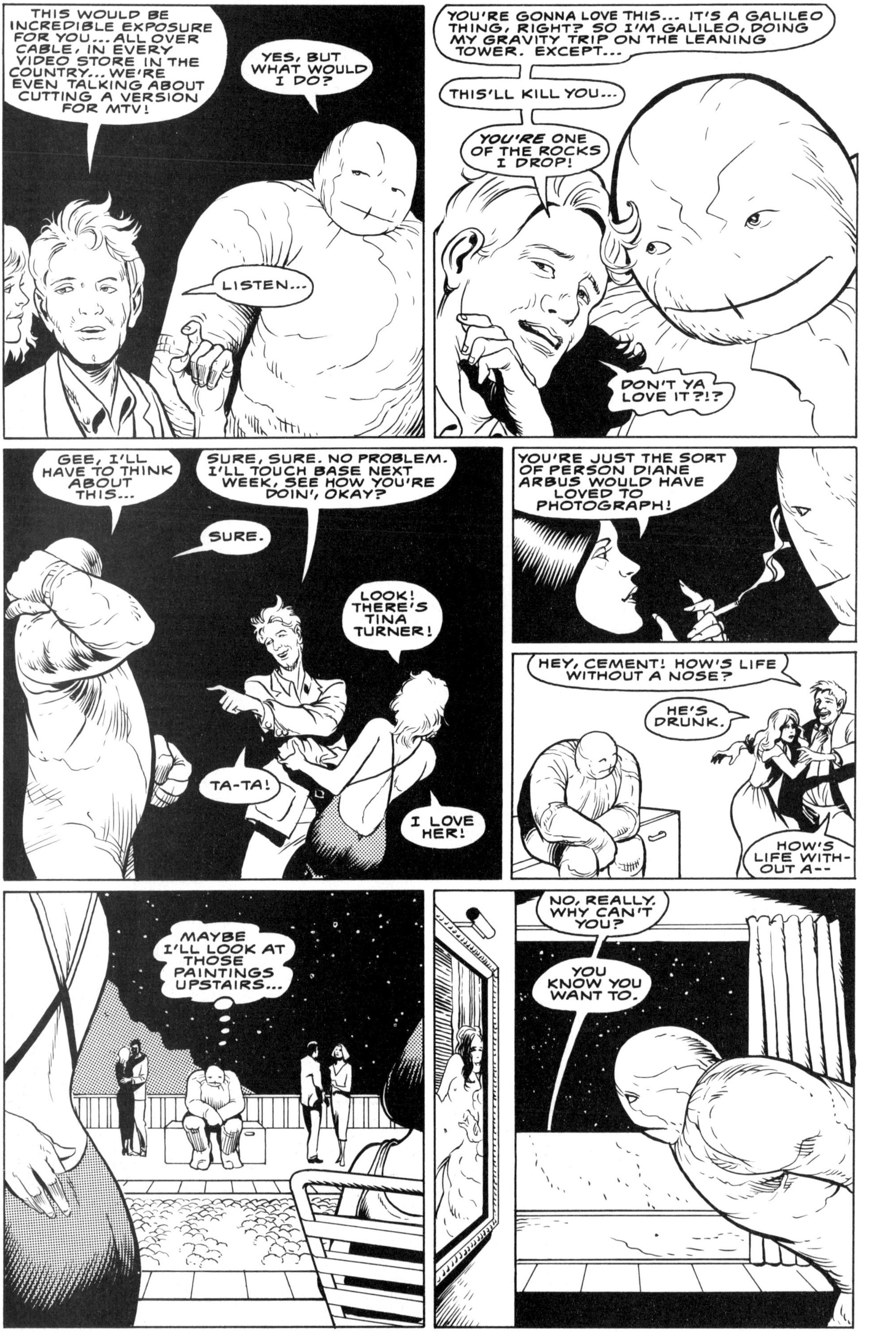

THIS WOULD BE INCREDIBLE EXPOSURE FOR YOU... ALL OVER CABLE, IN EVERY VIDEO STORE IN THE COUNTRY... WE'RE EVEN TALKING ABOUT CUTTING A VERSION FOR MTV!
YES, BUT WHAT WOULD I DO?
LISTEN...
YOU'RE GONNA LOVE THIS... IT'S A GALILEO THING, RIGHT? SO I'M GALILEO, DOING MY GRAVITY TRIP ON THE LEANING TOWER. EXCEPT...
THIS'LL KILL YOU...
YOU'RE ONE OF THE ROCKS I DROP!
DON'T YA LOVE IT?!?
GEE, I'LL HAVE TO THINK ABOUT THIS...
SURE, SURE. NO PROBLEM. I'LL TOUCH BASE NEXT WEEK, SEE HOW YOU'RE DOIN', OKAY?
SURE.
LOOK! THERE'S TINA TURNER!
TA-TA!
I LOVE HER!
YOU'RE JUST THE SORT OF PERSON DIANE ARBUS WOULD HAVE LOVED TO PHOTOGRAPH!
HEY, CEMENT! HOW'S LIFE WITHOUT A NOSE?
HE'S DRUNK.
HOW'S LIFE WITH-OUT A--
MAYBE I'LL LOOK AT THOSE PAINTINGS UPSTAIRS...
NO, REALLY. WHY CAN'T YOU?
YOU KNOW YOU WANT TO.

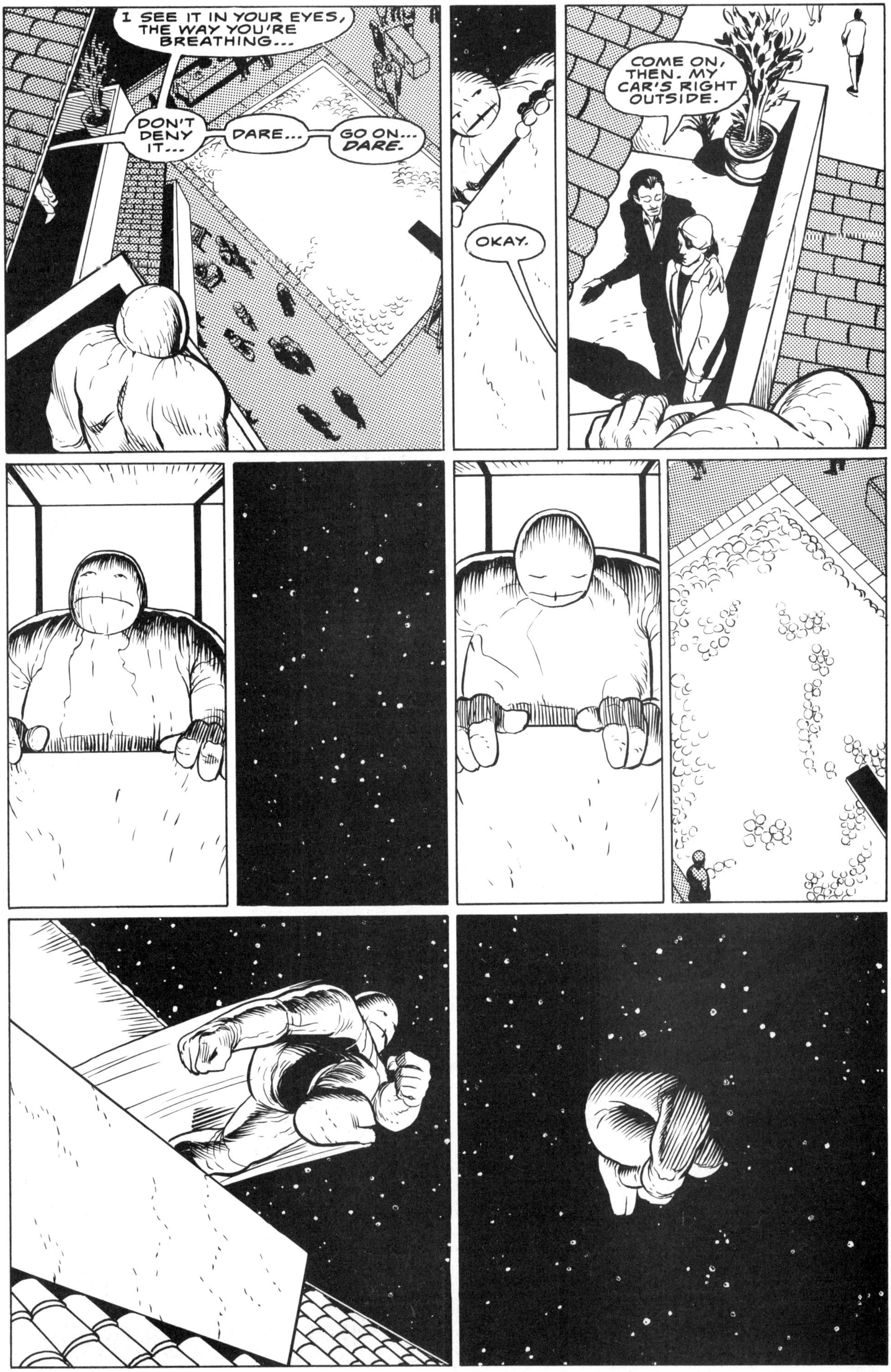
I SEE IT IN YOUR EYES, THE WAY YOU'RE BREATHING...
DON'T DENY IT...
DARE...
GO ON... DARE.
COME ON, THEN. MY CAR'S RIGHT OUTSIDE.
OKAY.

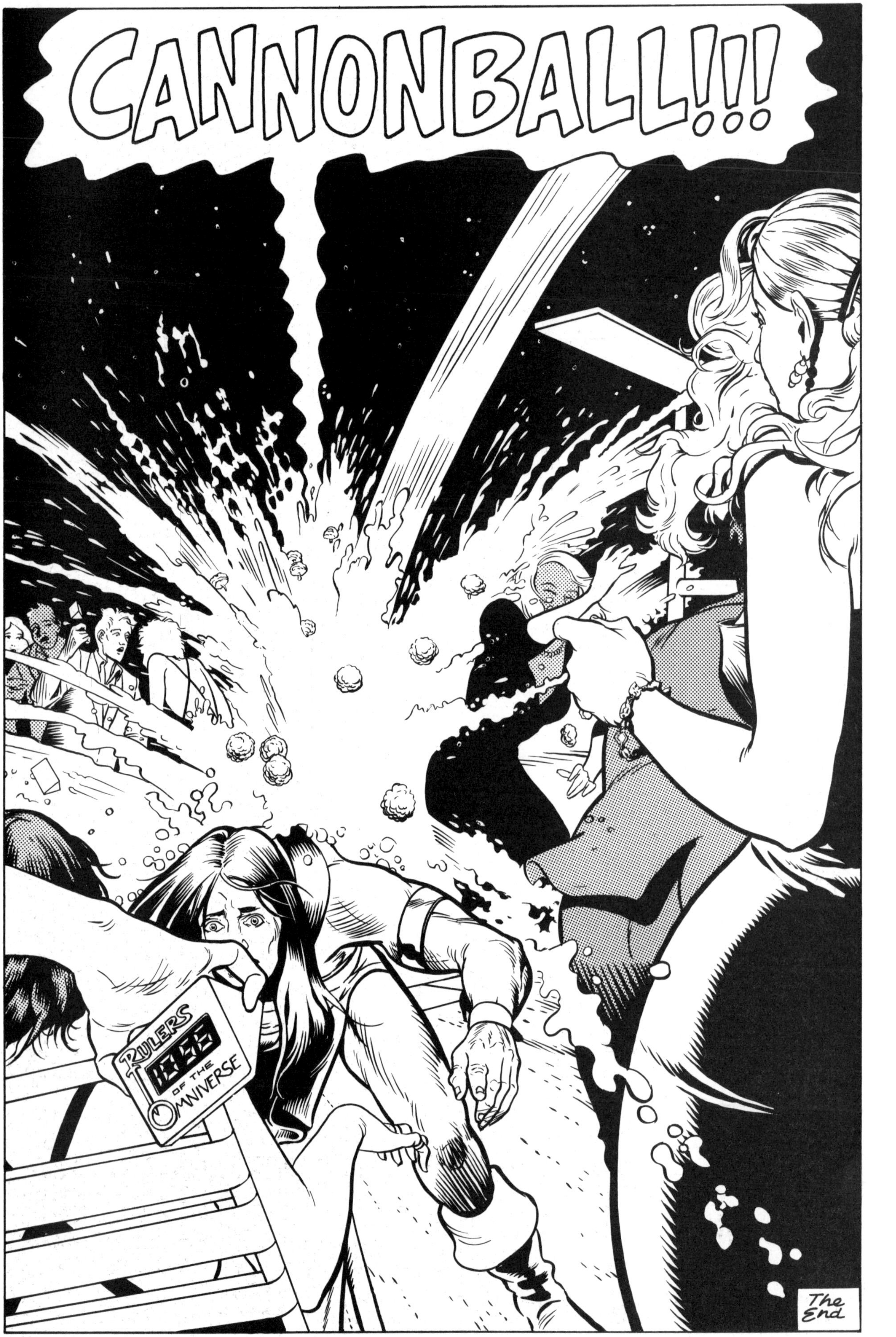
CANNONBALL!!!
RULERS OF THE OMNIVERSE
The End

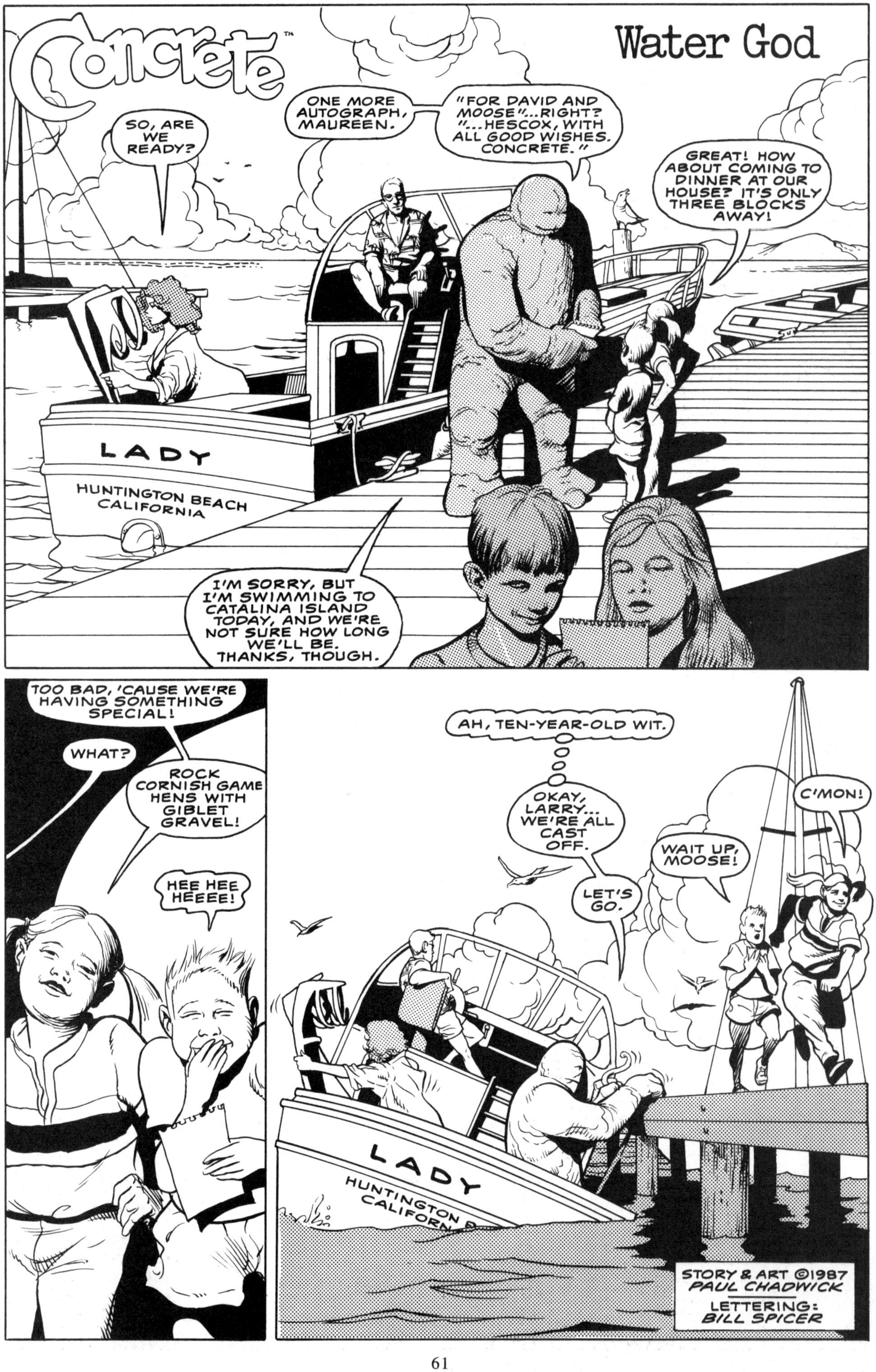
Concrete™
Water God
SO, ARE WE READY?
ONE MORE AUTOGRAPH, MAUREEN.
"FOR DAVID AND MOOSE"...RIGHT? "...HESCOX, WITH ALL GOOD WISHES. CONCRETE."
GREAT! HOW ABOUT COMING TO DINNER AT OUR HOUSE? IT'S ONLY THREE BLOCKS AWAY!
LADY
HUNTINGTON BEACH CALIFORNIA
I'M SORRY, BUT I'M SWIMMING TO CATALINA ISLAND TODAY, AND WE'RE NOT SURE HOW LONG WE'LL BE. THANKS, THOUGH.
TOO BAD, 'CAUSE WE'RE HAVING SOMETHING SPECIAL!
WHAT?
ROCK CORNISH GAME HENS WITH GIBLET GRAVEL!
HEE HEE HEEEE!
AH, TEN-YEAR-OLD WIT.
OKAY, LARRY... WE'RE ALL CAST OFF.
LET'S GO.
WAIT UP, MOOSE!
C'MON!
LADY
HUNTINGTON B
CALIFORN
STORY & ART ©1987 PAUL CHADWICK
LETTERING: BILL SPICER

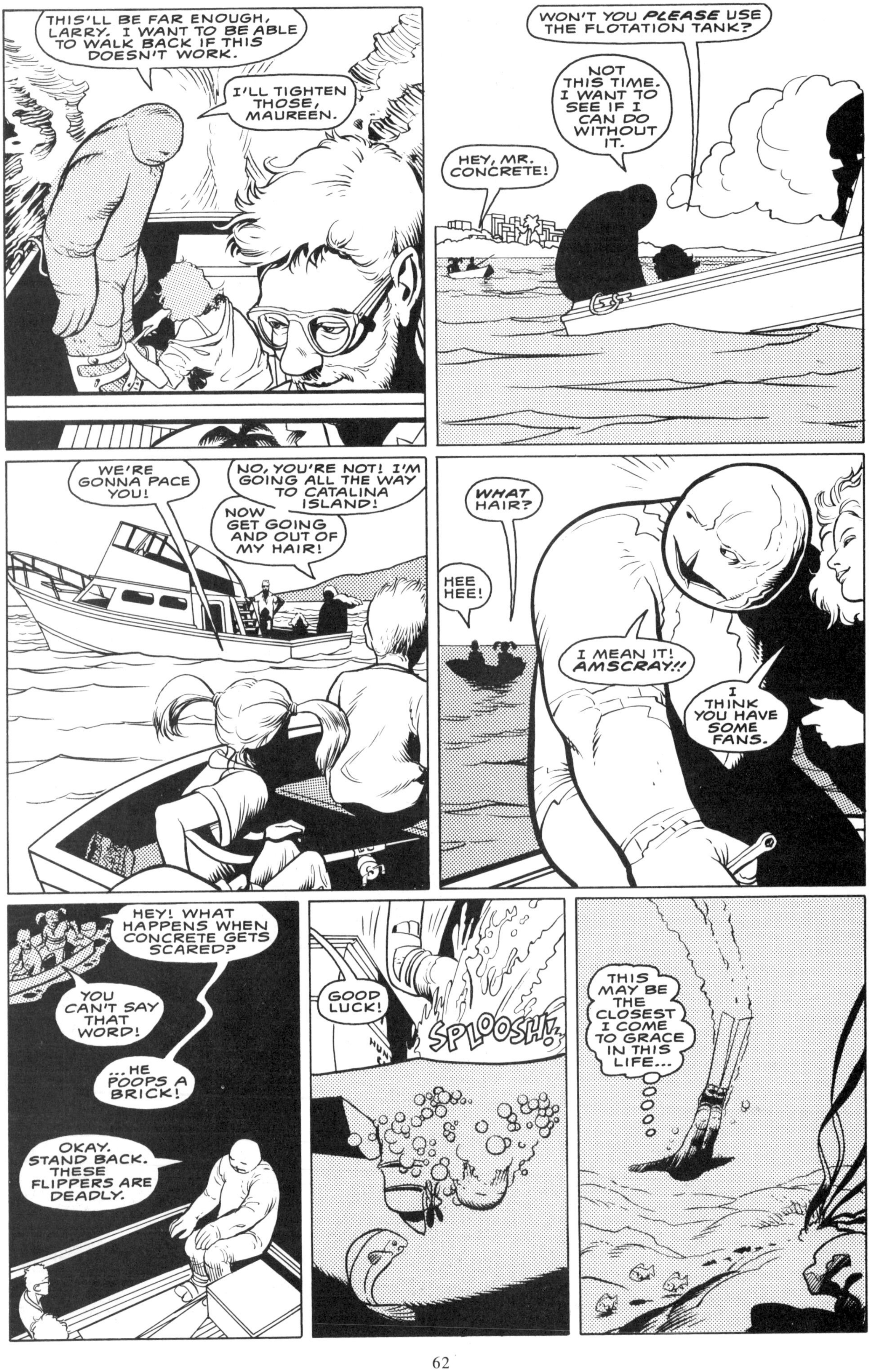
THIS'LL BE FAR ENOUGH, LARRY. I WANT TO BE ABLE TO WALK BACK IF THIS DOESN'T WORK.
I'LL TIGHTEN THOSE, MAUREEN.
WON'T YOU PLEASE USE THE FLOTATION TANK?
NOT THIS TIME. I WANT TO SEE IF I CAN DO WITHOUT IT.
HEY, MR. CONCRETE!
WE'RE GONNA PACE YOU!
NO, YOU'RE NOT! I'M GOING ALL THE WAY TO CATALINA ISLAND!
NOW GET GOING AND OUT OF MY HAIR!
WHAT HAIR?
HEE HEE!
I MEAN IT! AMSCRAY!!
I THINK YOU HAVE SOME FANS.
HEY! WHAT HAPPENS WHEN CONCRETE GETS SCARED?
YOU CAN'T SAY THAT WORD!
...HE POOPS A BRICK!
OKAY. STAND BACK. THESE FLIPPERS ARE DEADLY.
GOOD LUCK!
SPLOOSH!
THIS MAY BE THE CLOSEST I COME TO GRACE IN THIS LIFE...

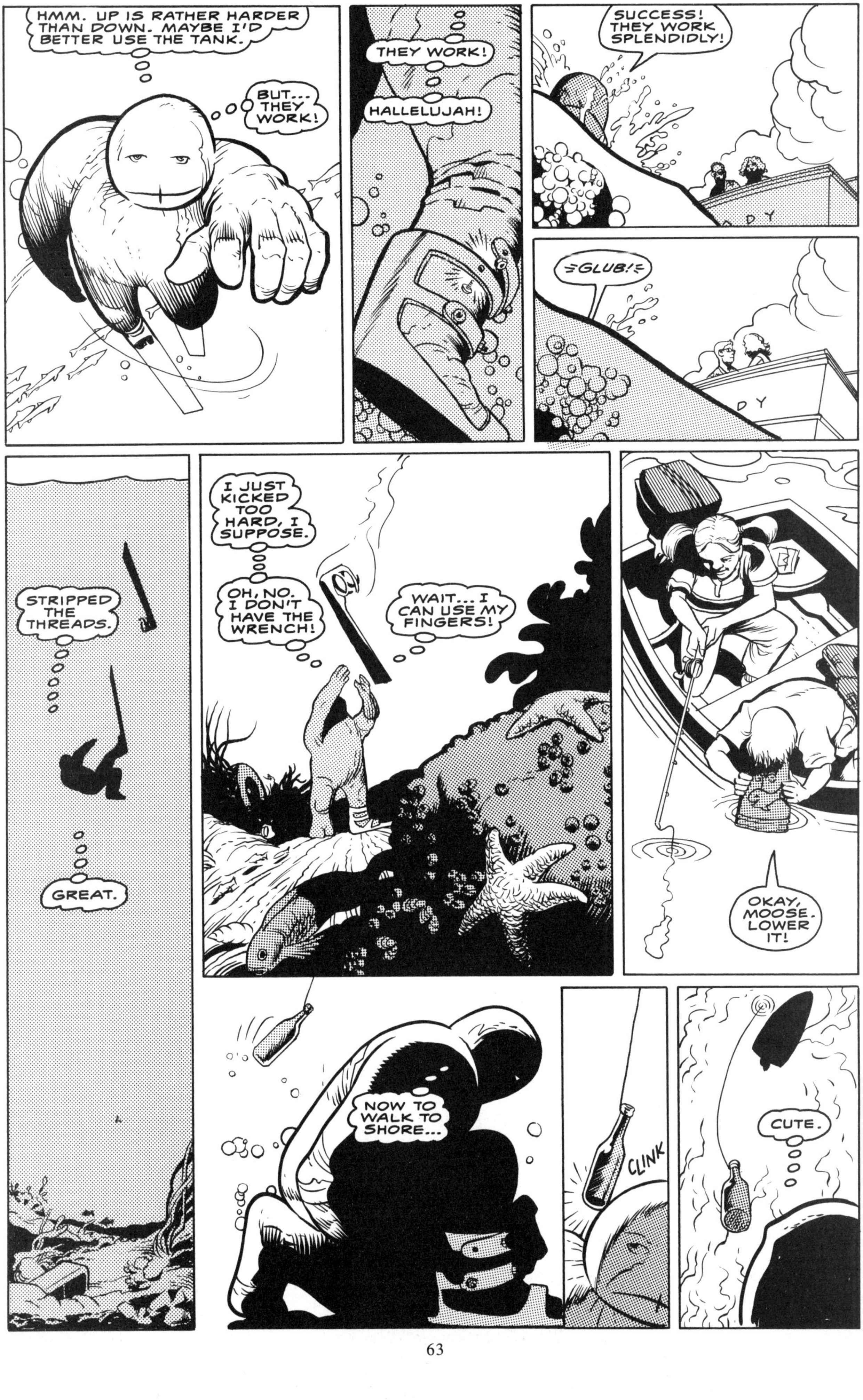
HMM. UP IS RATHER HARDER THAN DOWN. MAYBE I'D BETTER USE THE TANK.
BUT... THEY WORK!
THEY WORK!
HALLELUJAH!
SUCCESS! THEY WORK SPLENDIDLY!
GLUB!
STRIPPED THE THREADS.
GREAT.
I JUST KICKED TOO HARD, I SUPPOSE.
OH, NO. I DON'T HAVE THE WRENCH!
WAIT... I CAN USE MY FINGERS!
OKAY, MOOSE. LOWER IT!
NOW TO WALK TO SHORE...
CLINK
CUTE.

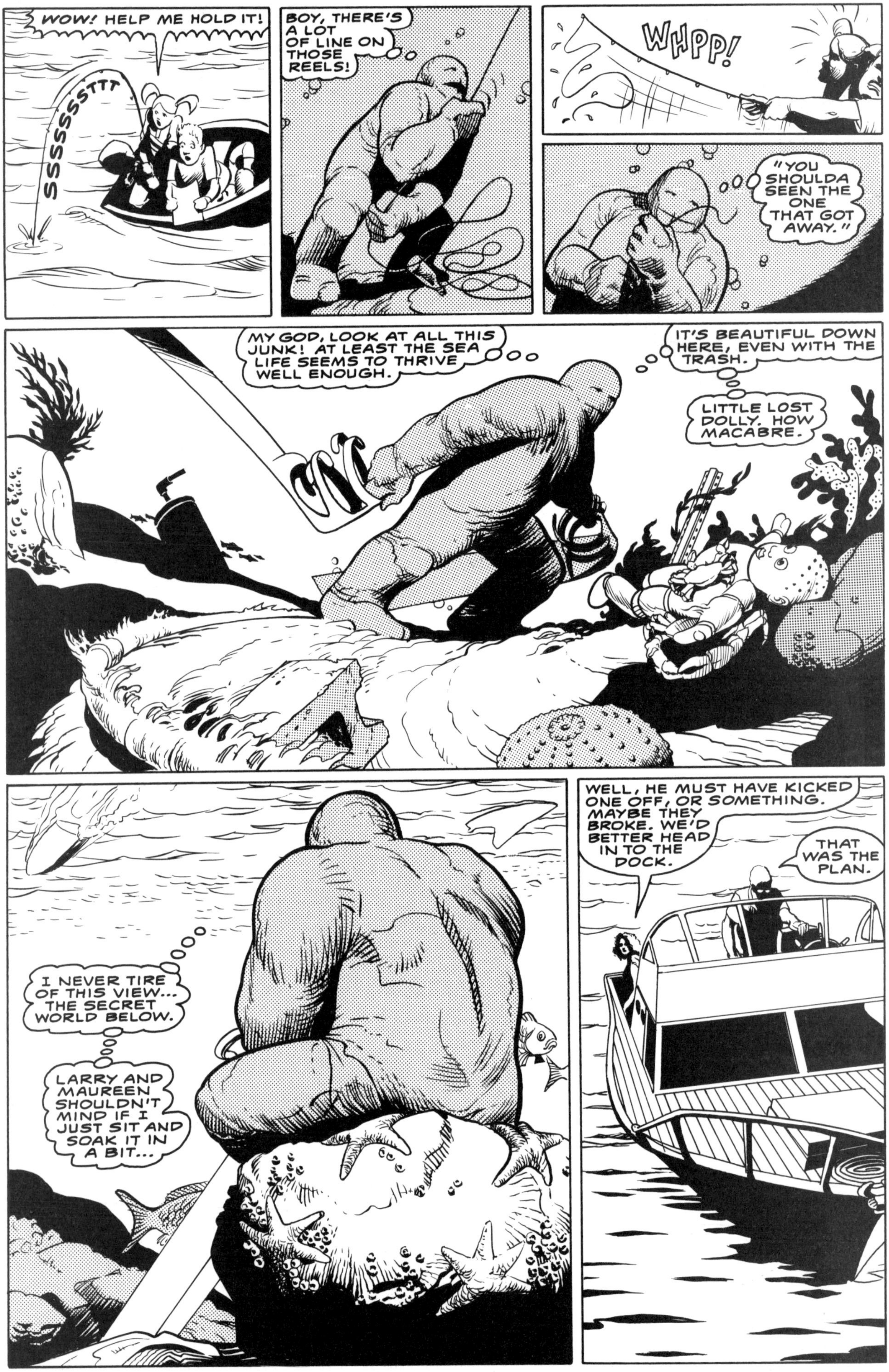
WOW! HELP ME HOLD IT!
SSSSSSSTTT
BOY, THERE'S A LOT OF LINE ON THOSE REELS!
WHPP!
"YOU SHOULDA SEEN THE ONE THAT GOT AWAY."
MY GOD, LOOK AT ALL THIS JUNK! AT LEAST THE SEA LIFE SEEMS TO THRIVE WELL ENOUGH.
IT'S BEAUTIFUL DOWN HERE, EVEN WITH THE TRASH.
LITTLE LOST DOLLY. HOW MACABRE.
I NEVER TIRE OF THIS VIEW... THE SECRET WORLD BELOW.
LARRY AND MAUREEN SHOULDN'T MIND IF I JUST SIT AND SOAK IT IN A BIT...
WELL, HE MUST HAVE KICKED ONE OFF, OR SOMETHING. MAYBE THEY BROKE. WE'D BETTER HEAD IN TO THE DOCK.
THAT WAS THE PLAN.

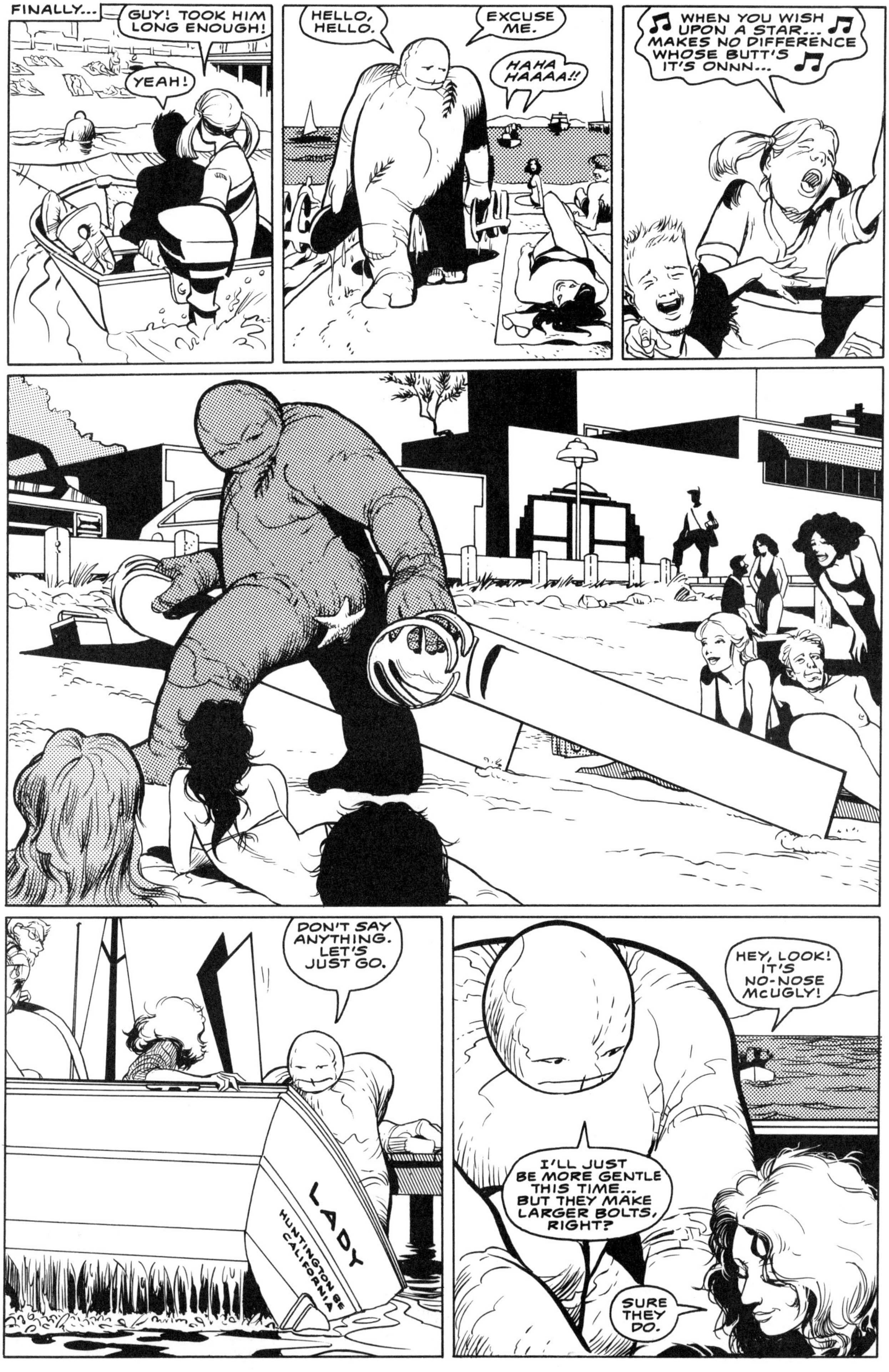
FINALLY...
GUY! TOOK HIM LONG ENOUGH!
YEAH!
HELLO, HELLO.
EXCUSE ME.
HAHA HAAAA!!
WHEN YOU WISH UPON A STAR... MAKES NO DIFFERENCE WHOSE BUTT'S IT'S ONNN...
DON'T SAY ANYTHING. LET'S JUST GO.
LADY
HUNTINGTON BE CALIFORNIA
HEY, LOOK! IT'S NO-NOSE McUGLY!
I'LL JUST BE MORE GENTLE THIS TIME... BUT THEY MAKE LARGER BOLTS, RIGHT?
SURE THEY DO.

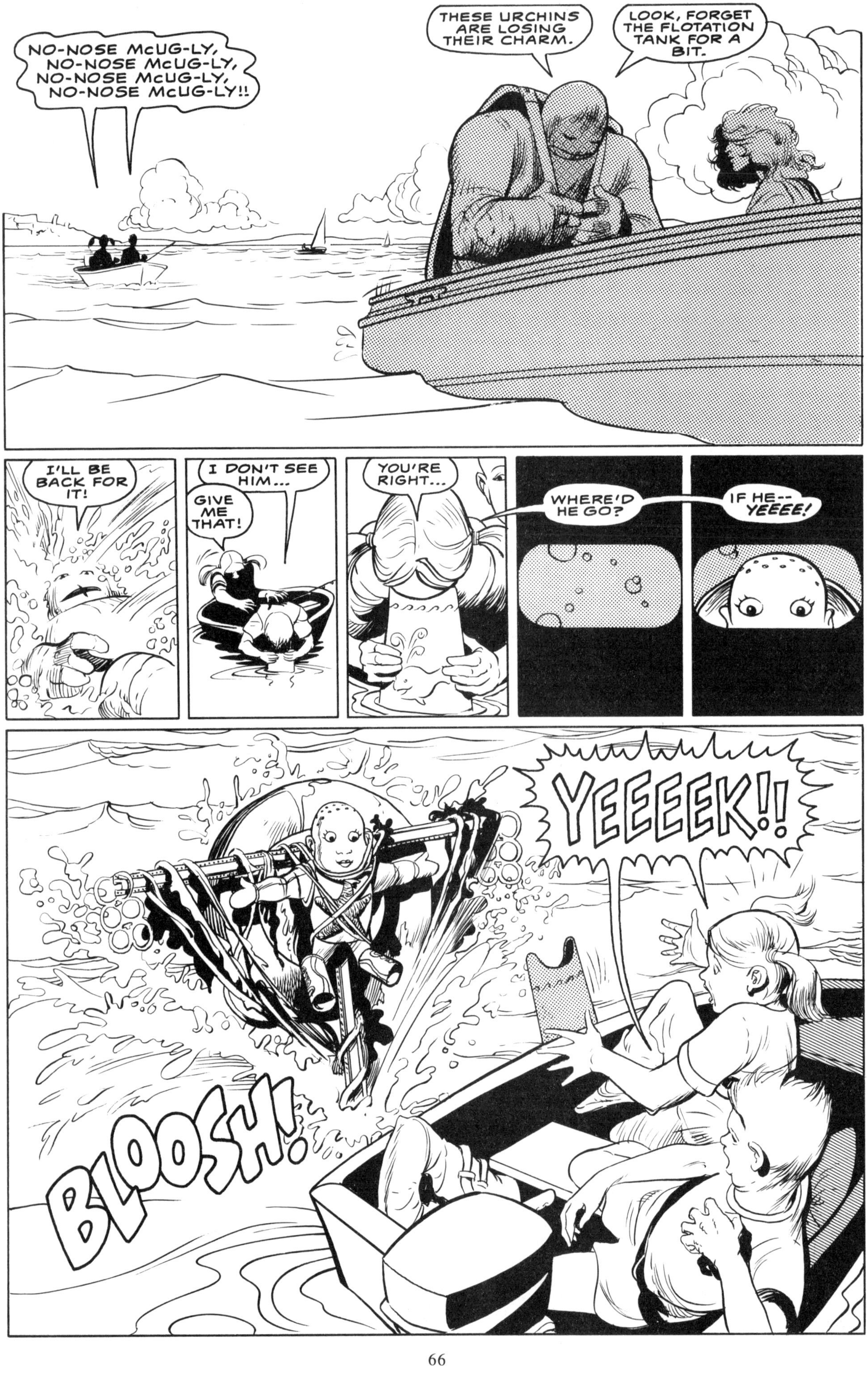
NO-NOSE McUG-LY, NO-NOSE McUG-LY, NO-NOSE McUG-LY, NO-NOSE McUG-LY!!
THESE URCHINS ARE LOSING THEIR CHARM.
LOOK, FORGET THE FLOTATION TANK FOR A BIT.
I'LL BE BACK FOR IT!
I DON'T SEE HIM...
GIVE ME THAT!
YOU'RE RIGHT...
WHERE'D HE GO?
IF HE-- YEEEE!
YEEEEK!!
BLOOSH!

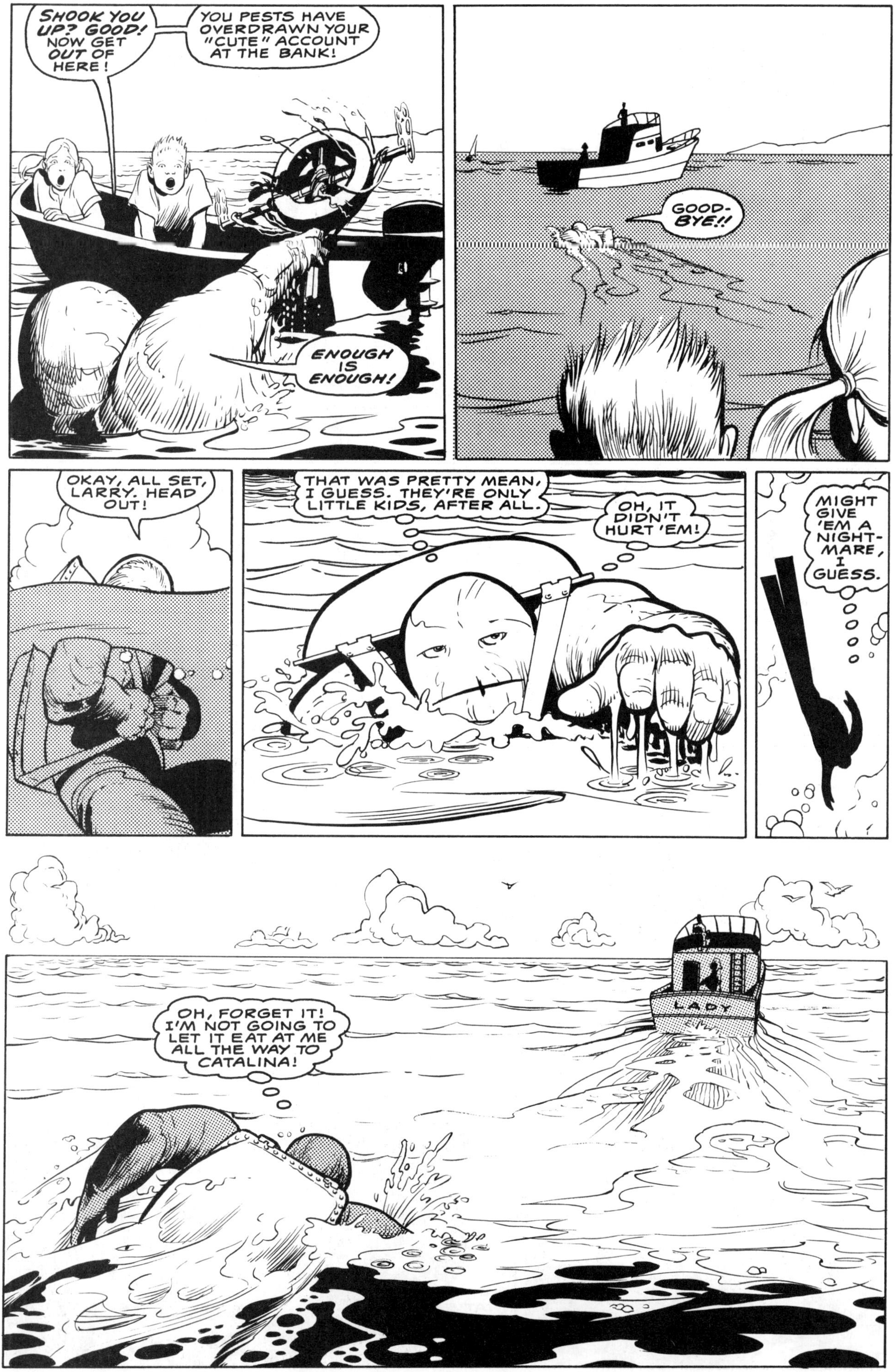
SHOOK YOU UP? GOOD! NOW GET OUT OF HERE!
YOU PESTS HAVE OVERDRAWN YOUR "CUTE" ACCOUNT AT THE BANK!
ENOUGH IS ENOUGH!
GOOD-BYE!!
OKAY, ALL SET, LARRY. HEAD OUT!
THAT WAS PRETTY MEAN, I GUESS. THEY'RE ONLY LITTLE KIDS, AFTER ALL.
OH, IT DIDN'T HURT 'EM!
MIGHT GIVE 'EM A NIGHT-MARE, I GUESS.
OH, FORGET IT! I'M NOT GOING TO LET IT EAT AT ME ALL THE WAY TO CATALINA!
LADY

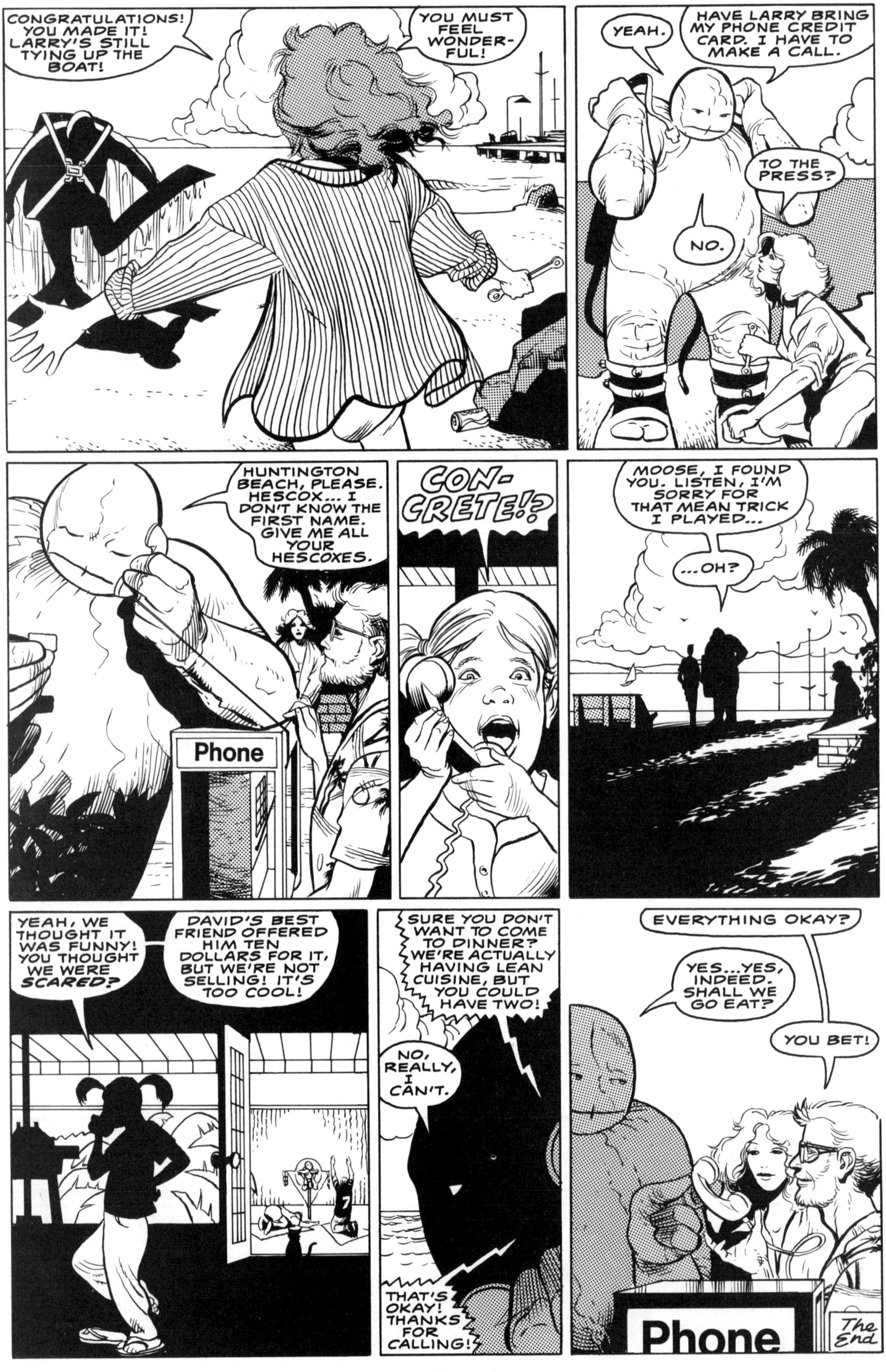
CONGRATULATIONS! YOU MADE IT! LARRY'S STILL TYING UP THE BOAT!
YOU MUST FEEL WONDERFUL!
YEAH.
HAVE LARRY BRING MY PHONE CREDIT CARD. I HAVE TO MAKE A CALL.
TO THE PRESS?
NO.
HUNTINGTON BEACH, PLEASE. HESCOX... I DON'T KNOW THE FIRST NAME. GIVE ME ALL YOUR HESCOXES.
Phone
CON-CRETE!?
MOOSE, I FOUND YOU. LISTEN, I'M SORRY FOR THAT MEAN TRICK I PLAYED...
...OH?
YEAH, WE THOUGHT IT WAS FUNNY! YOU THOUGHT WE WERE SCARED?
DAVID'S BEST FRIEND OFFERED HIM TEN DOLLARS FOR IT, BUT WE'RE NOT SELLING! IT'S TOO COOL!
SURE YOU DON'T WANT TO COME TO DINNER? WE'RE ACTUALLY HAVING LEAN CUISINE, BUT YOU COULD HAVE TWO!
NO, REALLY, I CAN'T.
THAT'S OKAY! THANKS FOR CALLING!
EVERYTHING OKAY?
YES...YES, INDEED. SHALL WE GO EAT?
YOU BET!
Phone
The End

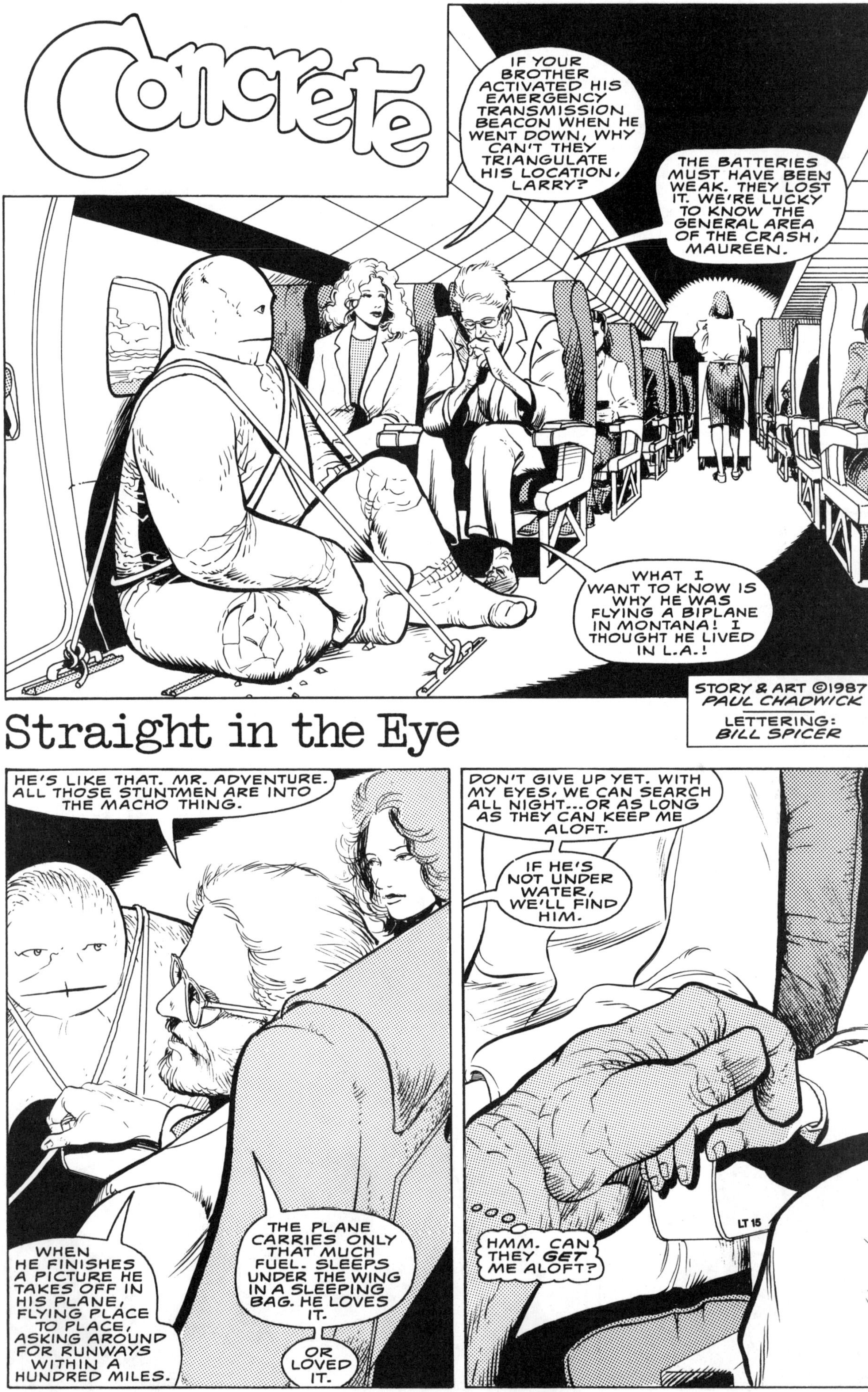
Concrete
IF YOUR BROTHER ACTIVATED HIS EMERGENCY TRANSMISSION BEACON WHEN HE WENT DOWN, WHY CAN'T THEY TRIANGULATE HIS LOCATION, LARRY?
THE BATTERIES MUST HAVE BEEN WEAK. THEY LOST IT. WE'RE LUCKY TO KNOW THE GENERAL AREA OF THE CRASH, MAUREEN.
WHAT I WANT TO KNOW IS WHY HE WAS FLYING A BIPLANE IN MONTANA! I THOUGHT HE LIVED IN L.A.!
STORY & ART ©1987 PAUL CHADWICK
LETTERING: BILL SPICER
Straight in the Eye
HE'S LIKE THAT. MR. ADVENTURE. ALL THOSE STUNTMEN ARE INTO THE MACHO THING.
WHEN HE FINISHES A PICTURE HE TAKES OFF IN HIS PLANE, FLYING PLACE TO PLACE, ASKING AROUND FOR RUNWAYS WITHIN A HUNDRED MILES.
THE PLANE CARRIES ONLY THAT MUCH FUEL. SLEEPS UNDER THE WING IN A SLEEPING BAG. HE LOVES IT.
OR LOVED IT.
DON'T GIVE UP YET. WITH MY EYES, WE CAN SEARCH ALL NIGHT...OR AS LONG AS THEY CAN KEEP ME ALOFT.
IF HE'S NOT UNDER WATER, WE'LL FIND HIM.
HMM. CAN THEY GET ME ALOFT?
LT 15

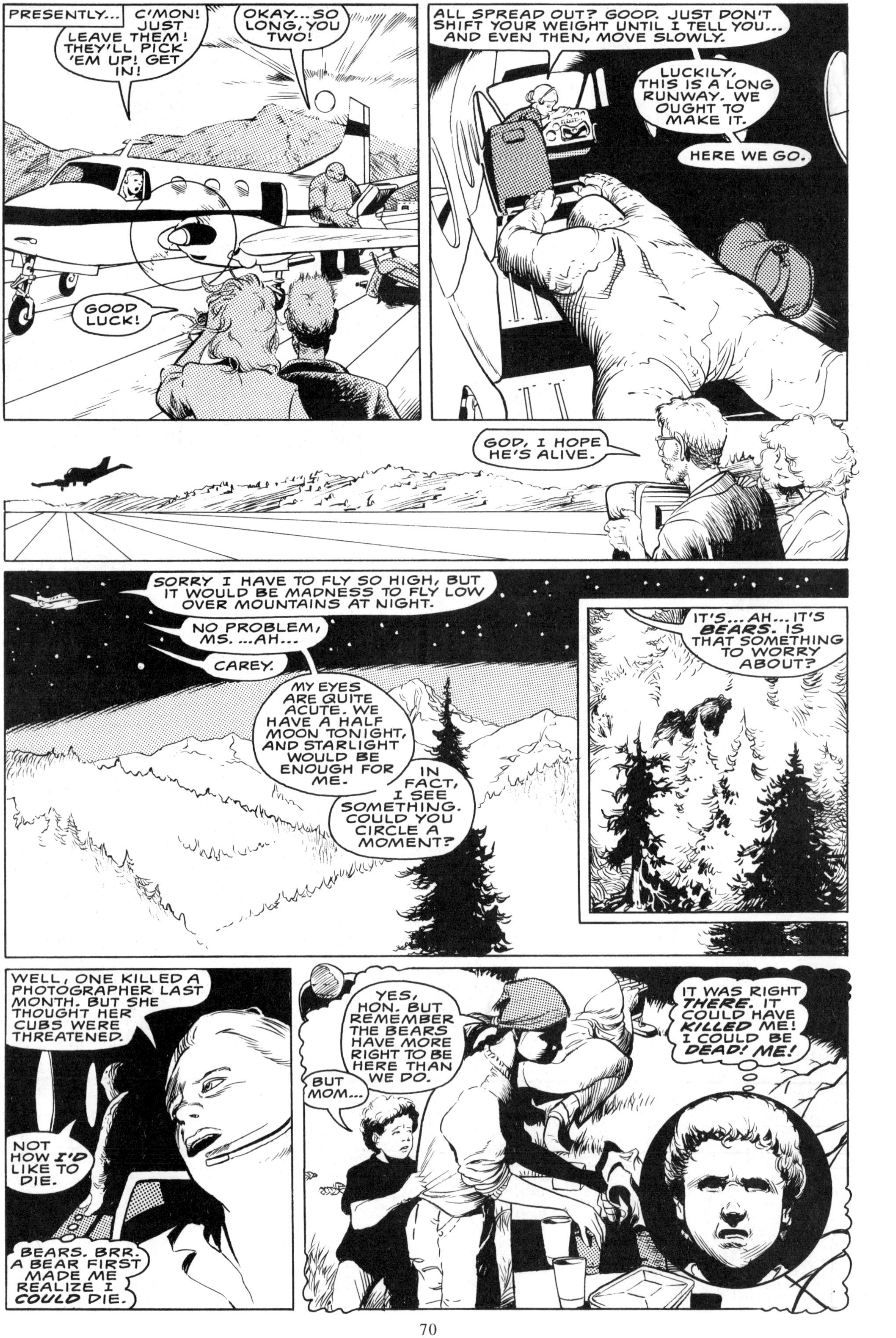
PRESENTLY...
C'MON! JUST LEAVE THEM! THEY'LL PICK 'EM UP! GET IN!
OKAY...SO LONG, YOU TWO!
GOOD LUCK!
ALL SPREAD OUT? GOOD. JUST DON'T SHIFT YOUR WEIGHT UNTIL I TELL YOU... AND EVEN THEN, MOVE SLOWLY.
LUCKILY, THIS IS A LONG RUNWAY. WE OUGHT TO MAKE IT.
HERE WE GO.
GOD, I HOPE HE'S ALIVE.
SORRY I HAVE TO FLY SO HIGH, BUT IT WOULD BE MADNESS TO FLY LOW OVER MOUNTAINS AT NIGHT.
NO PROBLEM, MS. ...AH...
CAREY.
MY EYES ARE QUITE ACUTE. WE HAVE A HALF MOON TONIGHT, AND STARLIGHT WOULD BE ENOUGH FOR ME.
IN FACT, I SEE SOMETHING. COULD YOU CIRCLE A MOMENT?
IT'S... AH... IT'S BEARS. IS THAT SOMETHING TO WORRY ABOUT?
WELL, ONE KILLED A PHOTOGRAPHER LAST MONTH. BUT SHE THOUGHT HER CUBS WERE THREATENED.
NOT HOW I'D LIKE TO DIE.
BEARS. BRR. A BEAR FIRST MADE ME REALIZE I COULD DIE.
YES, HON. BUT REMEMBER THE BEARS HAVE MORE RIGHT TO BE HERE THAN WE DO.
BUT MOM...
IT WAS RIGHT THERE. IT COULD HAVE KILLED ME! I COULD BE DEAD! ME!

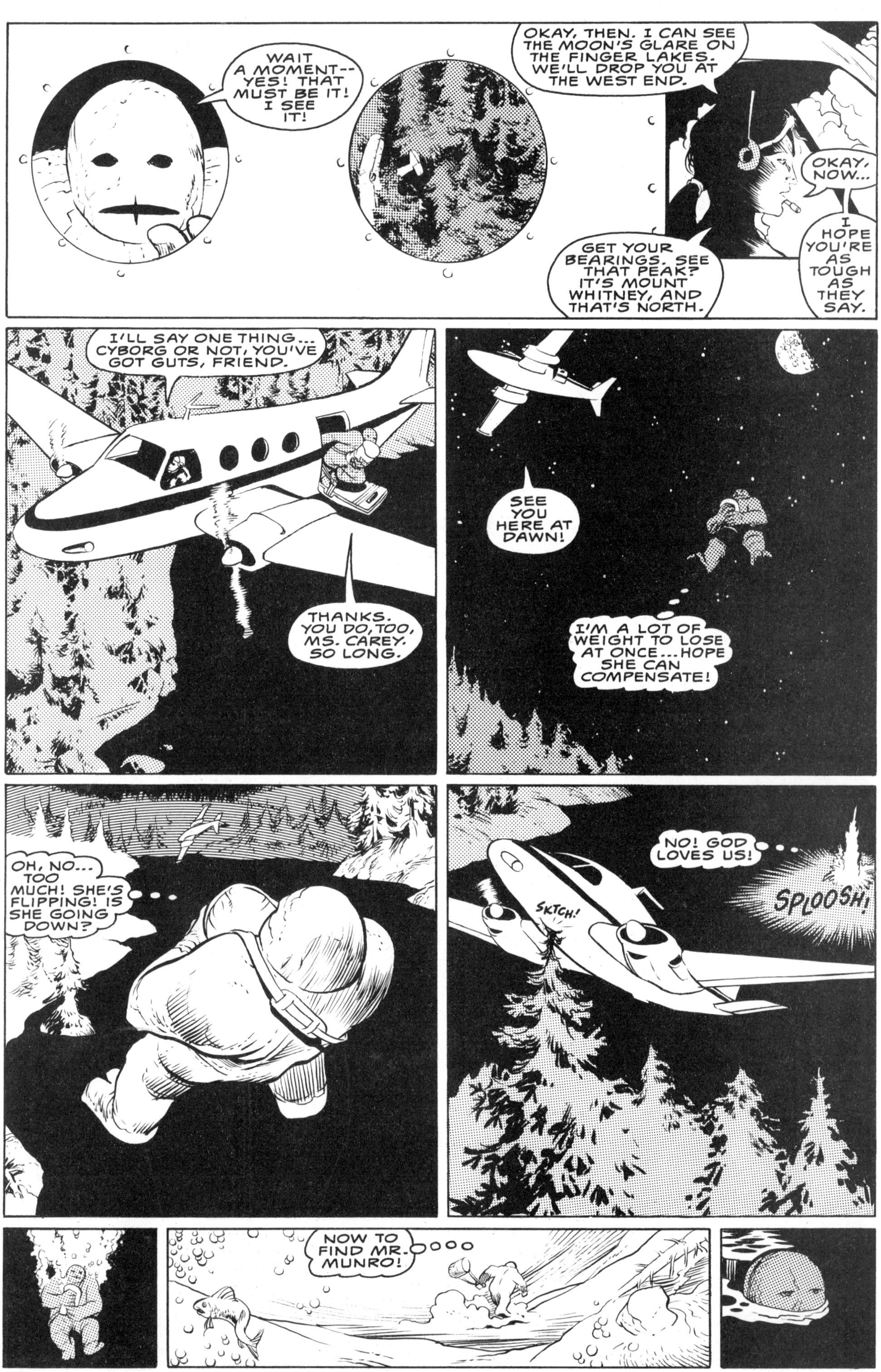
WAIT A MOMENT-- YES! THAT MUST BE IT! I SEE IT!
OKAY, THEN. I CAN SEE THE MOON'S GLARE ON THE FINGER LAKES. WE'LL DROP YOU AT THE WEST END.
OKAY, NOW...
GET YOUR BEARINGS. SEE THAT PEAK? IT'S MOUNT WHITNEY, AND THAT'S NORTH.
I HOPE YOU'RE AS TOUGH AS THEY SAY.
I'LL SAY ONE THING... CYBORG OR NOT, YOU'VE GOT GUTS, FRIEND.
THANKS. YOU DO, TOO, MS. CAREY. SO LONG.
SEE YOU HERE AT DAWN!
I'M A LOT OF WEIGHT TO LOSE AT ONCE... HOPE SHE CAN COMPENSATE!
OH, NO... TOO MUCH! SHE'S FLIPPING! IS SHE GOING DOWN?
NO! GOD LOVES US!
SKTCH!
SPLOOSH!
NOW TO FIND MR. MUNRO!

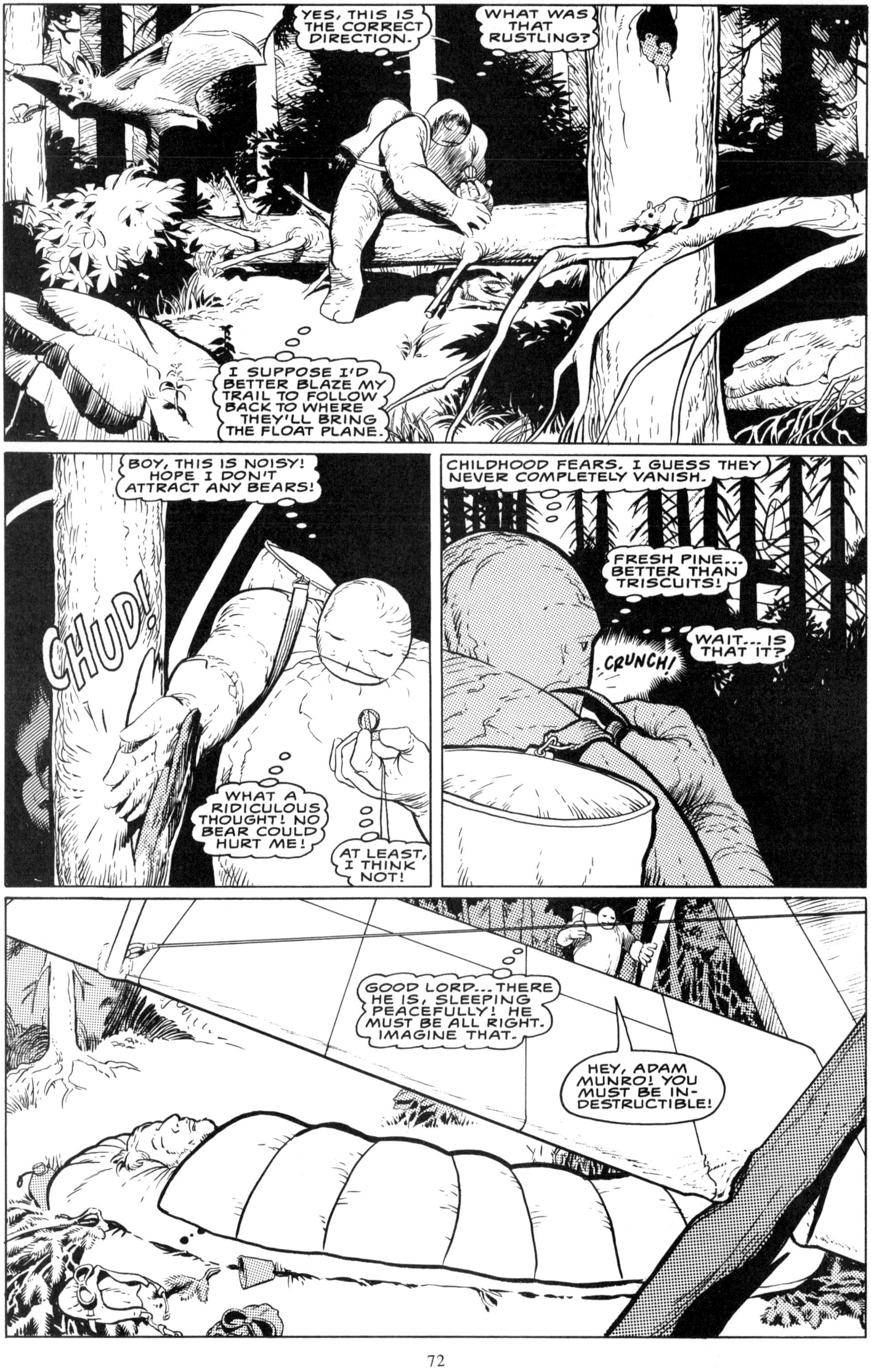
YES, THIS IS THE CORRECT DIRECTION.
WHAT WAS THAT RUSTLING?
I SUPPOSE I'D BETTER BLAZE MY TRAIL TO FOLLOW BACK TO WHERE THEY'LL BRING THE FLOAT PLANE.
BOY, THIS IS NOISY! HOPE I DON'T ATTRACT ANY BEARS!
CHUD!
WHAT A RIDICULOUS THOUGHT! NO BEAR COULD HURT ME!
AT LEAST, I THINK NOT!
CHILDHOOD FEARS. I GUESS THEY NEVER COMPLETELY VANISH.
FRESH PINE... BETTER THAN TRISCUITS!
CRUNCH!
WAIT... IS THAT IT?
GOOD LORD... THERE HE IS, SLEEPING PEACEFULLY! HE MUST BE ALL RIGHT. IMAGINE THAT.
HEY, ADAM MUNRO! YOU MUST BE IN-DESTRUCTIBLE!

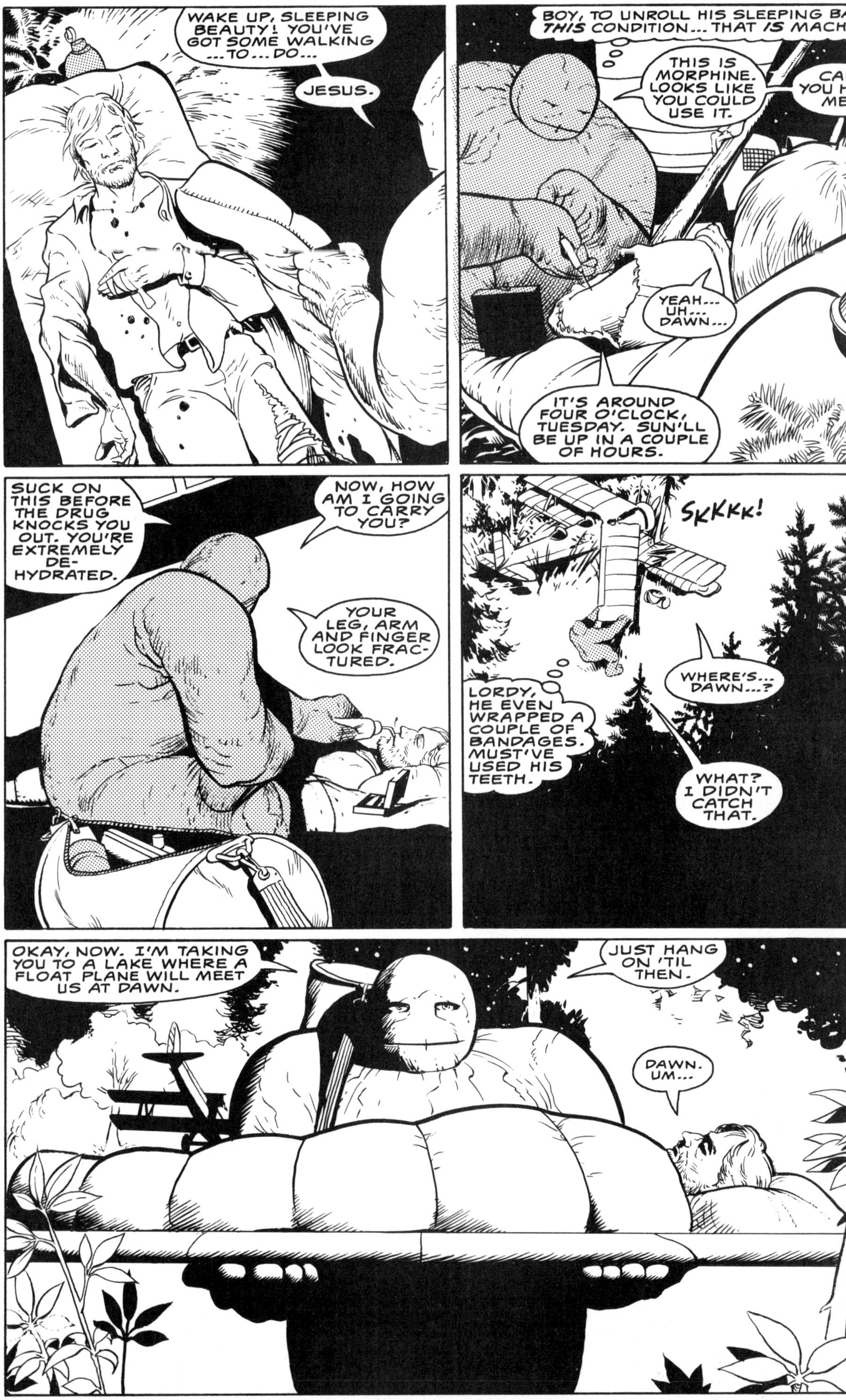
WAKE UP, SLEEPING BEAUTY! YOU'VE GOT SOME WALKING ...TO...DO...
JESUS.
BOY, TO UNROLL HIS SLEEPING BAG IN *THIS* CONDITION... THAT *IS* MACHO!
THIS IS MORPHINE. LOOKS LIKE YOU COULD USE IT.
CAN YOU HEAR ME?
YEAH... UH... DAWN...
IT'S AROUND FOUR O'CLOCK, TUESDAY. SUN'LL BE UP IN A COUPLE OF HOURS.
SUCK ON THIS BEFORE THE DRUG KNOCKS YOU OUT. YOU'RE EXTREMELY DE-HYDRATED.
NOW, HOW AM I GOING TO CARRY YOU?
YOUR LEG, ARM AND FINGER LOOK FRAC-TURED.
SKKKK!
WHERE'S... DAWN...?
LORDY, HE EVEN WRAPPED A COUPLE OF BANDAGES. MUST'VE USED HIS TEETH.
WHAT? I DIDN'T CATCH THAT.
OKAY, NOW. I'M TAKING YOU TO A LAKE WHERE A FLOAT PLANE WILL MEET US AT DAWN.
JUST HANG ON 'TIL THEN.
DAWN. UM...

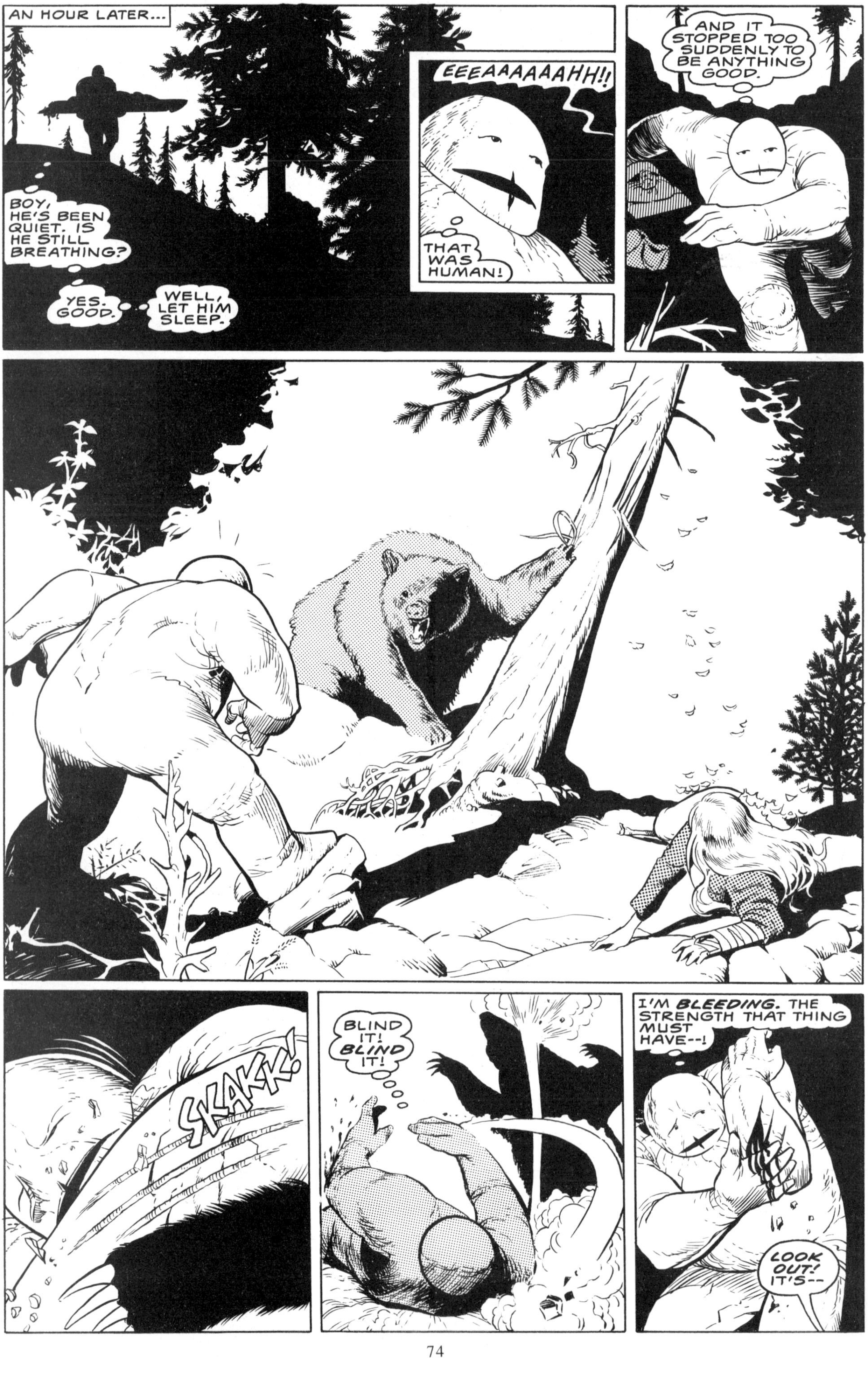
AN HOUR LATER...
BOY, HE'S BEEN QUIET. IS HE STILL BREATHING?
YES. GOOD.
WELL, LET HIM SLEEP.
EEEAAAAAAAHH!!
THAT WAS HUMAN!
AND IT STOPPED TOO SUDDENLY TO BE ANYTHING GOOD.
SKAKK!
BLIND IT! BLIND IT!
I'M BLEEDING. THE STRENGTH THAT THING MUST HAVE--!
LOOK OUT! IT'S--

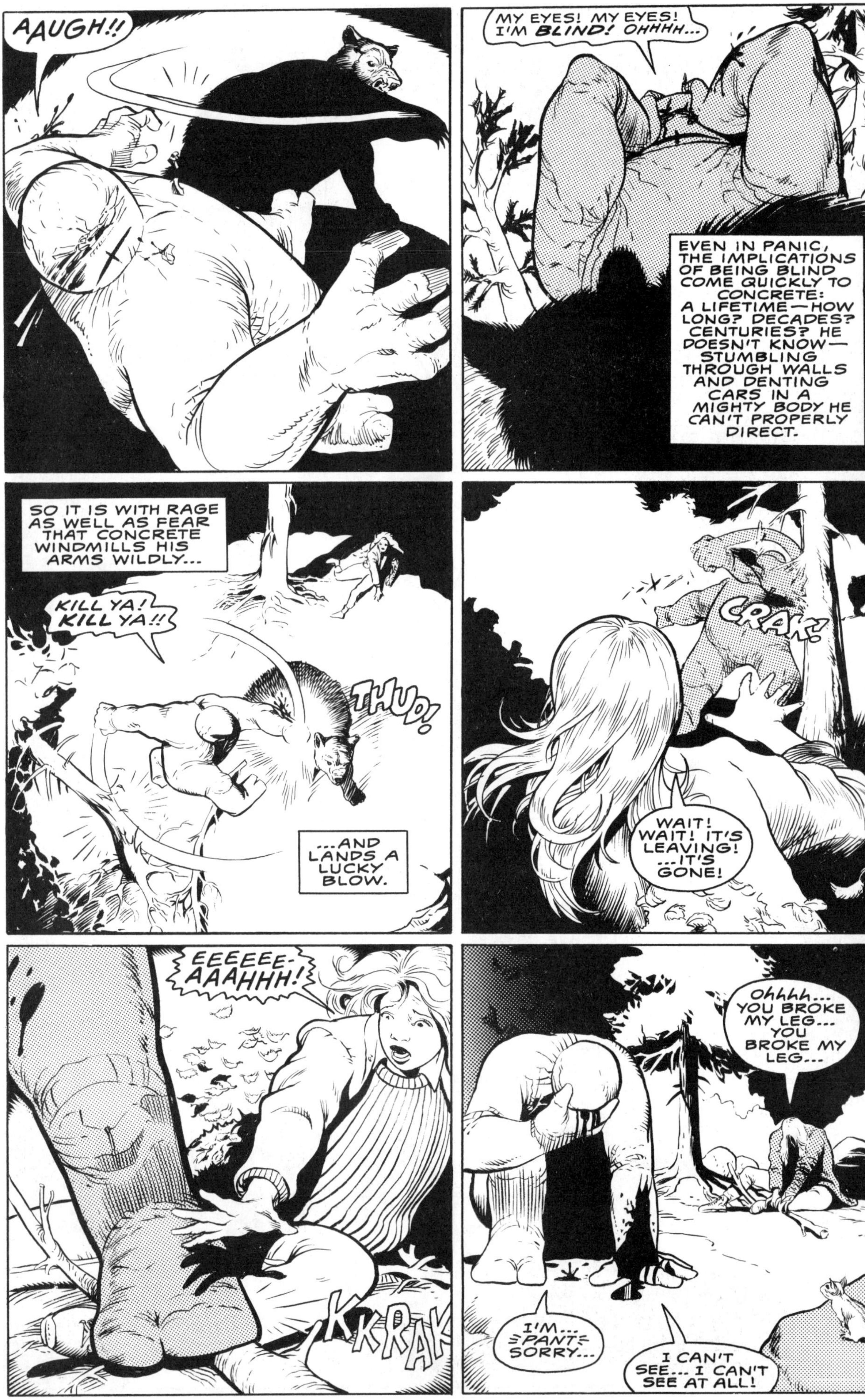
AAUGH!!
MY EYES! MY EYES! I'M BLIND! OHHHH...
EVEN IN PANIC, THE IMPLICATIONS OF BEING BLIND COME QUICKLY TO CONCRETE: A LIFETIME—HOW LONG? DECADES? CENTURIES? HE DOESN'T KNOW—STUMBLING THROUGH WALLS AND DENTING CARS IN A MIGHTY BODY HE CAN'T PROPERLY DIRECT.
SO IT IS WITH RAGE AS WELL AS FEAR THAT CONCRETE WINDMILLS HIS ARMS WILDLY...
KILL YA! KILL YA!!
THUD!
...AND LANDS A LUCKY BLOW.
CRAK!
WAIT! WAIT! IT'S LEAVING! ...IT'S GONE!
EEEEEE-AAAHHHH!
KKRAK
OHHHH... YOU BROKE MY LEG... YOU BROKE MY LEG...
I'M... PANT SORRY...
I CAN'T SEE... I CAN'T SEE AT ALL!

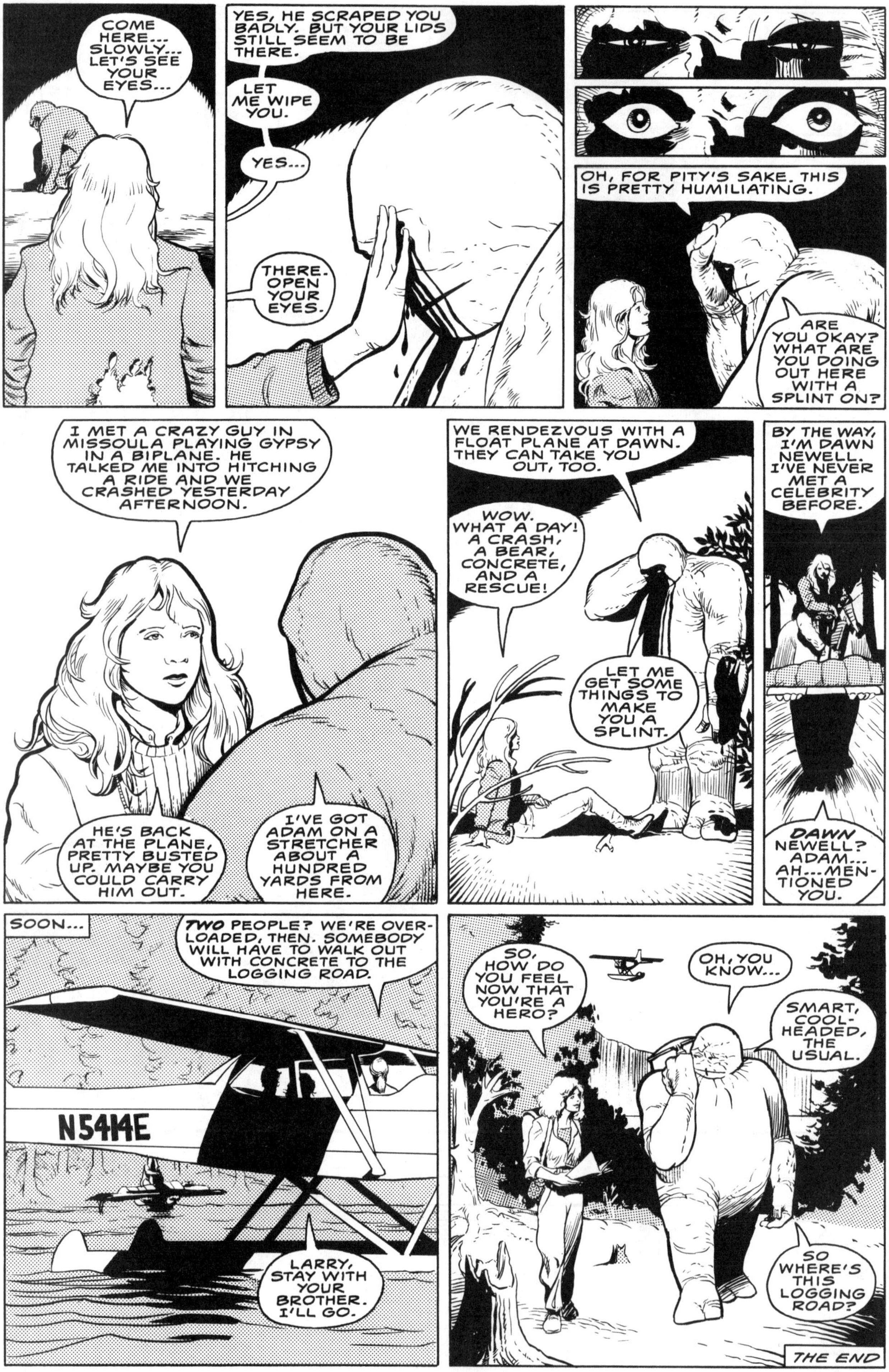
COME HERE... SLOWLY... LET'S SEE YOUR EYES...
YES, HE SCRAPED YOU BADLY. BUT YOUR LIDS STILL SEEM TO BE THERE.
LET ME WIPE YOU.
YES...
THERE. OPEN YOUR EYES.
OH, FOR PITY'S SAKE. THIS IS PRETTY HUMILIATING.
ARE YOU OKAY? WHAT ARE YOU DOING OUT HERE WITH A SPLINT ON?
I MET A CRAZY GUY IN MISSOULA PLAYING GYPSY IN A BIPLANE. HE TALKED ME INTO HITCHING A RIDE AND WE CRASHED YESTERDAY AFTERNOON.
HE'S BACK AT THE PLANE, PRETTY BUSTED UP. MAYBE YOU COULD CARRY HIM OUT.
I'VE GOT ADAM ON A STRETCHER ABOUT A HUNDRED YARDS FROM HERE.
WE RENDEZVOUS WITH A FLOAT PLANE AT DAWN. THEY CAN TAKE YOU OUT, TOO.
WOW. WHAT A DAY! A CRASH, A BEAR, CONCRETE, AND A RESCUE!
LET ME GET SOME THINGS TO MAKE YOU A SPLINT.
BY THE WAY, I'M DAWN NEWELL. I'VE NEVER MET A CELEBRITY BEFORE.
DAWN NEWELL? ADAM... AH... MENTIONED YOU.
SOON...
TWO PEOPLE? WE'RE OVERLOADED, THEN. SOMEBODY WILL HAVE TO WALK OUT WITH CONCRETE TO THE LOGGING ROAD.
N5414E
LARRY, STAY WITH YOUR BROTHER. I'LL GO.
SO, HOW DO YOU FEEL NOW THAT YOU'RE A HERO?
OH, YOU KNOW...
SMART, COOL-HEADED, THE USUAL.
SO WHERE'S THIS LOGGING ROAD?
THE END

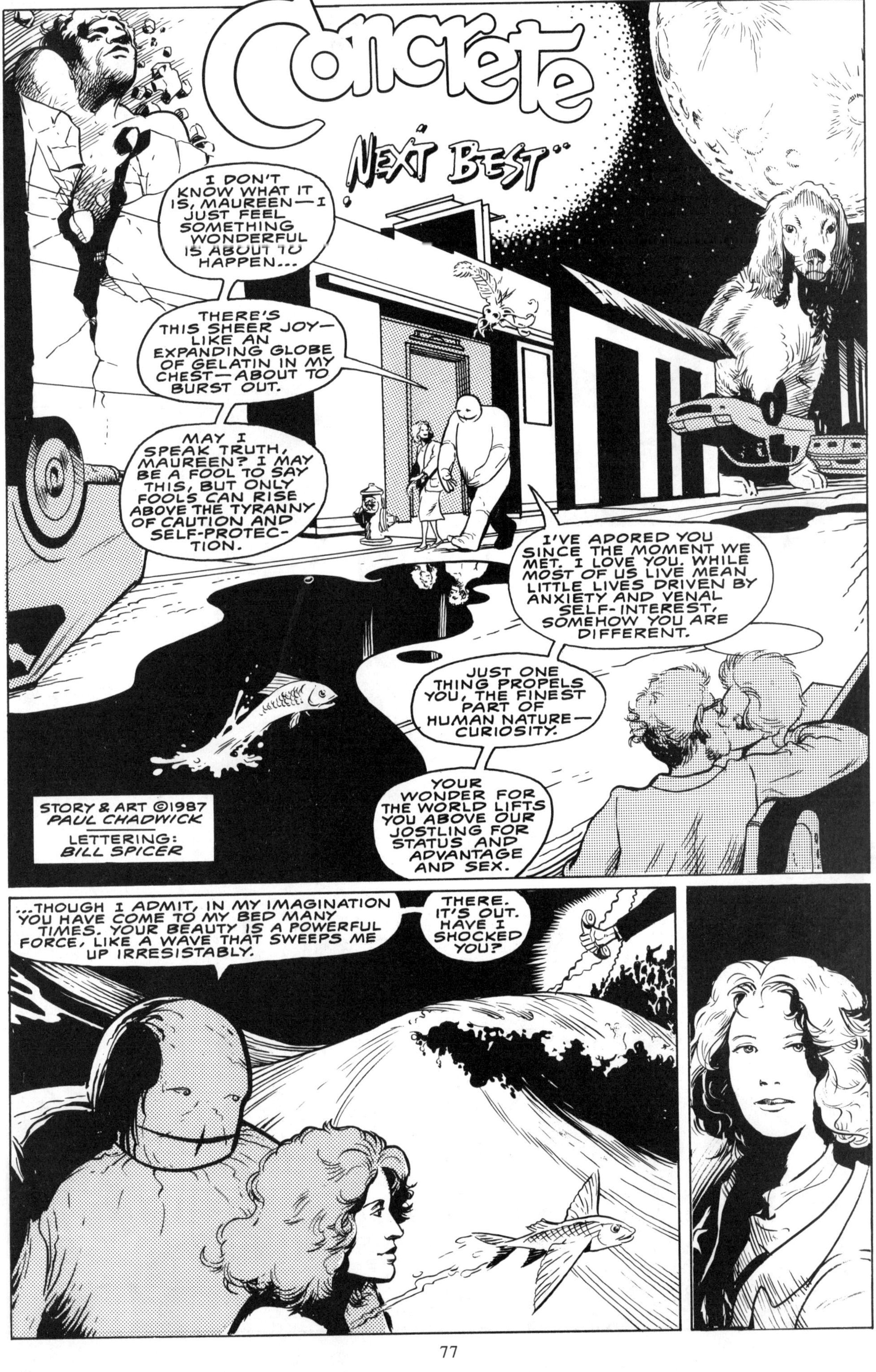
Concrete
"Next Best"
I DON'T KNOW WHAT IT IS, MAUREEN—I JUST FEEL SOMETHING WONDERFUL IS ABOUT TO HAPPEN...
THERE'S THIS SHEER JOY—LIKE AN EXPANDING GLOBE OF GELATIN IN MY CHEST—ABOUT TO BURST OUT.
MAY I SPEAK TRUTH, MAUREEN? I MAY BE A FOOL TO SAY THIS, BUT ONLY FOOLS CAN RISE ABOVE THE TYRANNY OF CAUTION AND SELF-PROTECTION.
I'VE ADORED YOU SINCE THE MOMENT WE MET. I LOVE YOU. WHILE MOST OF US LIVE MEAN LITTLE LIVES DRIVEN BY ANXIETY AND VENAL SELF-INTEREST, SOMEHOW YOU ARE DIFFERENT.
JUST ONE THING PROPELS YOU, THE FINEST PART OF HUMAN NATURE—CURIOSITY.
YOUR WONDER FOR THE WORLD LIFTS YOU ABOVE OUR JOSTLING FOR STATUS AND ADVANTAGE AND SEX.
STORY & ART ©1987 PAUL CHADWICK
LETTERING: BILL SPICER
...THOUGH I ADMIT, IN MY IMAGINATION YOU HAVE COME TO MY BED MANY TIMES. YOUR BEAUTY IS A POWERFUL FORCE, LIKE A WAVE THAT SWEEPS ME UP IRRESISTABLY.
THERE. IT'S OUT. HAVE I SHOCKED YOU?

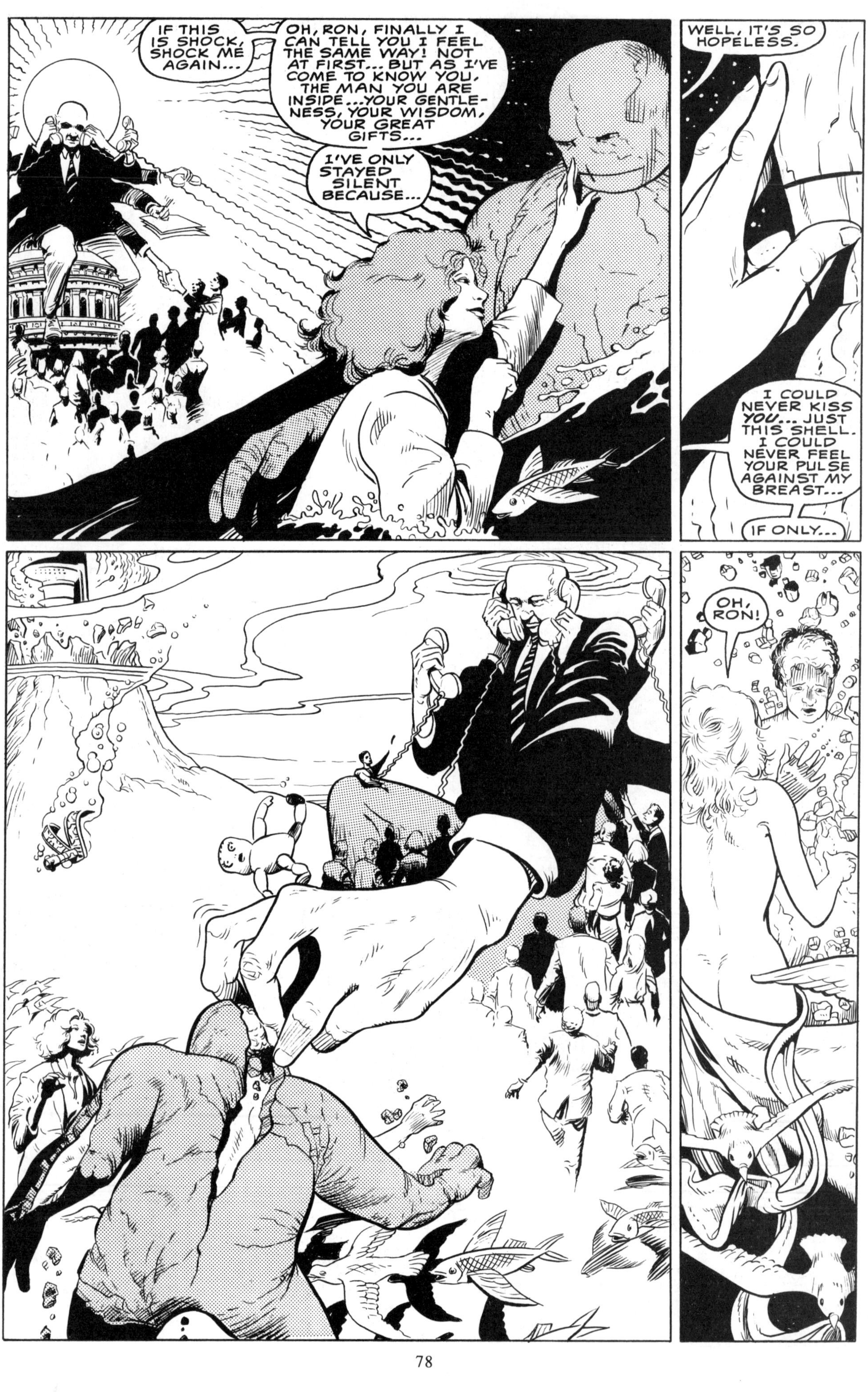
IF THIS IS SHOCK, SHOCK ME AGAIN...
OH, RON, FINALLY I CAN TELL YOU I FEEL THE SAME WAY! NOT AT FIRST... BUT AS I'VE COME TO KNOW YOU, THE MAN YOU ARE INSIDE... YOUR GENTLENESS, YOUR WISDOM, YOUR GREAT GIFTS...
I'VE ONLY STAYED SILENT BECAUSE...
WELL, IT'S SO HOPELESS.
I COULD NEVER KISS *YOU*... JUST THIS SHELL. I COULD NEVER FEEL YOUR PULSE AGAINST MY BREAST...
IF ONLY...
OH, RON!

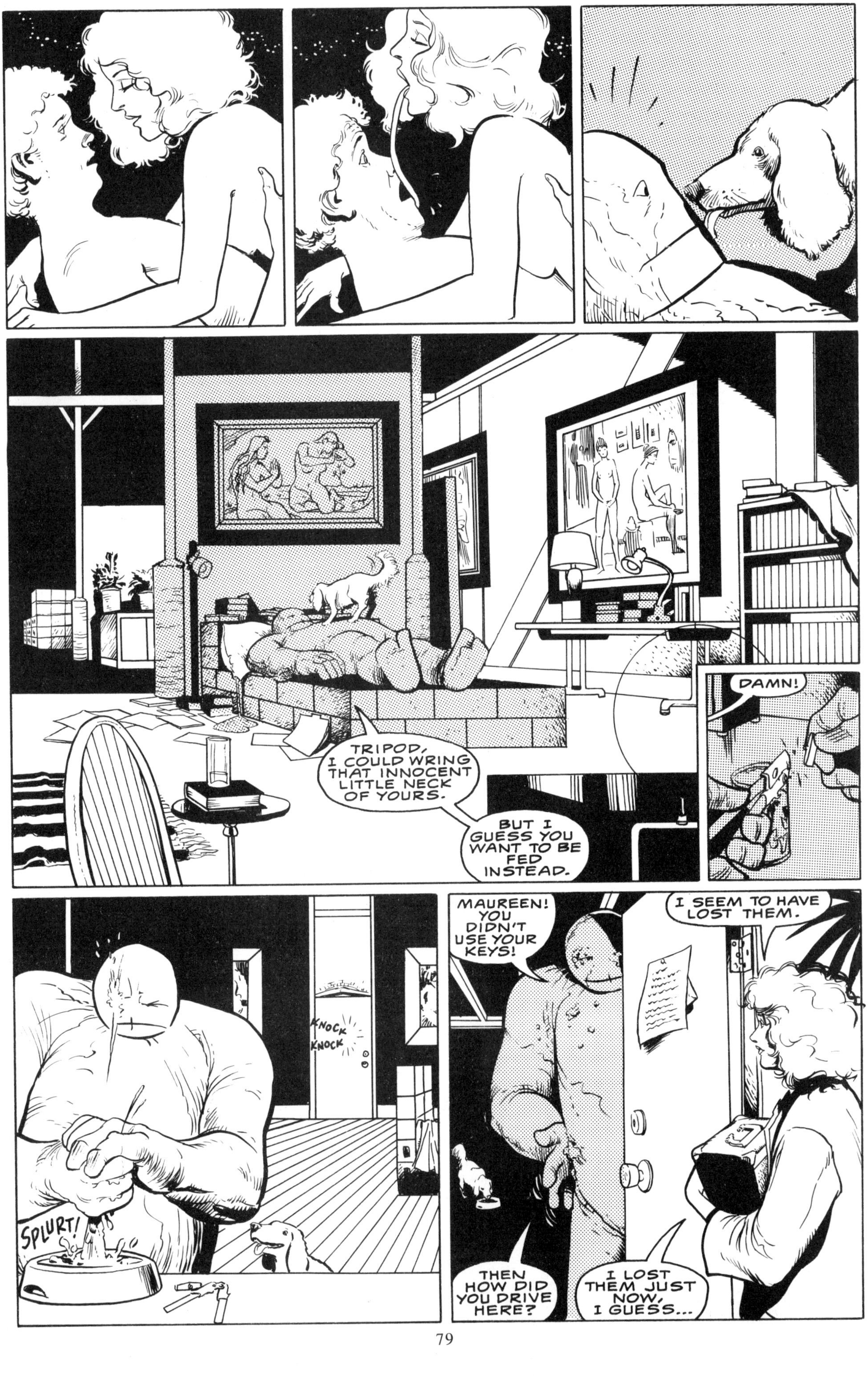
TRIPOD, I COULD WRING THAT INNOCENT LITTLE NECK OF YOURS.
BUT I GUESS YOU WANT TO BE FED INSTEAD.
DAMN!
KNOCK KNOCK
SPLURT!
MAUREEN! YOU DIDN'T USE YOUR KEYS!
I SEEM TO HAVE LOST THEM.
THEN HOW DID YOU DRIVE HERE?
I LOST THEM JUST NOW, I GUESS...

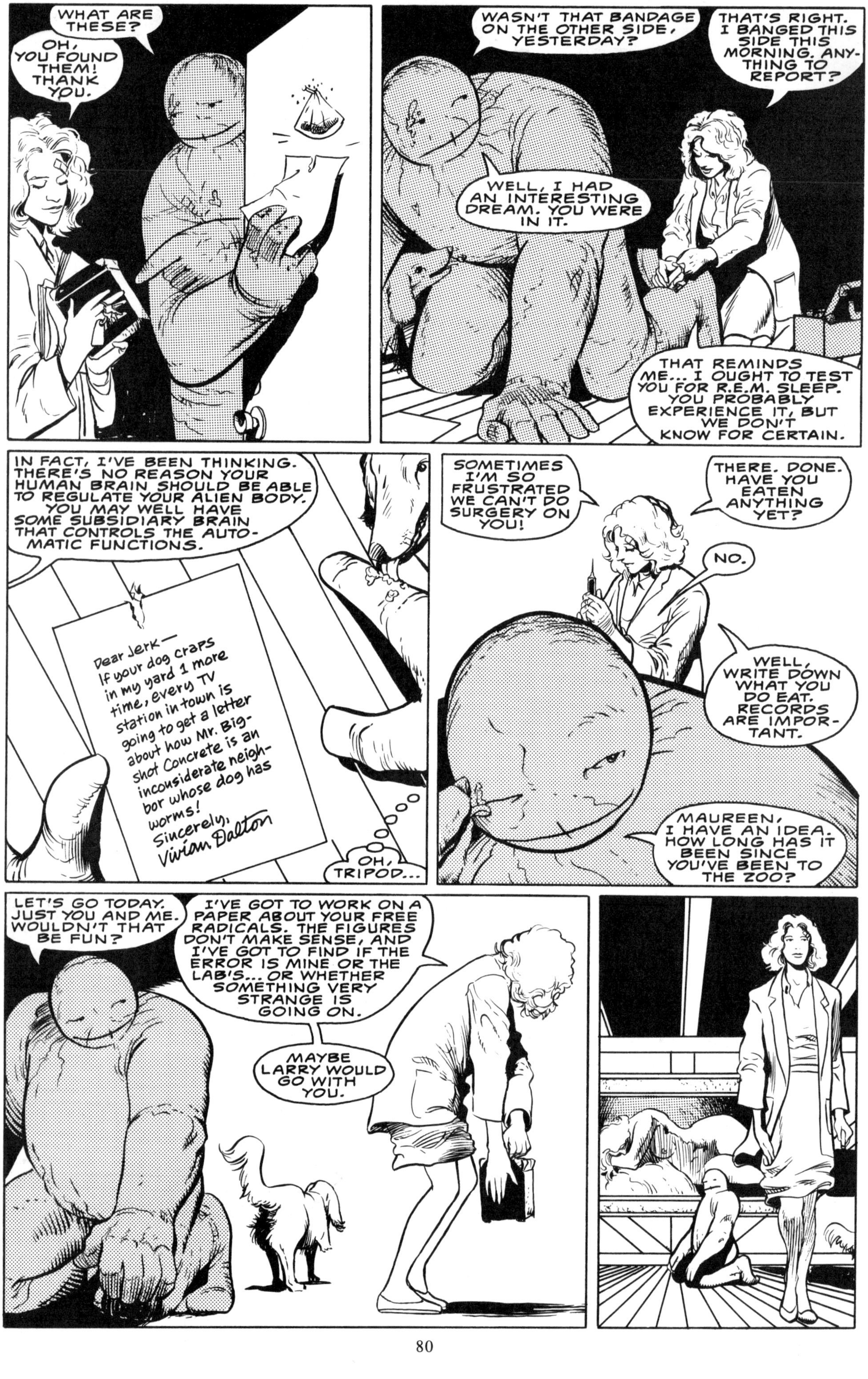
WHAT ARE THESE?
OH, YOU FOUND THEM! THANK YOU.
WASN'T THAT BANDAGE ON THE OTHER SIDE, YESTERDAY?
THAT'S RIGHT. I BANGED THIS SIDE THIS MORNING. ANYTHING TO REPORT?
WELL, I HAD AN INTERESTING DREAM. YOU WERE IN IT.
THAT REMINDS ME... I OUGHT TO TEST YOU FOR R.E.M. SLEEP. YOU PROBABLY EXPERIENCE IT, BUT WE DON'T KNOW FOR CERTAIN.
IN FACT, I'VE BEEN THINKING. THERE'S NO REASON YOUR HUMAN BRAIN SHOULD BE ABLE TO REGULATE YOUR ALIEN BODY. YOU MAY WELL HAVE SOME SUBSIDIARY BRAIN THAT CONTROLS THE AUTOMATIC FUNCTIONS.
Dear Jerk— If your dog craps in my yard 1 more time, every TV station in town is going to get a letter about how Mr. Big-shot Concrete is an inconsiderate neighbor whose dog has worms! Sincerely, Vivian Dalton
OH, TRIPOD...
SOMETIMES I'M SO FRUSTRATED WE CAN'T DO SURGERY ON YOU!
THERE. DONE. HAVE YOU EATEN ANYTHING YET?
NO.
WELL, WRITE DOWN WHAT YOU DO EAT. RECORDS ARE IMPORTANT.
MAUREEN, I HAVE AN IDEA. HOW LONG HAS IT BEEN SINCE YOU'VE BEEN TO THE ZOO?
LET'S GO TODAY. JUST YOU AND ME. WOULDN'T THAT BE FUN?
I'VE GOT TO WORK ON A PAPER ABOUT YOUR FREE RADICALS. THE FIGURES DON'T MAKE SENSE, AND I'VE GOT TO FIND IF THE ERROR IS MINE OR THE LAB'S... OR WHETHER SOMETHING VERY STRANGE IS GOING ON.
MAYBE LARRY WOULD GO WITH YOU.

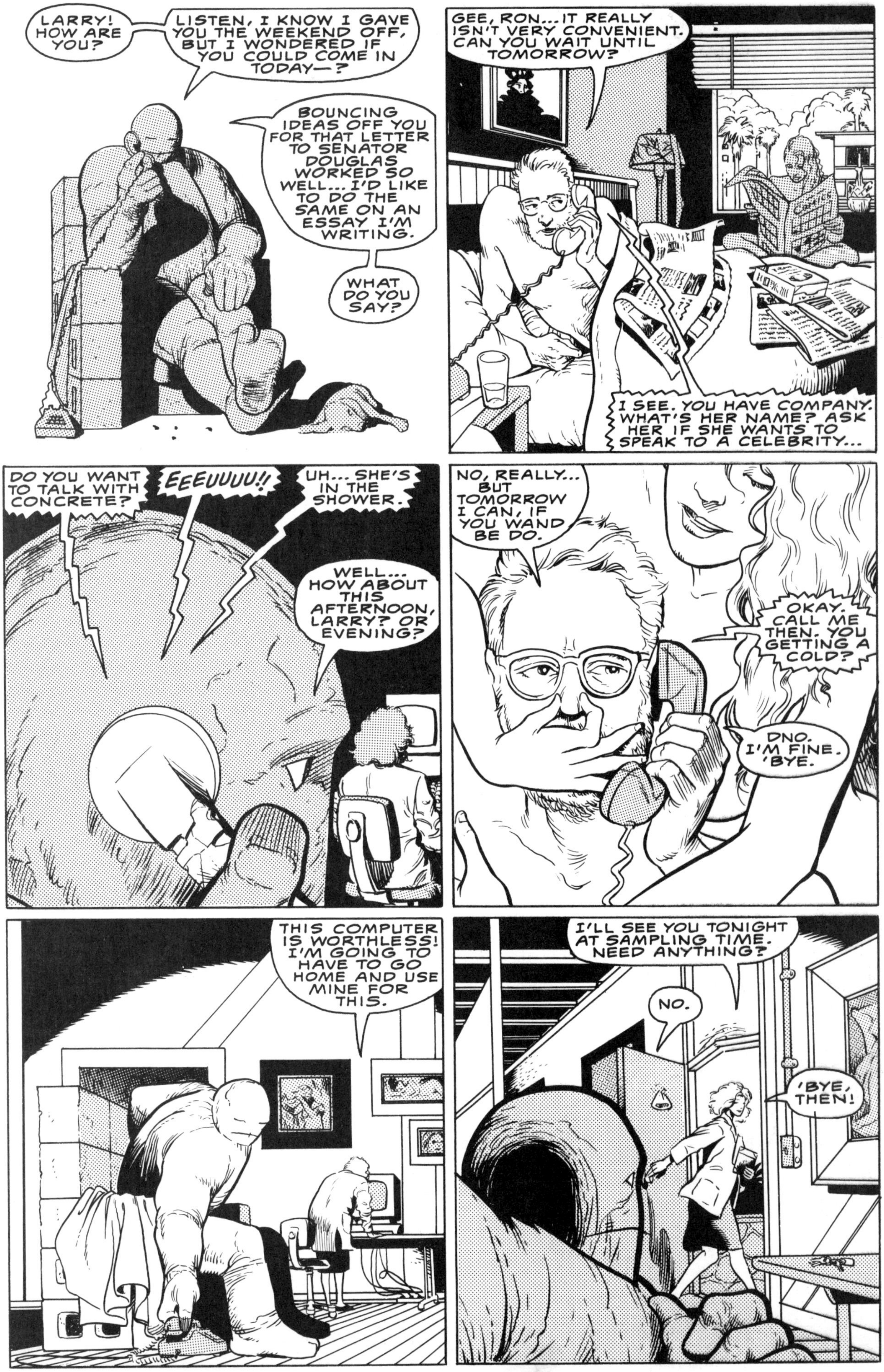
LARRY! HOW ARE YOU?
LISTEN, I KNOW I GAVE YOU THE WEEKEND OFF, BUT I WONDERED IF YOU COULD COME IN TODAY—?
BOUNCING IDEAS OFF YOU FOR THAT LETTER TO SENATOR DOUGLAS WORKED SO WELL... I'D LIKE TO DO THE SAME ON AN ESSAY I'M WRITING.
WHAT DO YOU SAY?
GEE, RON... IT REALLY ISN'T VERY CONVENIENT. CAN YOU WAIT UNTIL TOMORROW?
I SEE. YOU HAVE COMPANY. WHAT'S HER NAME? ASK HER IF SHE WANTS TO SPEAK TO A CELEBRITY...
DO YOU WANT TO TALK WITH CONCRETE?
EEEUUUU!!
UH... SHE'S IN THE SHOWER.
WELL... HOW ABOUT THIS AFTERNOON, LARRY? OR EVENING?
NO, REALLY... BUT TOMORROW I CAN, IF YOU WAND BE DO.
OKAY. CALL ME THEN. YOU GETTING A COLD?
DNO. I'M FINE. 'BYE.
THIS COMPUTER IS WORTHLESS! I'M GOING TO HAVE TO GO HOME AND USE MINE FOR THIS.
I'LL SEE YOU TONIGHT AT SAMPLING TIME. NEED ANYTHING?
NO.
'BYE, THEN!

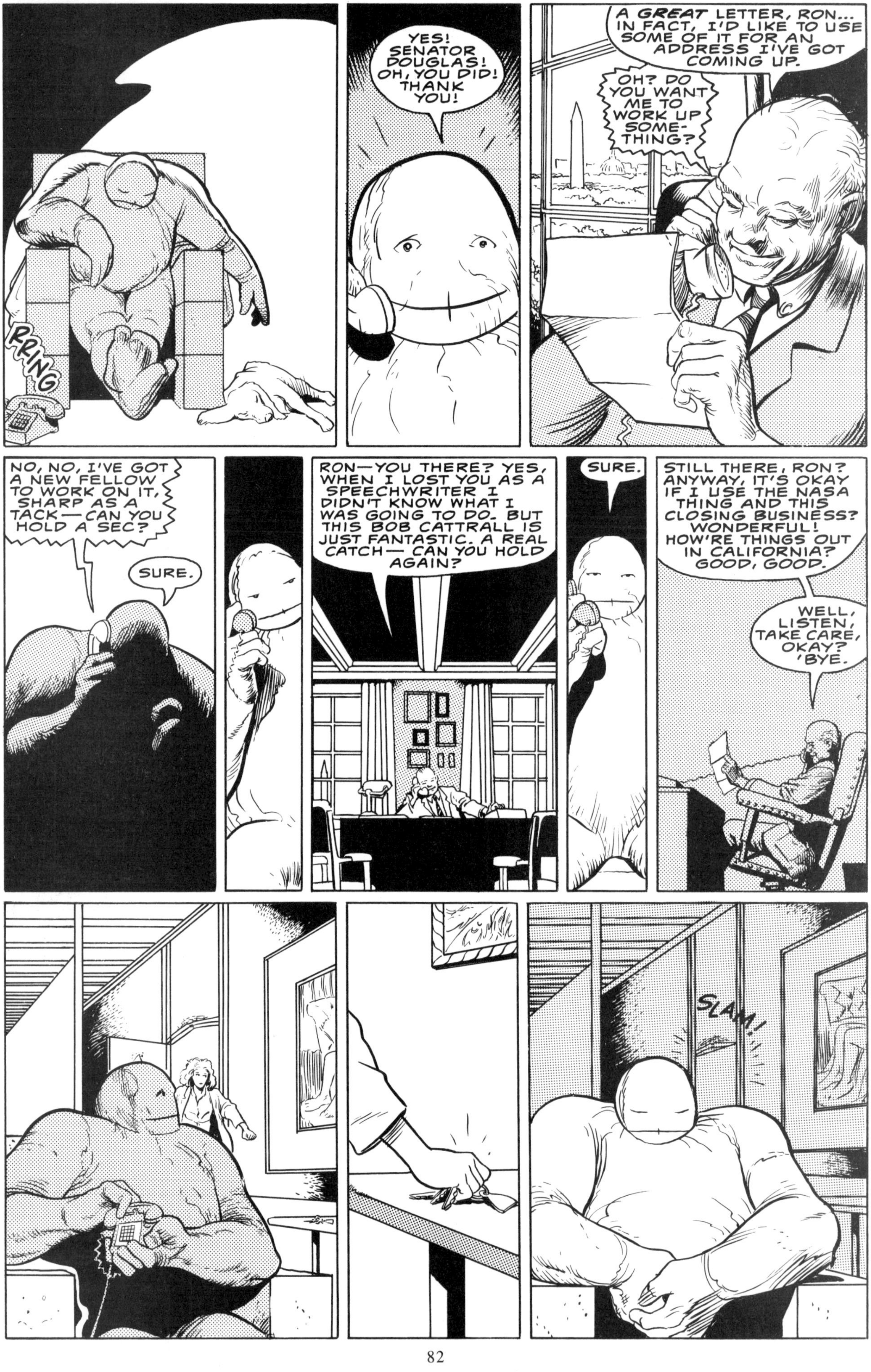
RRING
YES! SENATOR DOUGLAS! OH, YOU DID! THANK YOU!
A GREAT LETTER, RON... IN FACT, I'D LIKE TO USE SOME OF IT FOR AN ADDRESS I'VE GOT COMING UP.
OH? DO YOU WANT ME TO WORK UP SOME-THING?
NO, NO, I'VE GOT A NEW FELLOW TO WORK ON IT, SHARP AS A TACK— CAN YOU HOLD A SEC?
SURE.
RON—YOU THERE? YES, WHEN I LOST YOU AS A SPEECHWRITER I DIDN'T KNOW WHAT I WAS GOING TO DO. BUT THIS BOB CATTRALL IS JUST FANTASTIC. A REAL CATCH— CAN YOU HOLD AGAIN?
SURE.
STILL THERE, RON? ANYWAY, IT'S OKAY IF I USE THE NASA THING AND THIS CLOSING BUSINESS? WONDERFUL! HOW'RE THINGS OUT IN CALIFORNIA? GOOD, GOOD.
WELL, LISTEN, TAKE CARE, OKAY? 'BYE.
SLAM!

WELL, WHAT HAVE WE GOT HERE...

...MORE PICTURES FROM MS. STRANGEHANDS. LOVE THAT NAME.

OKAY, LARRY, WHEN YOU TYPE THESE UP *PLEASE* STICK REASONABLY CLOSE TO WHAT I SAY. I DON'T MIND A LITTLE POLISH, BUT FLIGHTS OF PROSE ARE A BIT MUCH.

FIRST, TO OUR FAITHFUL CORRESPONDENT MELISSA STRANGEHANDS...

THANK YOU FOR YOUR LATEST PICTURES. THIS CROPPING IDEA IS QUITE INTERESTING, AND I CONTINUE TO ENJOY YOUR ARTISTIC EVOLUTION. I REMAIN FLATTERED THAT YOU HAVE CHOSEN ME AS YOUR SUBJECT.

I'M SORRY TO DISAPPOINT YOU AGAIN, BUT I WILL NOT BE ABLE TO POSE FOR YOU IN THE NEAR FUTURE. SINCERELY...

I SWEAR, LARRY, ANY WOMAN SO FASCINATED WITH ME HAS TO BE SOME KIND OF KOOK.

AND NEXT...OH, LORDY!

OKAY... DEAR MR. JOHNSON: YOUR ACCUSATIONS OF MY INVOLVEMENT WITH ANY INTERNATIONAL JEWISH CONSPIRACY ARE ABSURD. MY WORK WITH THE TRILATERAL COMMISION AND THE SONS OF THE ILLUMINATI TAKES FAR TOO MUCH TIME TO ALLOW...

ON SECOND THOUGHT, DON'T ANSWER THIS ONE. JUST FILE IT UNDER "HOSTILE NUTS."

NOW WHAT'S THIS—?

"DEAR CONCRETE: I HOPE YOU DON'T THINK IT ODD THAT WE TURN TO YOU. I HOPE YOU WILL SEE THIS AS A CHANCE TO MAKE A DIFFERENCE. IT IS A CHANCE TO HELP SOME PEOPLE WHO NEED YOU. YOU HAVE IMPRESSED US EVEN ON THE MOST SUPERFICIAL, GLITZY TALK SHOWS...

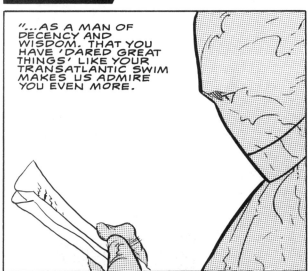

"...AS A MAN OF DECENCY AND WISDOM. THAT YOU HAVE 'DARED GREAT THINGS' LIKE YOUR TRANSATLANTIC SWIM MAKES US ADMIRE YOU EVEN MORE.

"YOU GIVE THE SENSE OF A MAN WHO KNOWS RIGHT FROM WRONG, AND WHO HAS THE MORAL COURAGE TO ACT ON WHAT HE SEES.

"THIS IS WHY WE TURN TO YOU.

GEE...

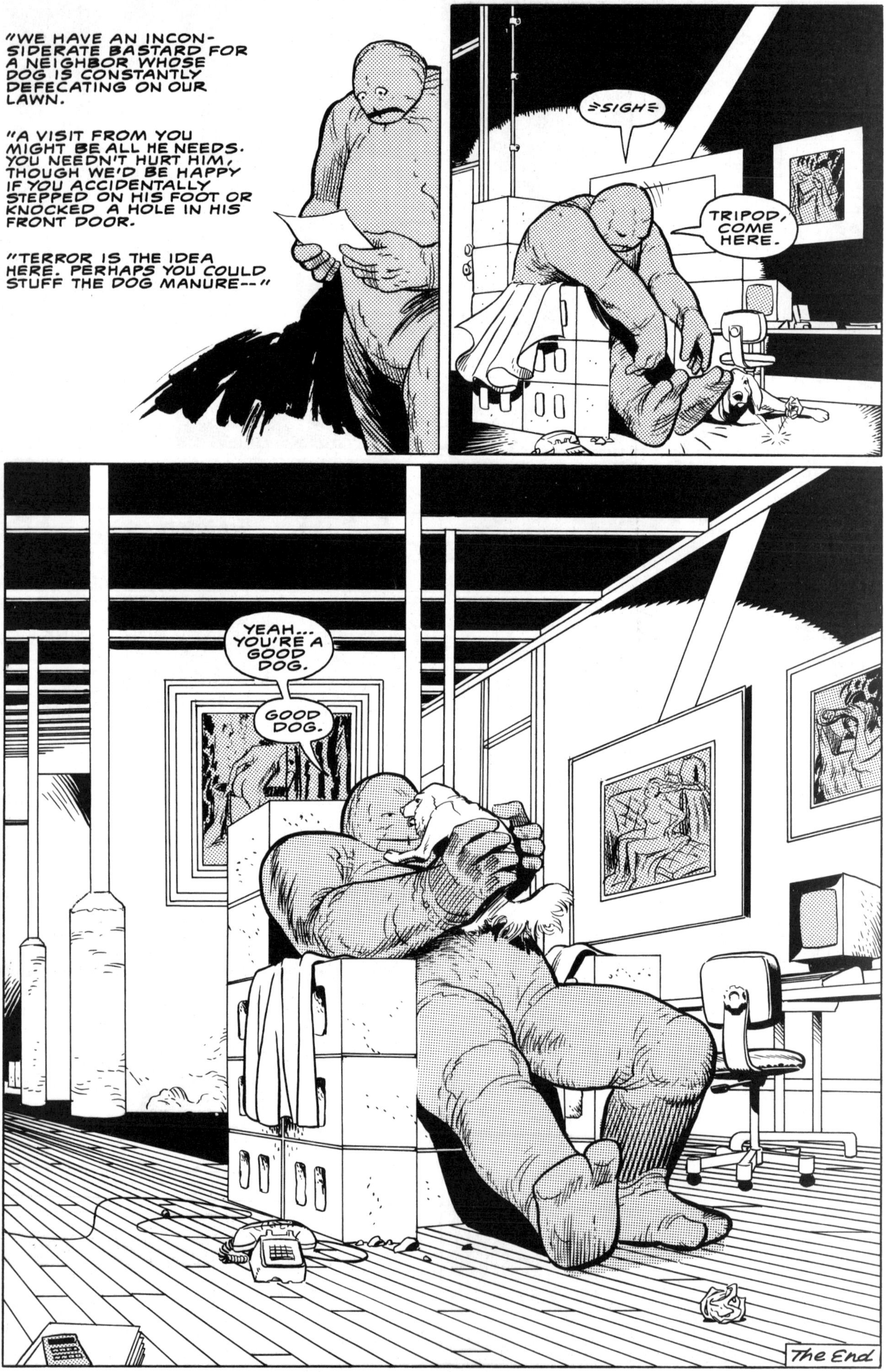
"WE HAVE AN INCON-SIDERATE BASTARD FOR A NEIGHBOR WHOSE DOG IS CONSTANTLY DEFECATING ON OUR LAWN.
"A VISIT FROM YOU MIGHT BE ALL HE NEEDS. YOU NEEDN'T HURT HIM, THOUGH WE'D BE HAPPY IF YOU ACCIDENTALLY STEPPED ON HIS FOOT OR KNOCKED A HOLE IN HIS FRONT DOOR.
"TERROR IS THE IDEA HERE. PERHAPS YOU COULD STUFF THE DOG MANURE--"
SIGH
TRIPOD, COME HERE.
YEAH... YOU'RE A GOOD DOG.
GOOD DOG.
The End

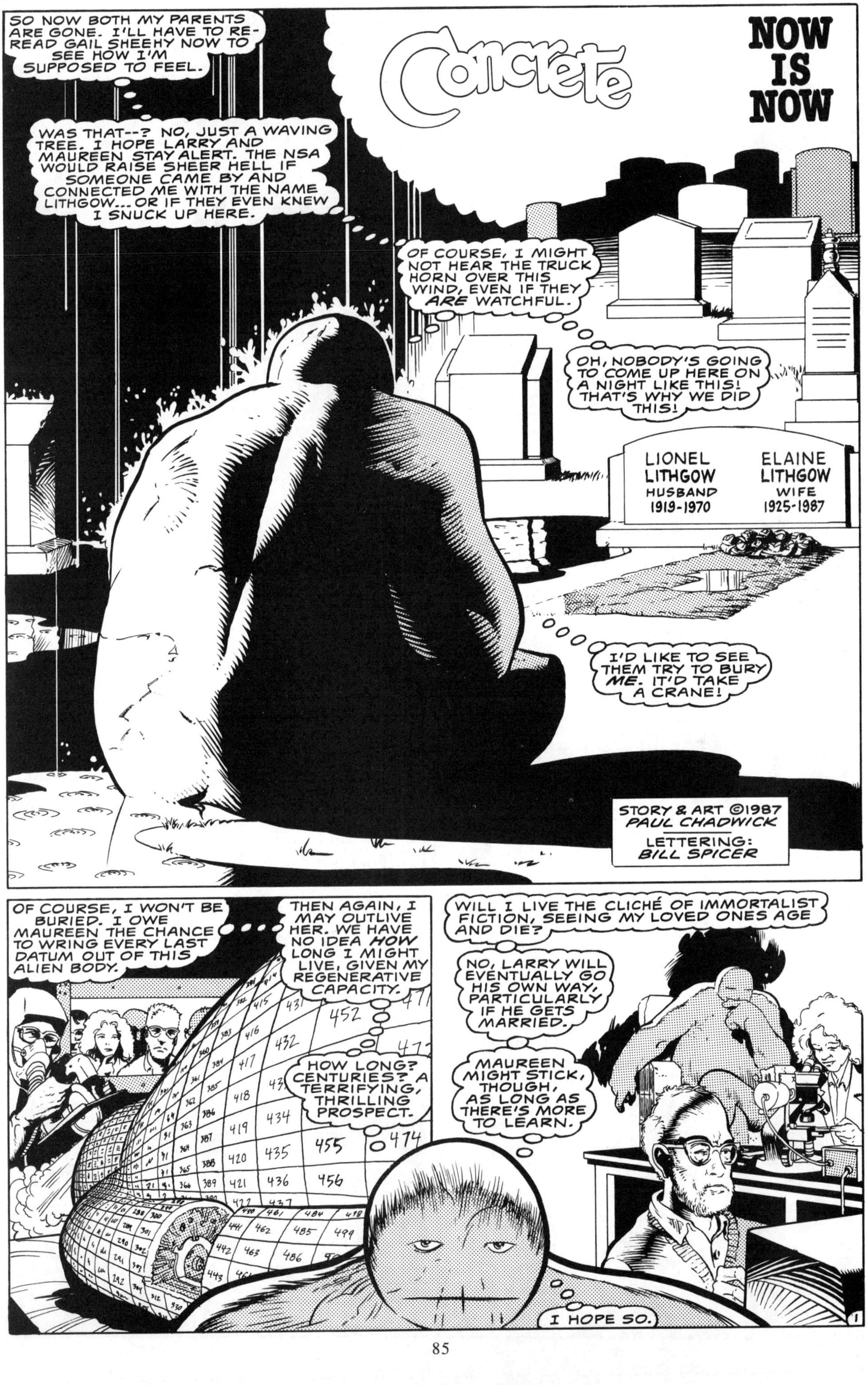
Concrete
NOW IS NOW
SO NOW BOTH MY PARENTS ARE GONE. I'LL HAVE TO RE-READ GAIL SHEEHY NOW TO SEE HOW I'M SUPPOSED TO FEEL.
WAS THAT--? NO, JUST A WAVING TREE. I HOPE LARRY AND MAUREEN STAY ALERT. THE NSA WOULD RAISE SHEER HELL IF SOMEONE CAME BY AND CONNECTED ME WITH THE NAME LITHGOW... OR IF THEY EVEN KNEW I SNUCK UP HERE.
OF COURSE, I MIGHT NOT HEAR THE TRUCK HORN OVER THIS WIND, EVEN IF THEY ARE WATCHFUL.
OH, NOBODY'S GOING TO COME UP HERE ON A NIGHT LIKE THIS! THAT'S WHY WE DID THIS!
LIONEL LITHGOW HUSBAND 1919-1970
ELAINE LITHGOW WIFE 1925-1987
I'D LIKE TO SEE THEM TRY TO BURY ME. IT'D TAKE A CRANE!
STORY & ART ©1987 PAUL CHADWICK
LETTERING: BILL SPICER
OF COURSE, I WON'T BE BURIED. I OWE MAUREEN THE CHANCE TO WRING EVERY LAST DATUM OUT OF THIS ALIEN BODY.
THEN AGAIN, I MAY OUTLIVE HER. WE HAVE NO IDEA HOW LONG I MIGHT LIVE, GIVEN MY REGENERATIVE CAPACITY.
HOW LONG? CENTURIES? A TERRIFYING, THRILLING PROSPECT.
WILL I LIVE THE CLICHÉ OF IMMORTALIST FICTION, SEEING MY LOVED ONES AGE AND DIE?
NO, LARRY WILL EVENTUALLY GO HIS OWN WAY, PARTICULARLY IF HE GETS MARRIED.
MAUREEN MIGHT STICK, THOUGH, AS LONG AS THERE'S MORE TO LEARN.
I HOPE SO.
1

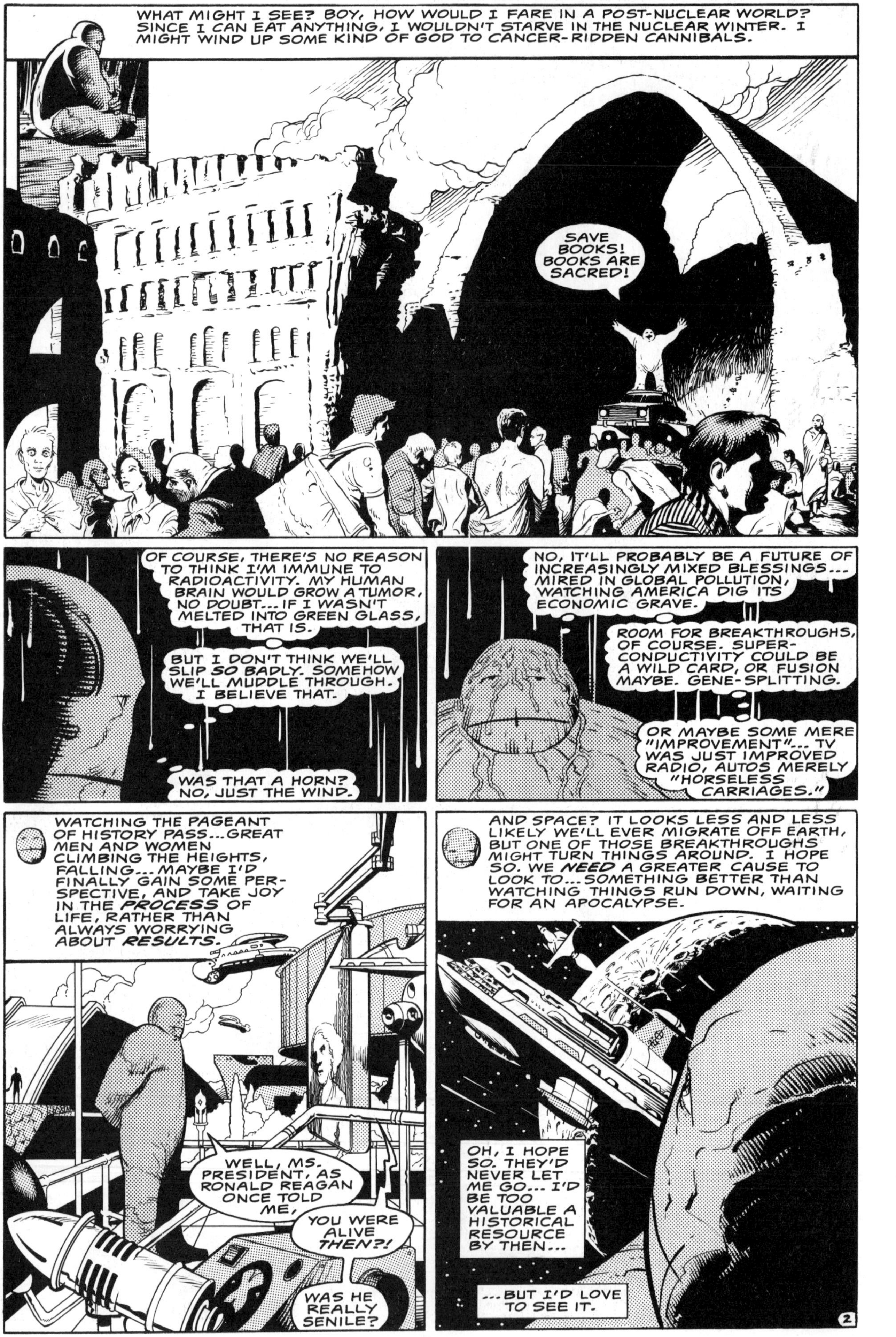
WHAT MIGHT I SEE? BOY, HOW WOULD I FARE IN A POST-NUCLEAR WORLD? SINCE I CAN EAT ANYTHING, I WOULDN'T STARVE IN THE NUCLEAR WINTER. I MIGHT WIND UP SOME KIND OF GOD TO CANCER-RIDDEN CANNIBALS.
SAVE BOOKS! BOOKS ARE SACRED!
OF COURSE, THERE'S NO REASON TO THINK I'M IMMUNE TO RADIOACTIVITY. MY HUMAN BRAIN WOULD GROW A TUMOR, NO DOUBT... IF I WASN'T MELTED INTO GREEN GLASS, THAT IS.
BUT I DON'T THINK WE'LL SLIP SO BADLY. SOMEHOW WE'LL MUDDLE THROUGH. I BELIEVE THAT.
WAS THAT A HORN? NO, JUST THE WIND.
NO, IT'LL PROBABLY BE A FUTURE OF INCREASINGLY MIXED BLESSINGS... MIRED IN GLOBAL POLLUTION, WATCHING AMERICA DIG ITS ECONOMIC GRAVE.
ROOM FOR BREAKTHROUGHS, OF COURSE. SUPER-CONDUCTIVITY COULD BE A WILD CARD, OR FUSION MAYBE. GENE-SPLITTING.
OR MAYBE SOME MERE "IMPROVEMENT"... TV WAS JUST IMPROVED RADIO, AUTOS MERELY "HORSELESS CARRIAGES."
WATCHING THE PAGEANT OF HISTORY PASS... GREAT MEN AND WOMEN CLIMBING THE HEIGHTS, FALLING... MAYBE I'D FINALLY GAIN SOME PERSPECTIVE, AND TAKE JOY IN THE PROCESS OF LIFE, RATHER THAN ALWAYS WORRYING ABOUT RESULTS.
WELL, MS. PRESIDENT, AS RONALD REAGAN ONCE TOLD ME,
YOU WERE ALIVE THEN?!
WAS HE REALLY SENILE?
AND SPACE? IT LOOKS LESS AND LESS LIKELY WE'LL EVER MIGRATE OFF EARTH, BUT ONE OF THOSE BREAKTHROUGHS MIGHT TURN THINGS AROUND. I HOPE SO. WE NEED A GREATER CAUSE TO LOOK TO... SOMETHING BETTER THAN WATCHING THINGS RUN DOWN, WAITING FOR AN APOCALYPSE.
OH, I HOPE SO. THEY'D NEVER LET ME GO... I'D BE TOO VALUABLE A HISTORICAL RESOURCE BY THEN...
...BUT I'D LOVE TO SEE IT.
2

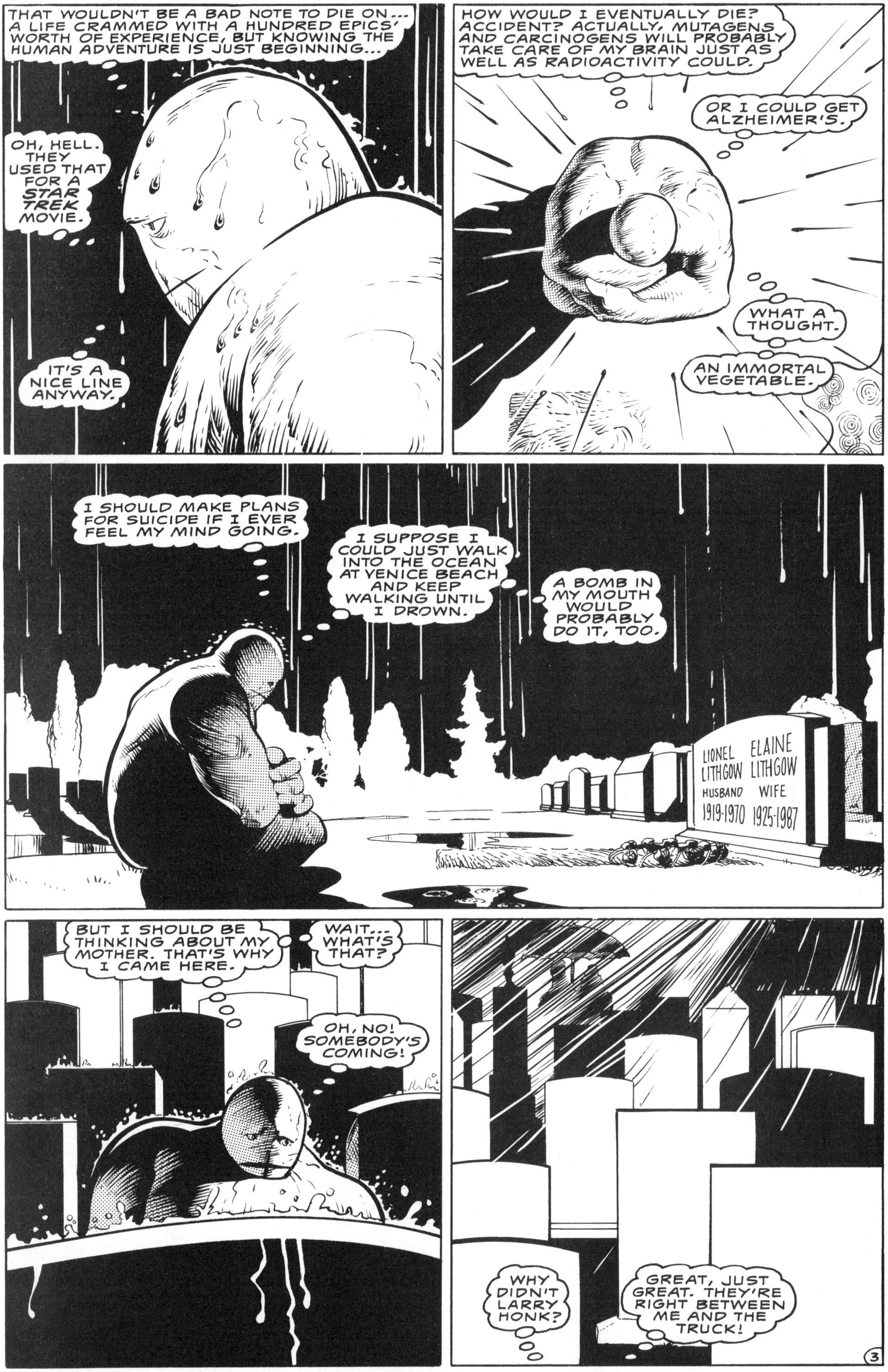
THAT WOULDN'T BE A BAD NOTE TO DIE ON... A LIFE CRAMMED WITH A HUNDRED EPICS' WORTH OF EXPERIENCE, BUT KNOWING THE HUMAN ADVENTURE IS JUST BEGINNING...
OH, HELL. THEY USED THAT FOR A STAR TREK MOVIE.
IT'S A NICE LINE ANYWAY.
HOW WOULD I EVENTUALLY DIE? ACCIDENT? ACTUALLY, MUTAGENS AND CARCINOGENS WILL PROBABLY TAKE CARE OF MY BRAIN JUST AS WELL AS RADIOACTIVITY COULD.
OR I COULD GET ALZHEIMER'S.
WHAT A THOUGHT.
AN IMMORTAL VEGETABLE.
I SHOULD MAKE PLANS FOR SUICIDE IF I EVER FEEL MY MIND GOING.
I SUPPOSE I COULD JUST WALK INTO THE OCEAN AT VENICE BEACH AND KEEP WALKING UNTIL I DROWN.
A BOMB IN MY MOUTH WOULD PROBABLY DO IT, TOO.
LIONEL LITHGOW HUSBAND 1919-1970
ELAINE LITHGOW WIFE 1925-1987
BUT I SHOULD BE THINKING ABOUT MY MOTHER. THAT'S WHY I CAME HERE.
WAIT... WHAT'S THAT?
OH, NO! SOMEBODY'S COMING!
WHY DIDN'T LARRY HONK?
GREAT, JUST GREAT. THEY'RE RIGHT BETWEEN ME AND THE TRUCK!
3

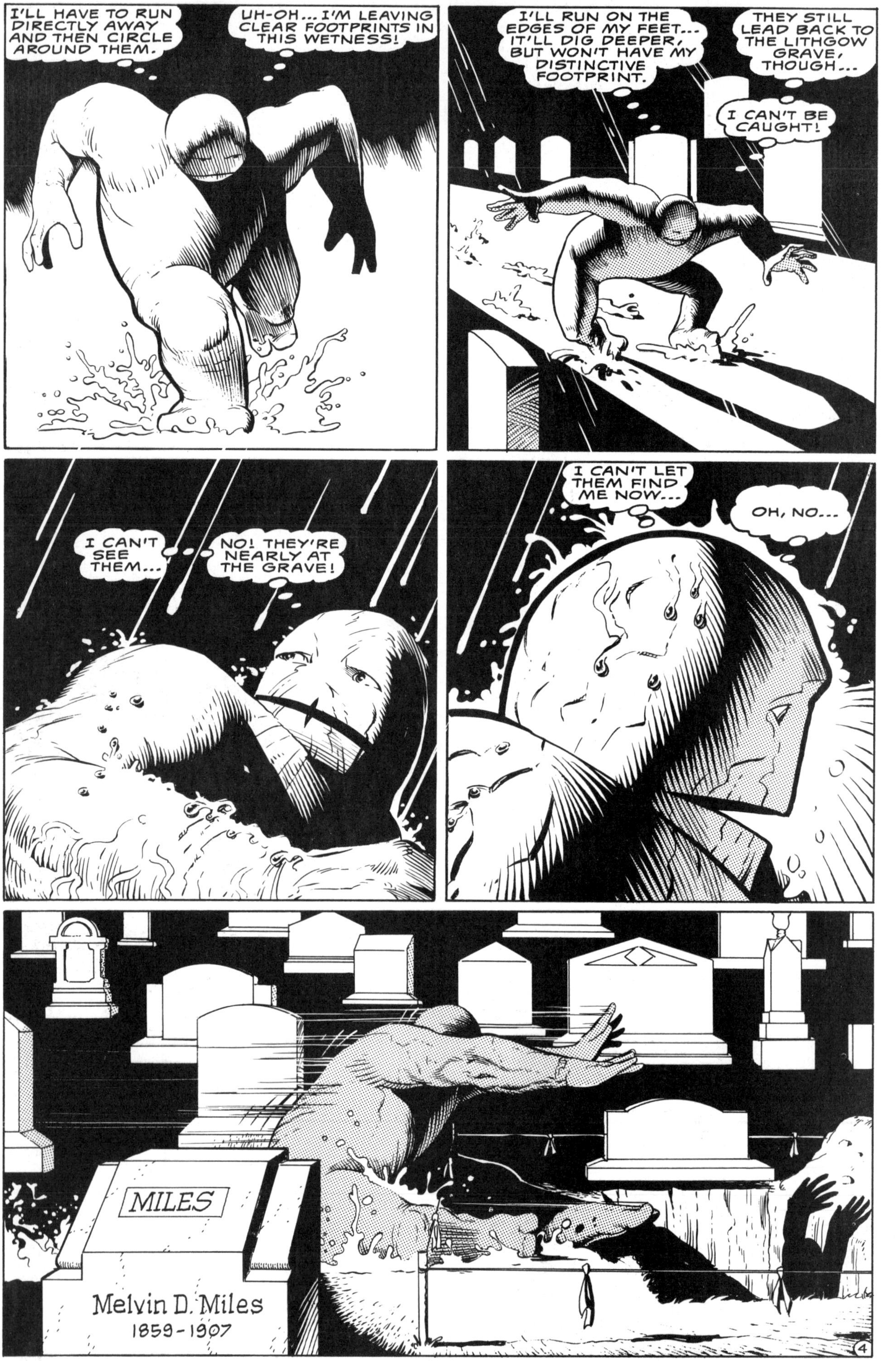
I'LL HAVE TO RUN DIRECTLY AWAY AND THEN CIRCLE AROUND THEM.
UH-OH... I'M LEAVING CLEAR FOOTPRINTS IN THIS WETNESS!
I'LL RUN ON THE EDGES OF MY FEET... IT'LL DIG DEEPER, BUT WON'T HAVE MY DISTINCTIVE FOOTPRINT.
THEY STILL LEAD BACK TO THE LITHGOW GRAVE, THOUGH...
I CAN'T BE CAUGHT!
I CAN'T SEE THEM...
NO! THEY'RE NEARLY AT THE GRAVE!
I CAN'T LET THEM FIND ME NOW...
OH, NO...
MILES
Melvin D. Miles
1859-1907
4

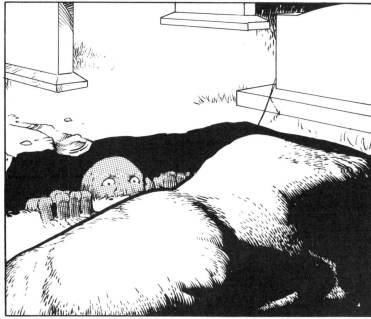

NOW STAY CALM! IT *IS* PRETTY MUCKY, BUT THE EDGE IS JUST ABOVE MY EYES. I'LL GET A GOOD PURCHASE, AND JUST PULL MYSELF OUT.

NOW DIG IN COMPLETELY...

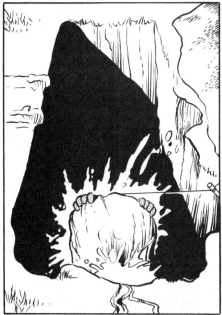

PLAN "B"...

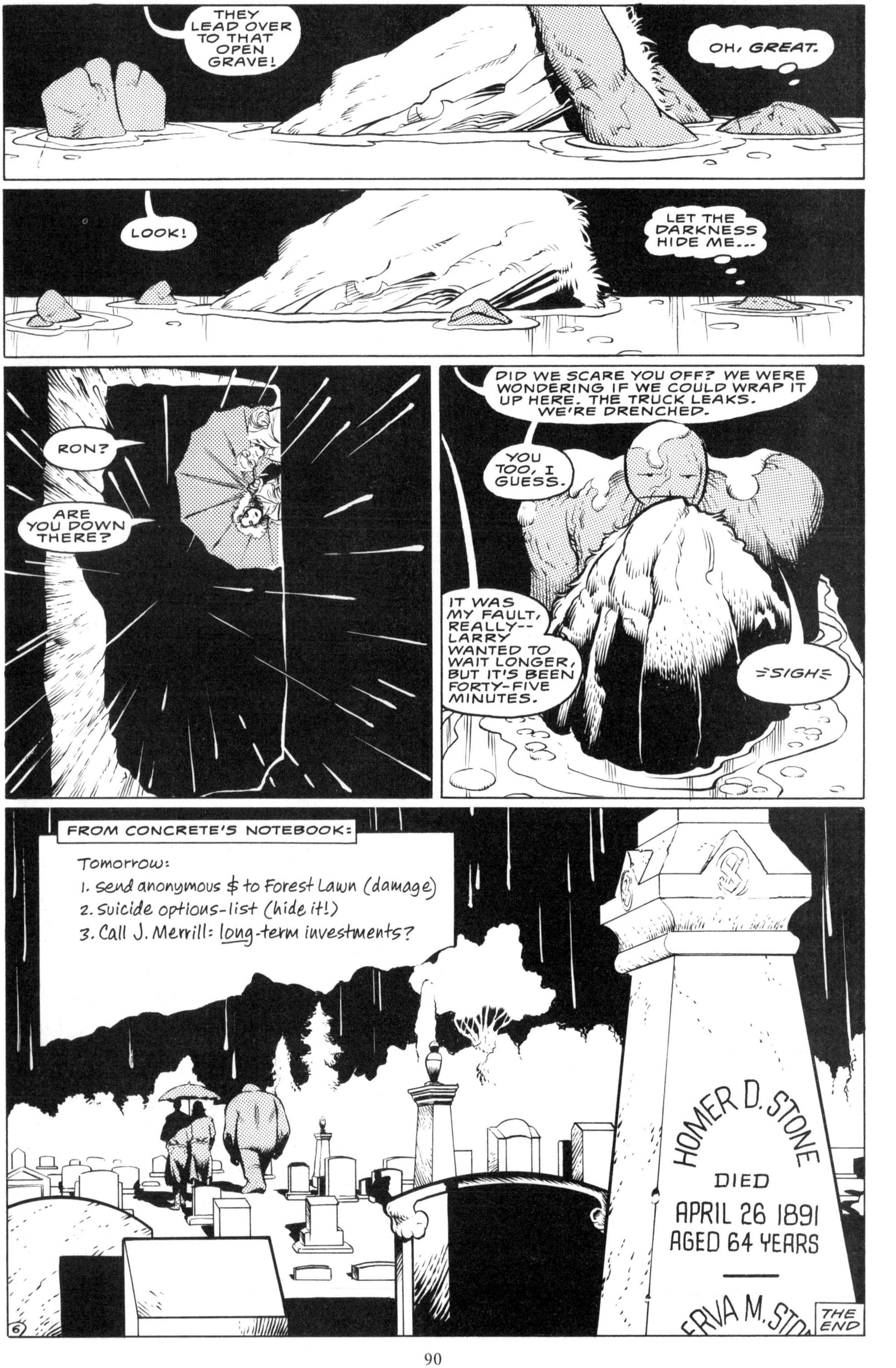
THEY LEAD OVER TO THAT OPEN GRAVE!
OH, GREAT.
LOOK!
LET THE DARKNESS HIDE ME...
RON?
ARE YOU DOWN THERE?
DID WE SCARE YOU OFF? WE WERE WONDERING IF WE COULD WRAP IT UP HERE. THE TRUCK LEAKS. WE'RE DRENCHED.
YOU TOO, I GUESS.
IT WAS MY FAULT, REALLY-- LARRY WANTED TO WAIT LONGER, BUT IT'S BEEN FORTY-FIVE MINUTES.
=SIGH=
FROM CONCRETE'S NOTEBOOK:
Tomorrow:
1. send anonymous $ to Forest Lawn (damage)
2. suicide options-list (hide it!)
3. Call J. Merrill: long-term investments?
HOMER D. STONE
DIED
APRIL 26 1891
AGED 64 YEARS
ERVA M. STO
6
THE END

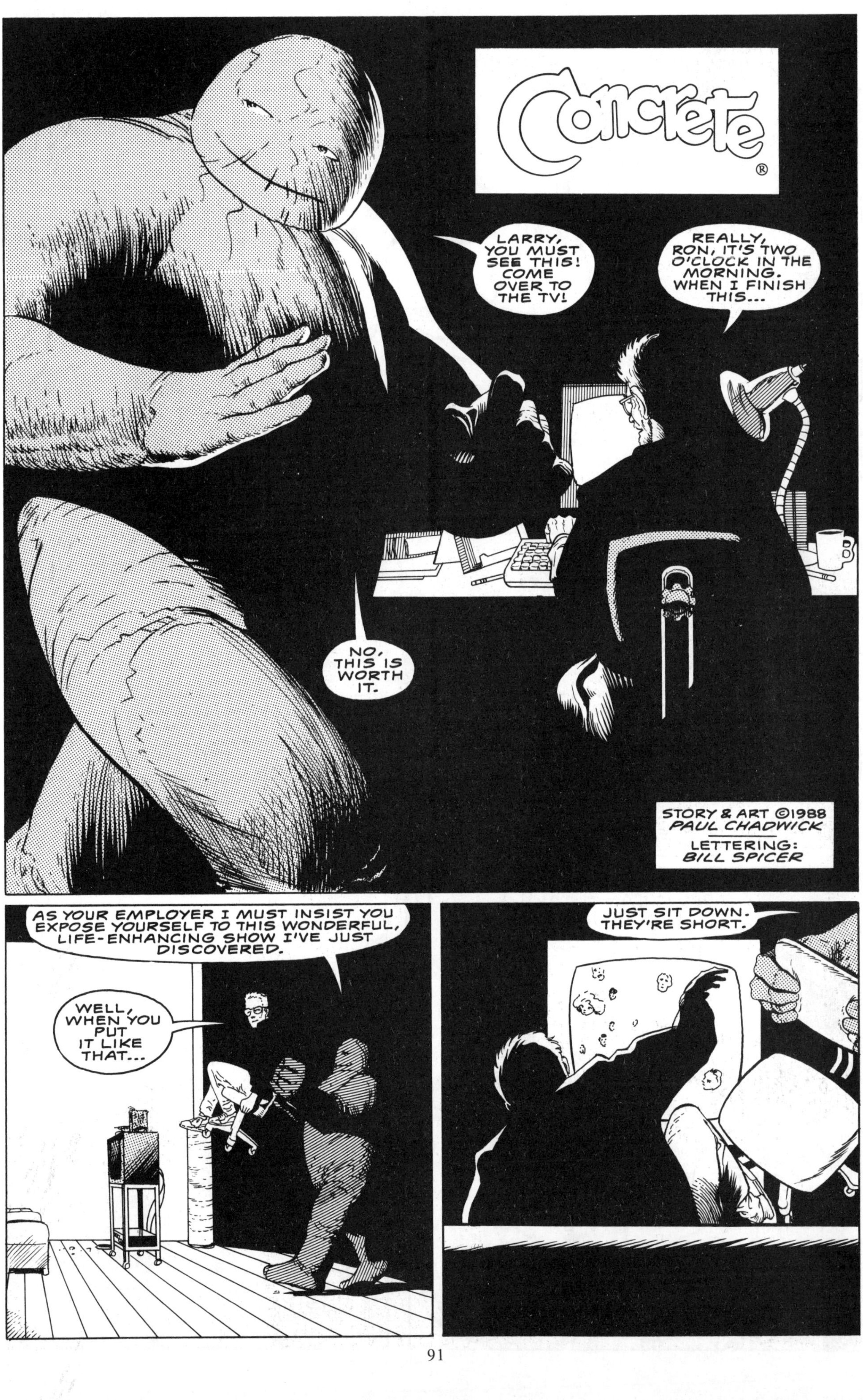
Concrete®
LARRY, YOU MUST SEE THIS! COME OVER TO THE TV!
REALLY, RON, IT'S TWO O'CLOCK IN THE MORNING. WHEN I FINISH THIS...
NO, THIS IS WORTH IT.
STORY & ART ©1988 PAUL CHADWICK
LETTERING: BILL SPICER
AS YOUR EMPLOYER I MUST INSIST YOU EXPOSE YOURSELF TO THIS WONDERFUL, LIFE-ENHANCING SHOW I'VE JUST DISCOVERED.
WELL, WHEN YOU PUT IT LIKE THAT...
JUST SIT DOWN. THEY'RE SHORT.

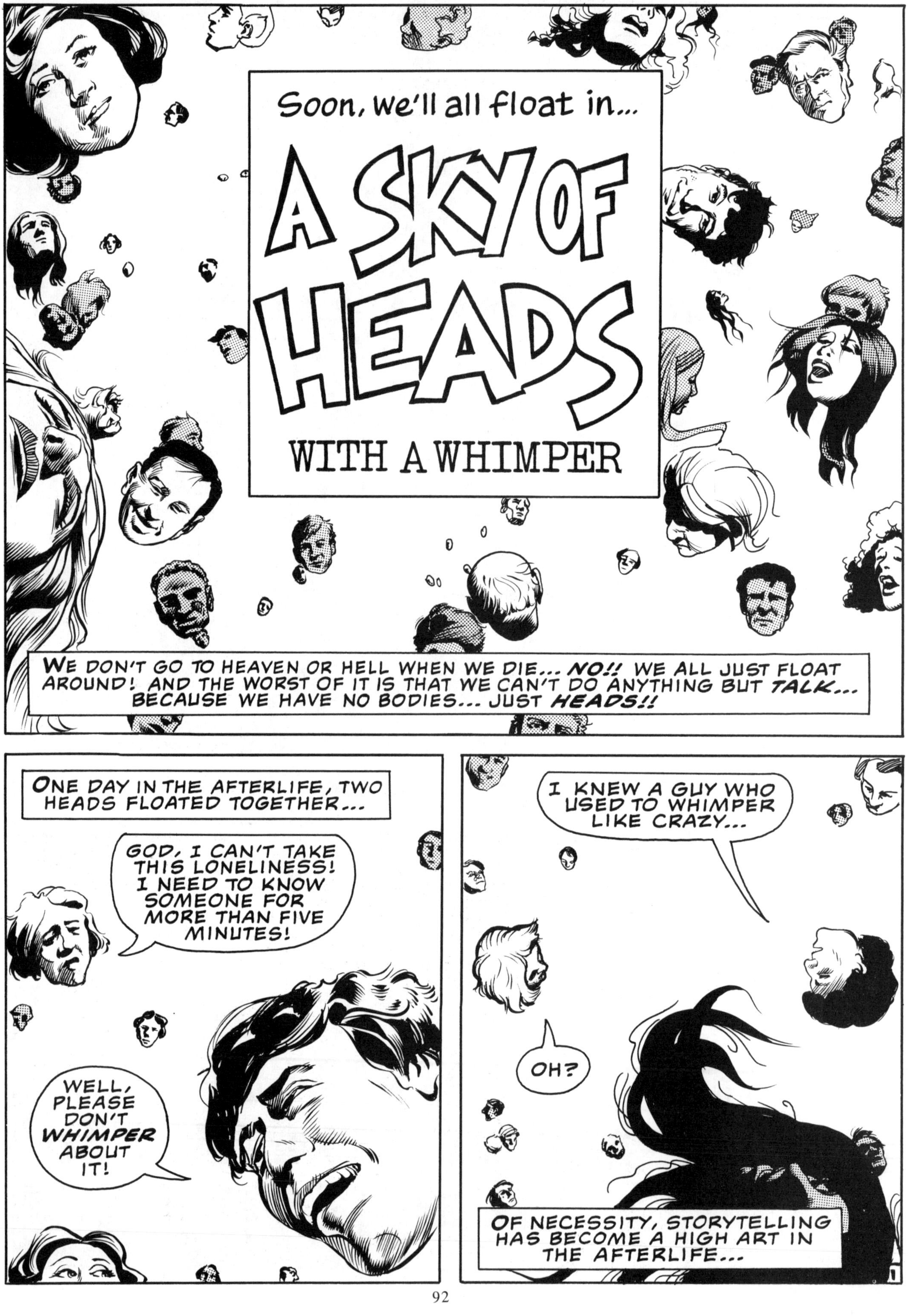
Soon, we'll all float in...
A SKY OF HEADS
WITH A WHIMPER
WE DON'T GO TO HEAVEN OR HELL WHEN WE DIE... NO!! WE ALL JUST FLOAT AROUND! AND THE WORST OF IT IS THAT WE CAN'T DO ANYTHING BUT TALK... BECAUSE WE HAVE NO BODIES... JUST HEADS!!
ONE DAY IN THE AFTERLIFE, TWO HEADS FLOATED TOGETHER...
GOD, I CAN'T TAKE THIS LONELINESS! I NEED TO KNOW SOMEONE FOR MORE THAN FIVE MINUTES!
WELL, PLEASE DON'T WHIMPER ABOUT IT!
I KNEW A GUY WHO USED TO WHIMPER LIKE CRAZY...
OH?
OF NECESSITY, STORYTELLING HAS BECOME A HIGH ART IN THE AFTERLIFE...

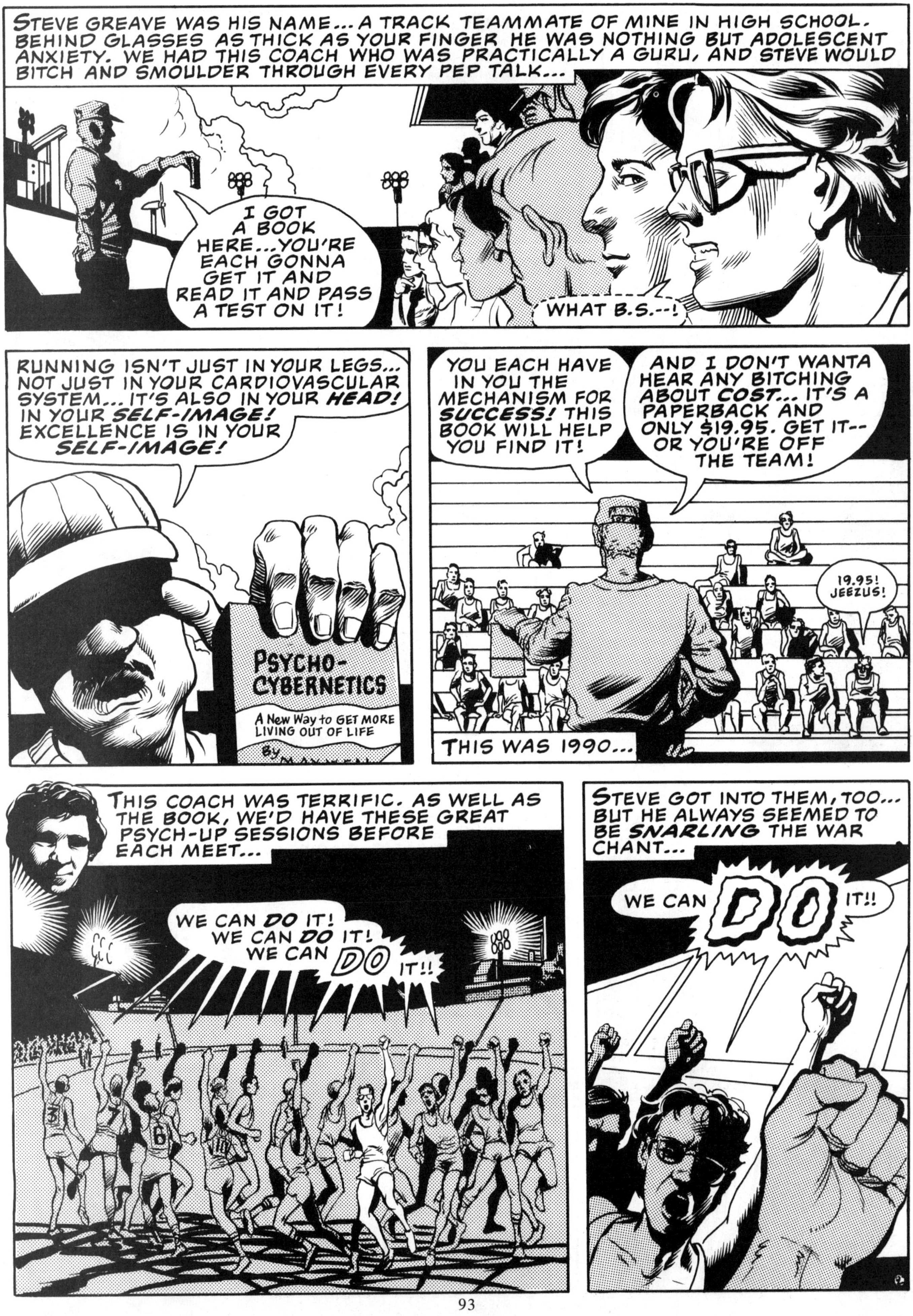
STEVE GREAVE WAS HIS NAME... A TRACK TEAMMATE OF MINE IN HIGH SCHOOL. BEHIND GLASSES AS THICK AS YOUR FINGER HE WAS NOTHING BUT ADOLESCENT ANXIETY. WE HAD THIS COACH WHO WAS PRACTICALLY A GURU, AND STEVE WOULD BITCH AND SMOULDER THROUGH EVERY PEP TALK...
I GOT A BOOK HERE... YOU'RE EACH GONNA GET IT AND READ IT AND PASS A TEST ON IT!
WHAT B.S.--!
RUNNING ISN'T JUST IN YOUR LEGS... NOT JUST IN YOUR CARDIOVASCULAR SYSTEM... IT'S ALSO IN YOUR HEAD! IN YOUR SELF-IMAGE! EXCELLENCE IS IN YOUR SELF-IMAGE!
PSYCHO-CYBERNETICS
A New Way to GET MORE LIVING OUT OF LIFE
By
YOU EACH HAVE IN YOU THE MECHANISM FOR SUCCESS! THIS BOOK WILL HELP YOU FIND IT!
AND I DON'T WANTA HEAR ANY BITCHING ABOUT COST... IT'S A PAPERBACK AND ONLY $19.95. GET IT-- OR YOU'RE OFF THE TEAM!
19.95! JEEZUS!
THIS WAS 1990...
THIS COACH WAS TERRIFIC. AS WELL AS THE BOOK, WE'D HAVE THESE GREAT PSYCH-UP SESSIONS BEFORE EACH MEET...
WE CAN DO IT! WE CAN DO IT! WE CAN DO IT!!
STEVE GOT INTO THEM, TOO... BUT HE ALWAYS SEEMED TO BE SNARLING THE WAR CHANT...
WE CAN DO IT!!

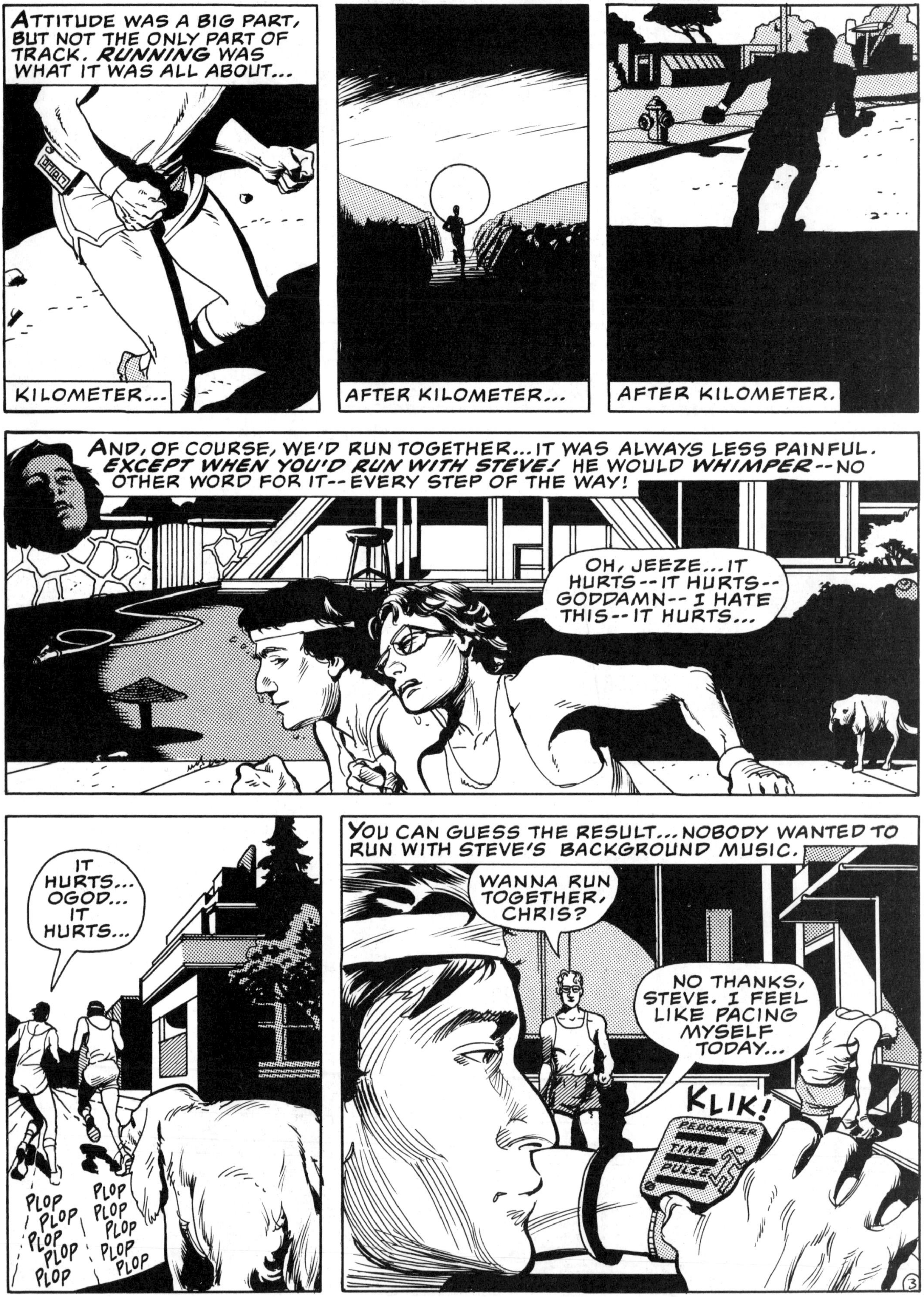
ATTITUDE WAS A BIG PART, BUT NOT THE ONLY PART OF TRACK. *RUNNING* WAS WHAT IT WAS ALL ABOUT...
KILOMETER...
AFTER KILOMETER...
AFTER KILOMETER.
AND, OF COURSE, WE'D RUN TOGETHER... IT WAS ALWAYS LESS PAINFUL. *EXCEPT WHEN YOU'D RUN WITH STEVE!* HE WOULD *WHIMPER*--NO OTHER WORD FOR IT--EVERY STEP OF THE WAY!
OH, JEEZE... IT HURTS--IT HURTS--GODDAMN--I HATE THIS--IT HURTS...
IT HURTS... OGOD... IT HURTS...
PLOP PLOP PLOP PLOP PLOP
PLOP PLOP PLOP PLOP PLOP PLOP
YOU CAN GUESS THE RESULT... NOBODY WANTED TO RUN WITH STEVE'S BACKGROUND MUSIC.
WANNA RUN TOGETHER, CHRIS?
NO THANKS, STEVE. I FEEL LIKE PACING MYSELF TODAY...
KLIK!
TIME
PULSE
3

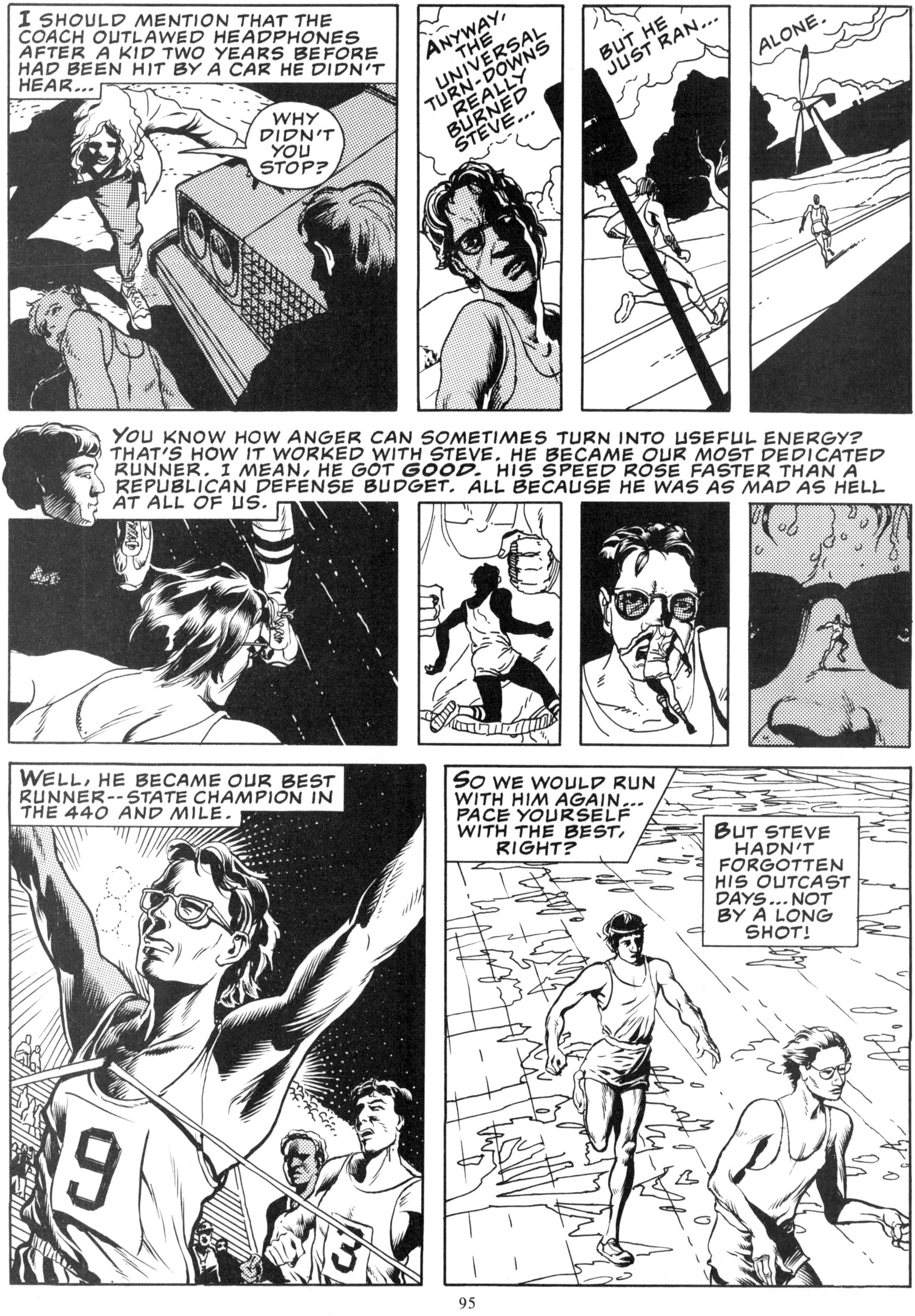

I SHOULD MENTION THAT THE COACH OUTLAWED HEADPHONES AFTER A KID TWO YEARS BEFORE HAD BEEN HIT BY A CAR HE DIDN'T HEAR...
WHY DIDN'T YOU STOP?
ANYWAY, THE UNIVERSAL TURN-DOWNS REALLY BURNED STEVE...
BUT HE JUST RAN...
ALONE.
YOU KNOW HOW ANGER CAN SOMETIMES TURN INTO USEFUL ENERGY? THAT'S HOW IT WORKED WITH STEVE. HE BECAME OUR MOST DEDICATED RUNNER. I MEAN, HE GOT **GOOD.** HIS SPEED ROSE FASTER THAN A REPUBLICAN DEFENSE BUDGET. ALL BECAUSE HE WAS AS MAD AS HELL AT ALL OF US.
WELL, HE BECAME OUR BEST RUNNER--STATE CHAMPION IN THE 440 AND MILE.
9
3
SO WE WOULD RUN WITH HIM AGAIN... PACE YOURSELF WITH THE BEST, RIGHT?
BUT STEVE HADN'T FORGOTTEN HIS OUTCAST DAYS...NOT BY A LONG SHOT!

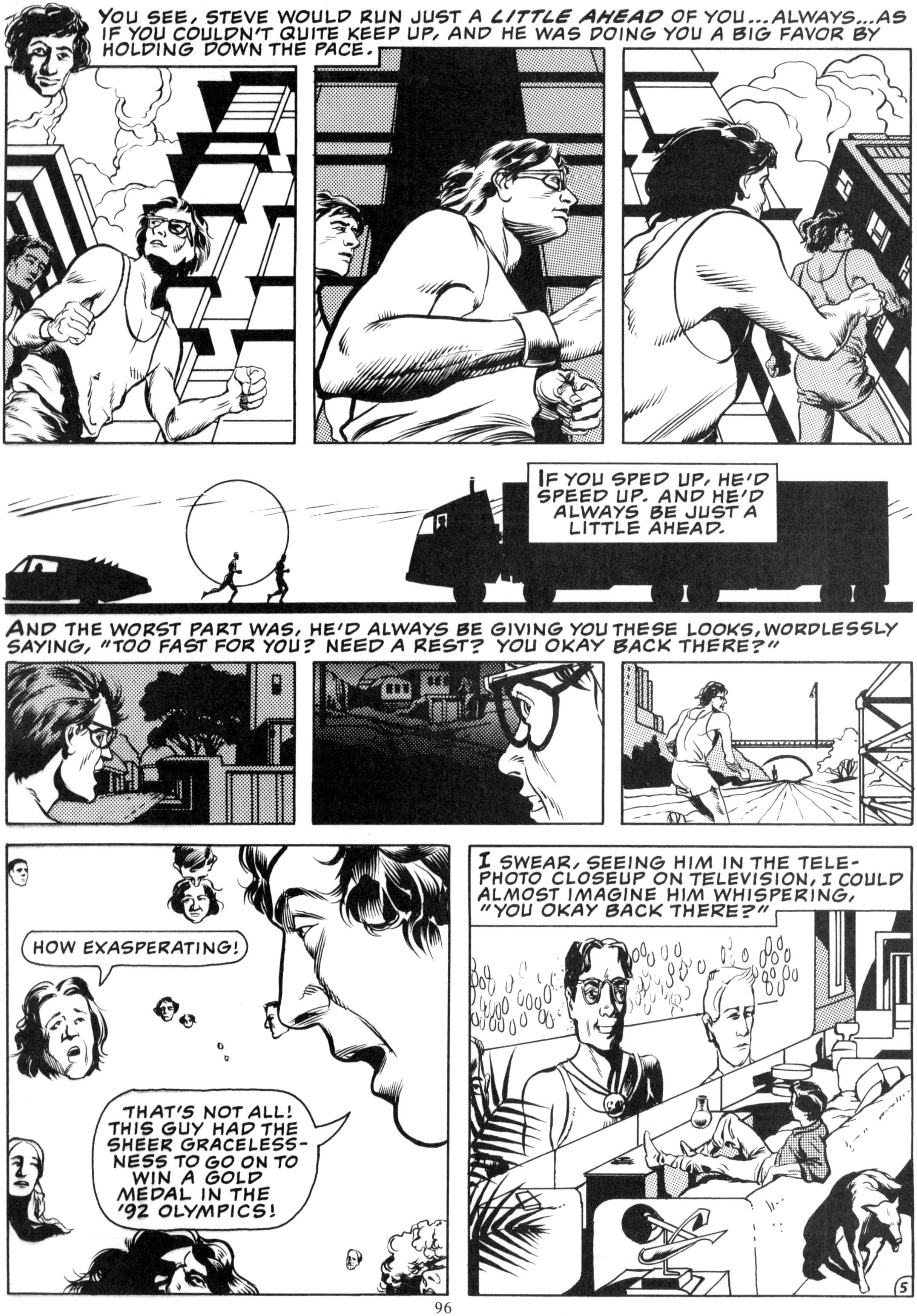
YOU SEE, STEVE WOULD RUN JUST A *LITTLE AHEAD* OF YOU... ALWAYS... AS IF YOU COULDN'T QUITE KEEP UP, AND HE WAS DOING YOU A BIG FAVOR BY HOLDING DOWN THE PACE.
IF YOU SPED UP, HE'D SPEED UP. AND HE'D ALWAYS BE JUST A LITTLE AHEAD.
AND THE WORST PART WAS, HE'D ALWAYS BE GIVING YOU THESE LOOKS, WORDLESSLY SAYING, "TOO FAST FOR YOU? NEED A REST? YOU OKAY BACK THERE?"
HOW EXASPERATING!
THAT'S NOT ALL! THIS GUY HAD THE SHEER GRACELESS-NESS TO GO ON TO WIN A GOLD MEDAL IN THE '92 OLYMPICS!
I SWEAR, SEEING HIM IN THE TELE-PHOTO CLOSEUP ON TELEVISION, I COULD ALMOST IMAGINE HIM WHISPERING, "YOU OKAY BACK THERE?"
5

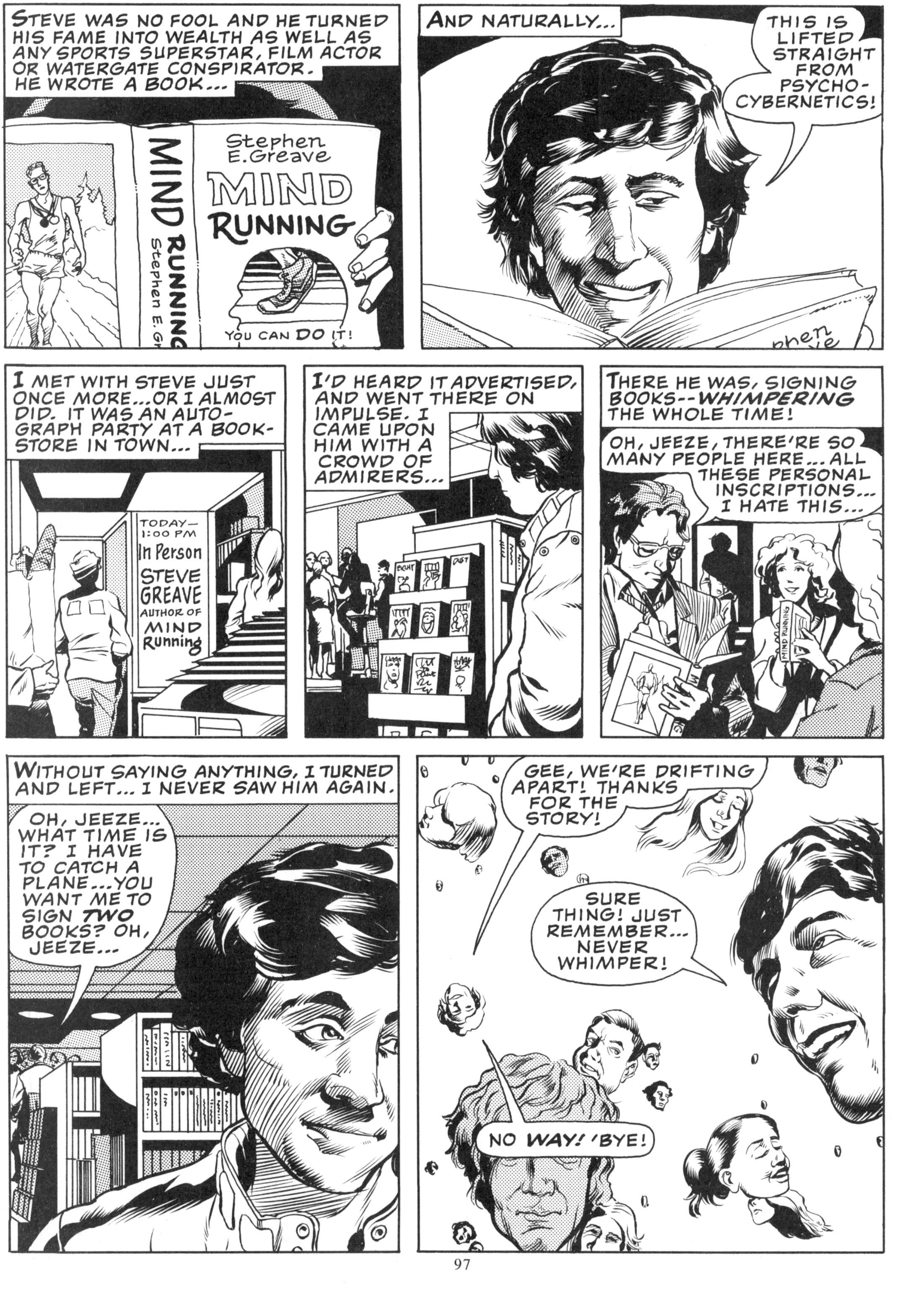
STEVE WAS NO FOOL AND HE TURNED HIS FAME INTO WEALTH AS WELL AS ANY SPORTS SUPERSTAR, FILM ACTOR OR WATERGATE CONSPIRATOR. HE WROTE A BOOK...
MIND RUNNING Stephen E. G
Stephen E.Greave
MIND RUNNING
YOU CAN DO IT!
AND NATURALLY...
THIS IS LIFTED STRAIGHT FROM PSYCHO-CYBERNETICS!
I MET WITH STEVE JUST ONCE MORE... OR I ALMOST DID. IT WAS AN AUTO-GRAPH PARTY AT A BOOK-STORE IN TOWN...
TODAY— 1:00 PM
In Person
STEVE GREAVE
AUTHOR OF
MIND Running
I'D HEARD IT ADVERTISED, AND WENT THERE ON IMPULSE. I CAME UPON HIM WITH A CROWD OF ADMIRERS...
THERE HE WAS, SIGNING BOOKS--WHIMPERING THE WHOLE TIME!
OH, JEEZE, THERE'RE SO MANY PEOPLE HERE... ALL THESE PERSONAL INSCRIPTIONS... I HATE THIS...
MIND RUNNING
WITHOUT SAYING ANYTHING, I TURNED AND LEFT... I NEVER SAW HIM AGAIN.
OH, JEEZE... WHAT TIME IS IT? I HAVE TO CATCH A PLANE... YOU WANT ME TO SIGN TWO BOOKS? OH, JEEZE...
GEE, WE'RE DRIFTING APART! THANKS FOR THE STORY!
SURE THING! JUST REMEMBER... NEVER WHIMPER!
NO WAY! 'BYE!

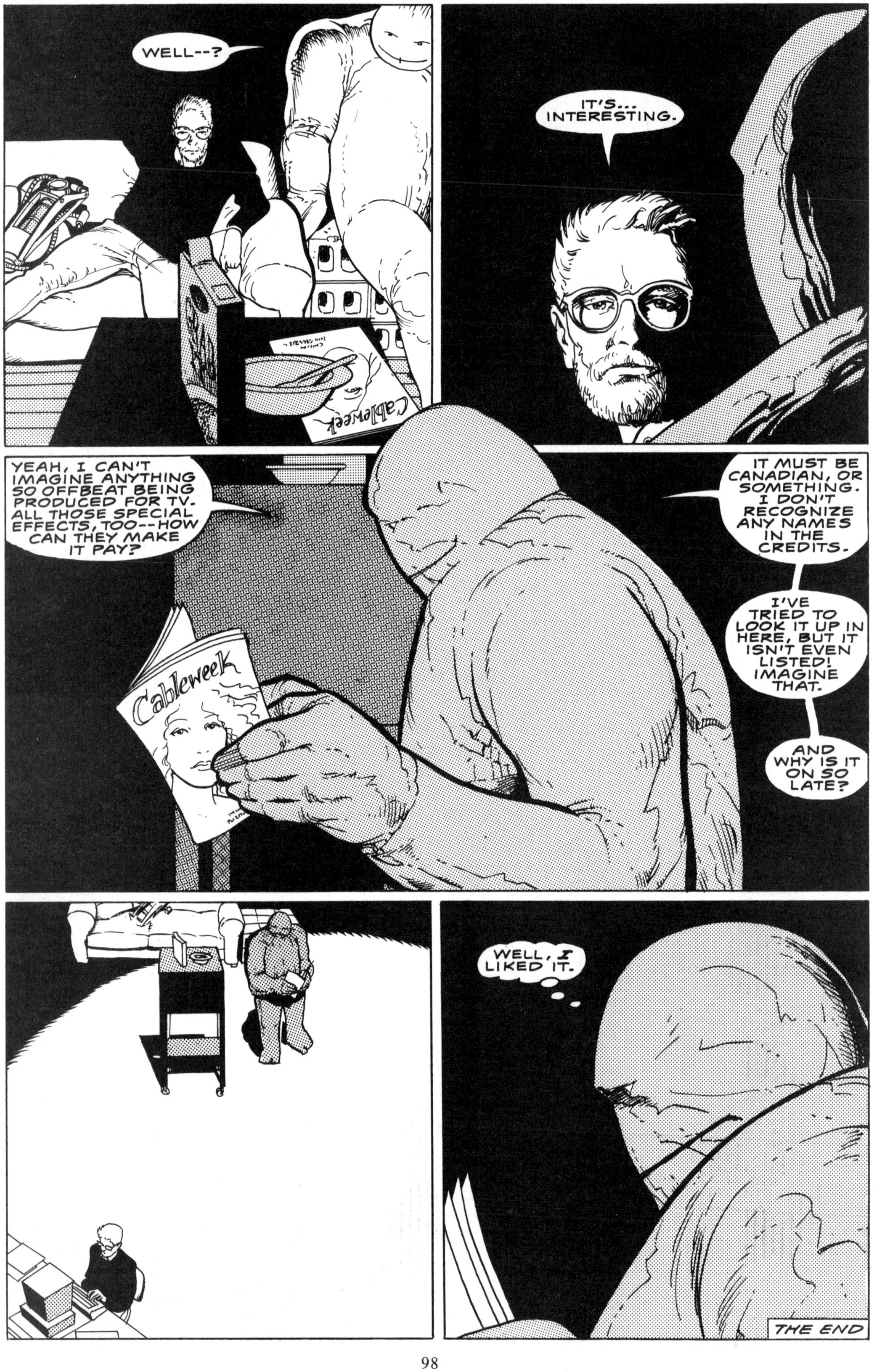

WELL--?
IT'S... INTERESTING.
Cableweek
YEAH, I CAN'T IMAGINE ANYTHING SO OFFBEAT BEING PRODUCED FOR TV. ALL THOSE SPECIAL EFFECTS, TOO--HOW CAN THEY MAKE IT PAY?
IT MUST BE CANADIAN, OR SOMETHING. I DON'T RECOGNIZE ANY NAMES IN THE CREDITS.
I'VE TRIED TO LOOK IT UP IN HERE, BUT IT ISN'T EVEN LISTED! IMAGINE THAT.
AND WHY IS IT ON SO LATE?
WELL, I LIKED IT.
THE END

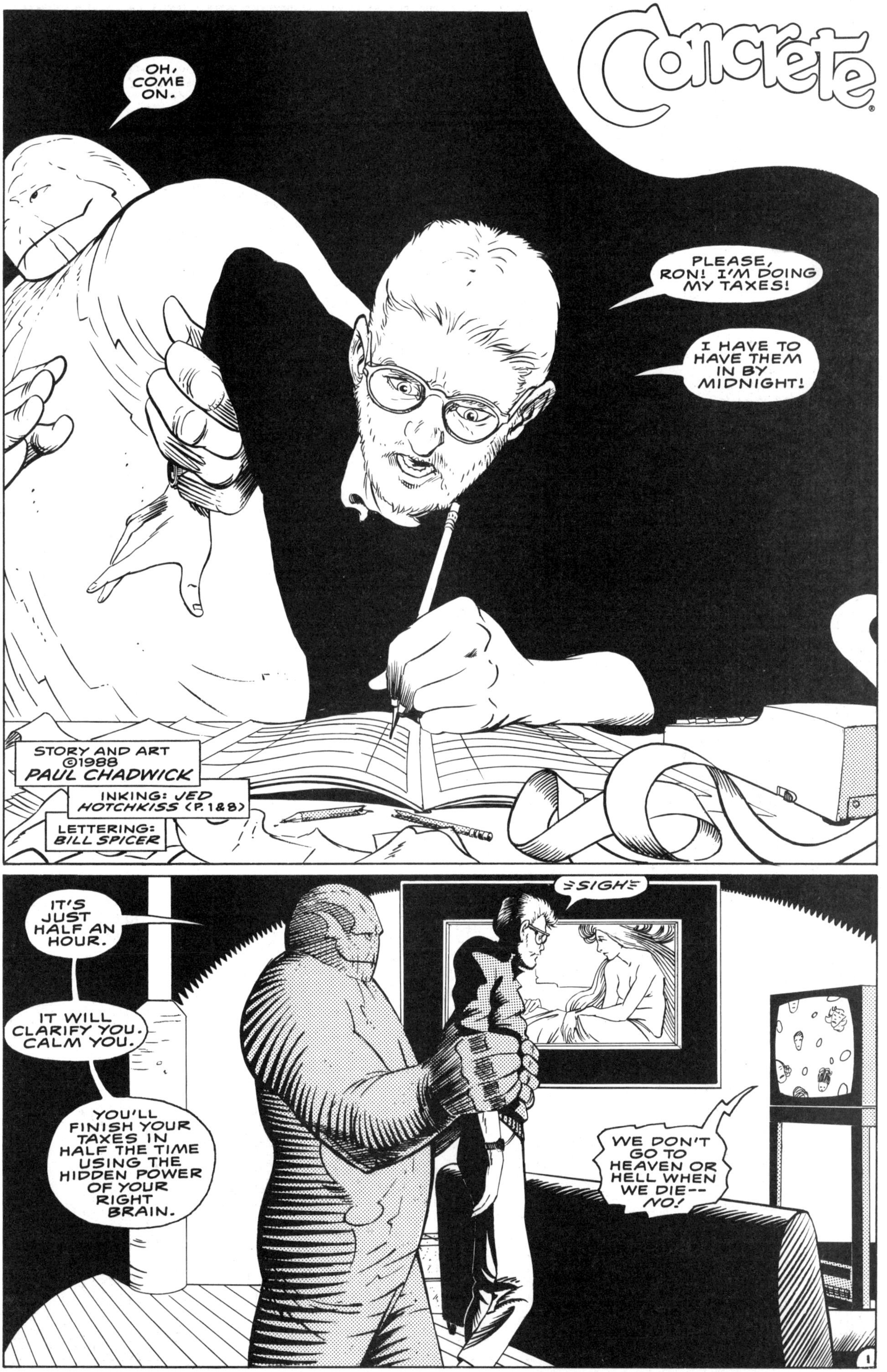
Concrete
OH, COME ON.
PLEASE, RON! I'M DOING MY TAXES!
I HAVE TO HAVE THEM IN BY MIDNIGHT!
STORY AND ART ©1988 PAUL CHADWICK
INKING: JED HOTCHKISS (P.1&8)
LETTERING: BILL SPICER
IT'S JUST HALF AN HOUR.
SIGH
IT WILL CLARIFY YOU. CALM YOU.
YOU'LL FINISH YOUR TAXES IN HALF THE TIME USING THE HIDDEN POWER OF YOUR RIGHT BRAIN.
WE DON'T GO TO HEAVEN OR HELL WHEN WE DIE-- NO!
1

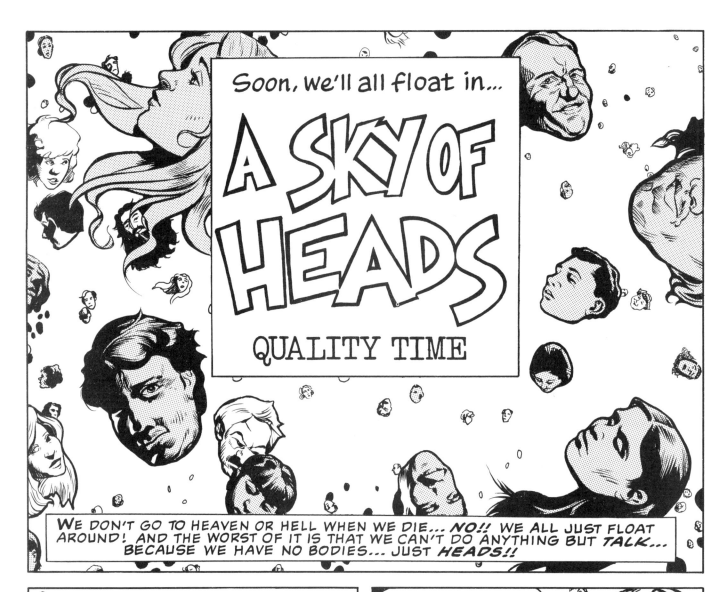

Soon, we'll all float in...

A SKY OF HEADS

QUALITY TIME

WE DON'T GO TO HEAVEN OR HELL WHEN WE DIE... *NO!!* WE ALL JUST FLOAT AROUND! AND THE WORST OF IT IS THAT WE CAN'T DO ANYTHING BUT *TALK*... BECAUSE WE HAVE NO BODIES... JUST *HEADS!!*

ONE DAY IN THE AFTERLIFE, TWO HEADS FLOATED TOGETHER...

WHEN WILL WE BE RELEASED FROM THIS TORMENT OF BOREDOM? *WHEN?*

DON'T TALK LIKE THAT! *YOU* MAKE IT BORING! YOU GOTTA MAKE EVERY MOMENT COUNT!

WHY, WHEN I WAS ALIVE, I MADE IT A *SCIENCE* TO MAKE EVERY MOMENT COUNT!

FOR EXAMPLE, I ALWAYS HAD A PAPERBACK BOOK TO READ WHEN I HAD TO WAIT IN LINE!

I KEPT AN ALWAYS UP-TO-DATE INDEX CARD OF FOREIGN LANGUAGE VOCABULARY WORDS IN MY SHIRT POCKET!

OH?

PEOPLE JUST DON'T THINK OF THESE THINGS!

②

WHEN I WAS YOUNG, I'D PUMP IRON WITH MY FREE ARM AS I BRUSHED MY TEETH...

WHEN COMMUTING TO WORK, I'D LISTEN TO TAPES OF NOVELS I DIDN'T HAVE TIME TO READ...

AT BORING DINNER PARTIES I'D PRACTICE SLEIGHT-OF-HAND TRICKS UNDER THE TABLE...

GOT PRETTY GOOD, TOO.

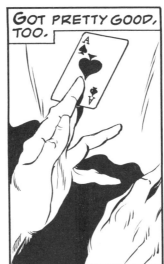

YES, I'D SAY I SPENT MY TIME WELL, ALL THE WAY UP TO MY DYING BREATH!

OH, COME ON... YOUR DYING BREATH? WHAT'S THE POINT OF SELF-IMPROVEMENT THEN?

NOT SELF-IMPROVEMENT! BUT TIME WELL SPENT NONETHELESS! IT WAS LATE AT NIGHT IN THE SANTA MONICA MALL SUBLEVEL TRANSPORT STATION. IT WAS ALMOST DESERTED.

CHRISTMAS NIGHT.

I'D FINISHED SOME CRITICAL WORK ON THE COMPUTER SYSTEM AT A DEPARTMENT STORE.

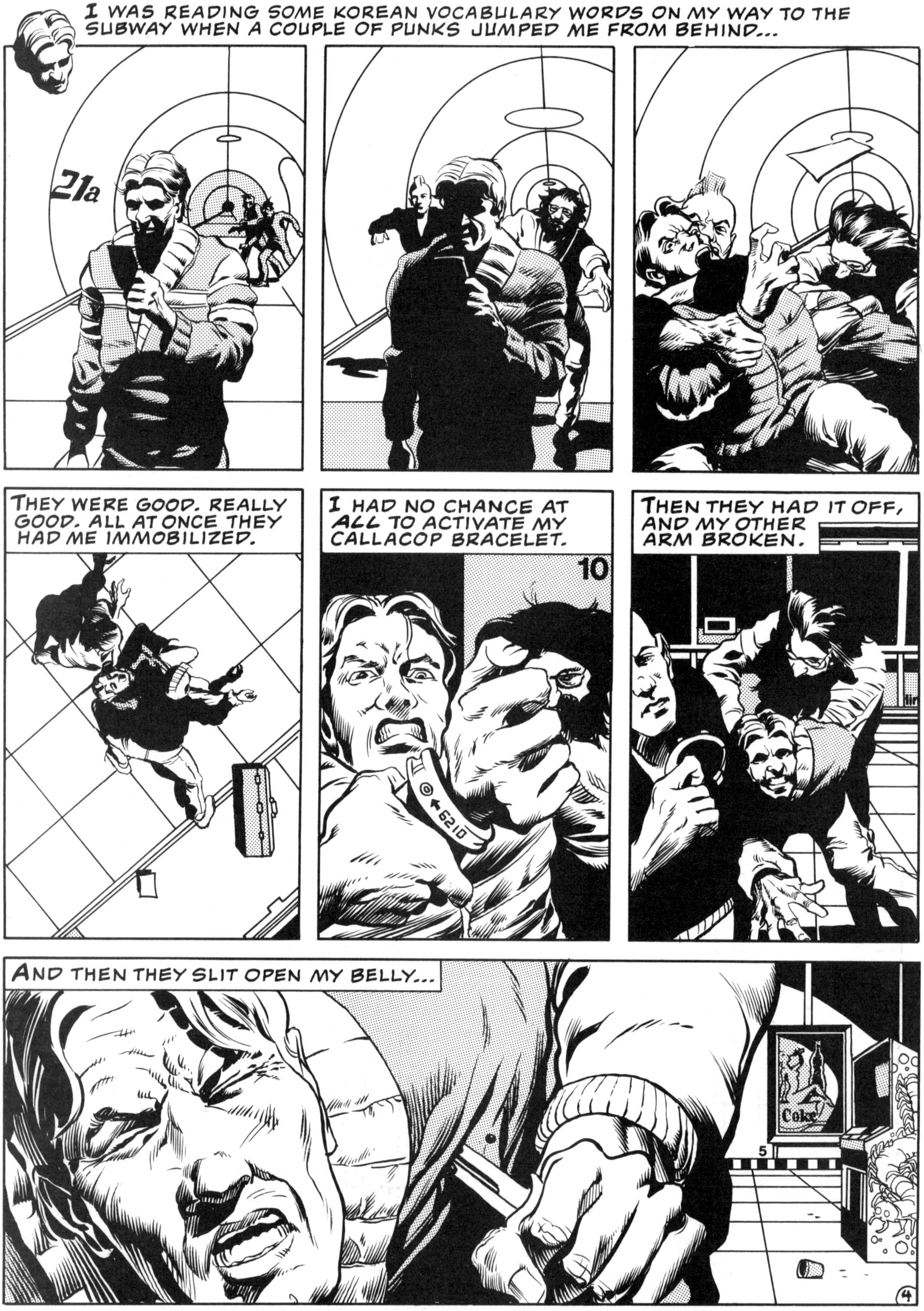
I WAS READING SOME KOREAN VOCABULARY WORDS ON MY WAY TO THE SUBWAY WHEN A COUPLE OF PUNKS JUMPED ME FROM BEHIND...
21a
THEY WERE GOOD. REALLY GOOD. ALL AT ONCE THEY HAD ME IMMOBILIZED.
I HAD NO CHANCE AT ALL TO ACTIVATE MY CALLACOP BRACELET.
10
6210
THEN THEY HAD IT OFF, AND MY OTHER ARM BROKEN.
AND THEN THEY SLIT OPEN MY BELLY...
Coke
5
4

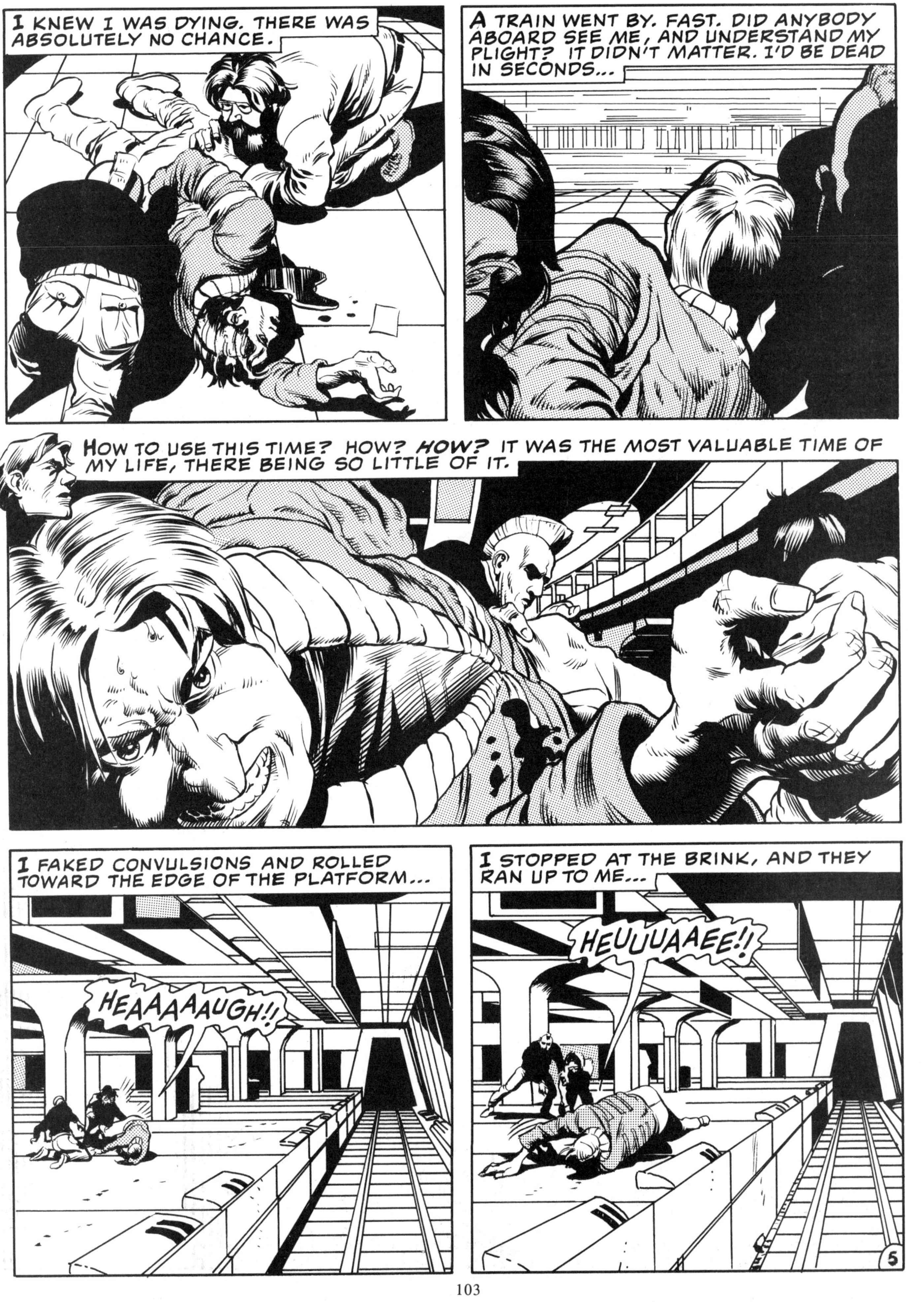
I KNEW I WAS DYING. THERE WAS ABSOLUTELY NO CHANCE.
A TRAIN WENT BY. FAST. DID ANYBODY ABOARD SEE ME, AND UNDERSTAND MY PLIGHT? IT DIDN'T MATTER. I'D BE DEAD IN SECONDS...
HOW TO USE THIS TIME? HOW? *HOW?* IT WAS THE MOST VALUABLE TIME OF MY LIFE, THERE BEING SO LITTLE OF IT.
I FAKED CONVULSIONS AND ROLLED TOWARD THE EDGE OF THE PLATFORM...
HEAAAAAUGH!!
I STOPPED AT THE BRINK, AND THEY RAN UP TO ME...
HEUUUAAEE!!
5

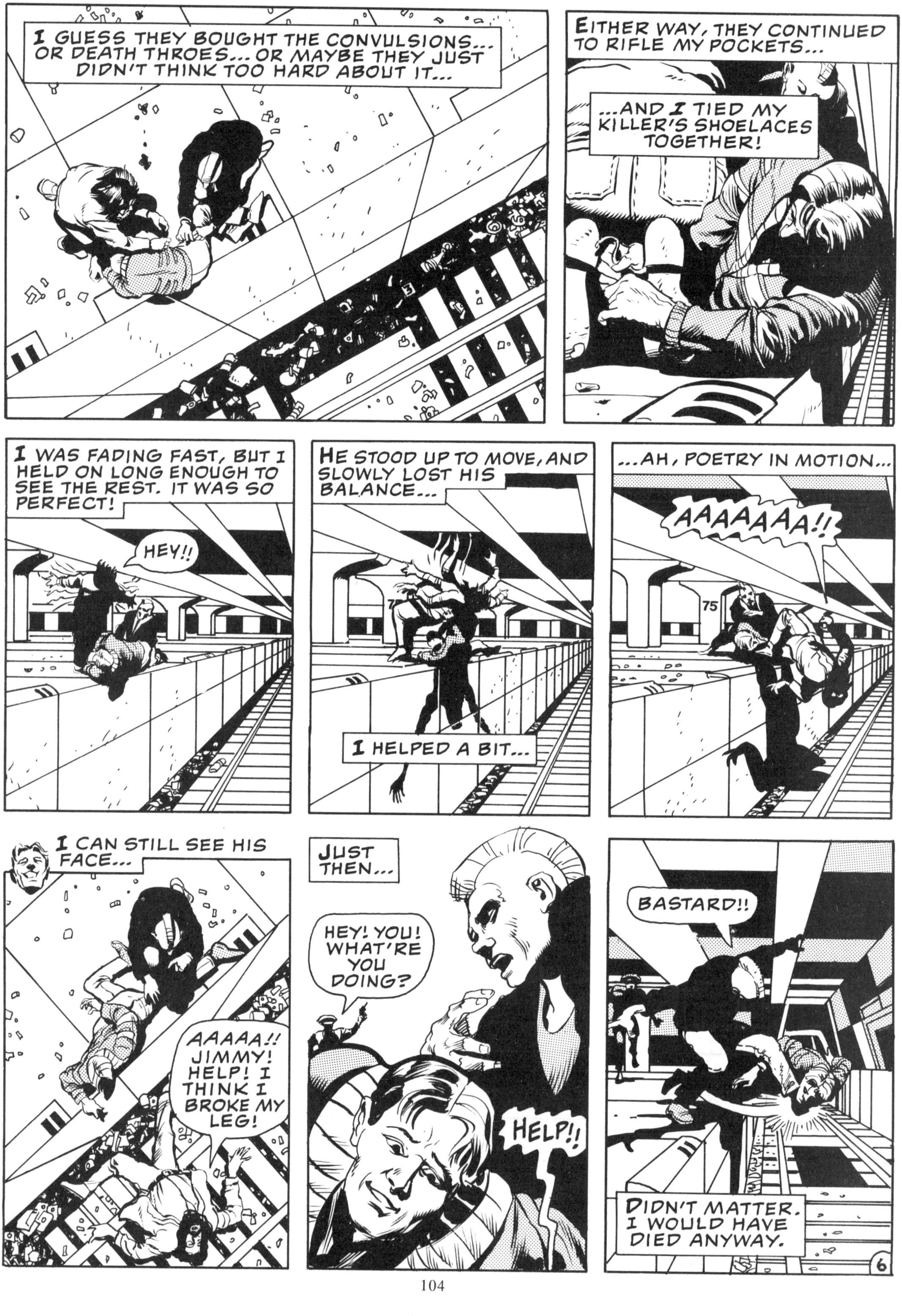
I GUESS THEY BOUGHT THE CONVULSIONS... OR DEATH THROES... OR MAYBE THEY JUST DIDN'T THINK TOO HARD ABOUT IT...
EITHER WAY, THEY CONTINUED TO RIFLE MY POCKETS...
...AND I TIED MY KILLER'S SHOELACES TOGETHER!
I WAS FADING FAST, BUT I HELD ON LONG ENOUGH TO SEE THE REST. IT WAS SO PERFECT!
HEY!!
HE STOOD UP TO MOVE, AND SLOWLY LOST HIS BALANCE...
I HELPED A BIT...
...AH, POETRY IN MOTION...
AAAAAAA!!
75
I CAN STILL SEE HIS FACE...
AAAAA!! JIMMY! HELP! I THINK I BROKE MY LEG!
JUST THEN...
HEY! YOU! WHAT'RE YOU DOING?
HELP!!
BASTARD!!
DIDN'T MATTER. I WOULD HAVE DIED ANYWAY.
6

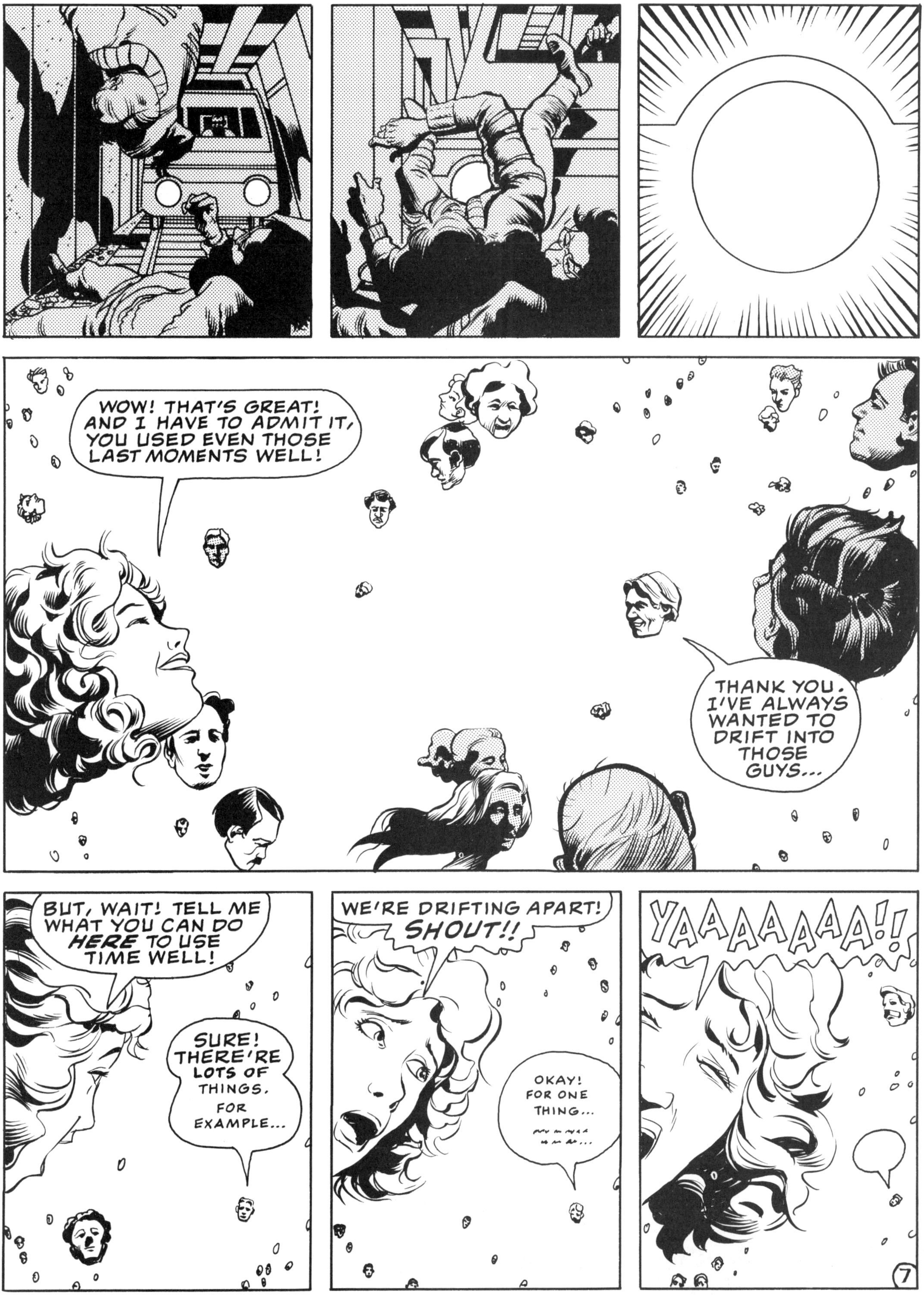
WOW! THAT'S GREAT! AND I HAVE TO ADMIT IT, YOU USED EVEN THOSE LAST MOMENTS WELL!
THANK YOU. I'VE ALWAYS WANTED TO DRIFT INTO THOSE GUYS...
BUT, WAIT! TELL ME WHAT YOU CAN DO HERE TO USE TIME WELL!
SURE! THERE'RE LOTS OF THINGS. FOR EXAMPLE...
WE'RE DRIFTING APART! SHOUT!!
OKAY! FOR ONE THING...
YAAAAAAA!!
7

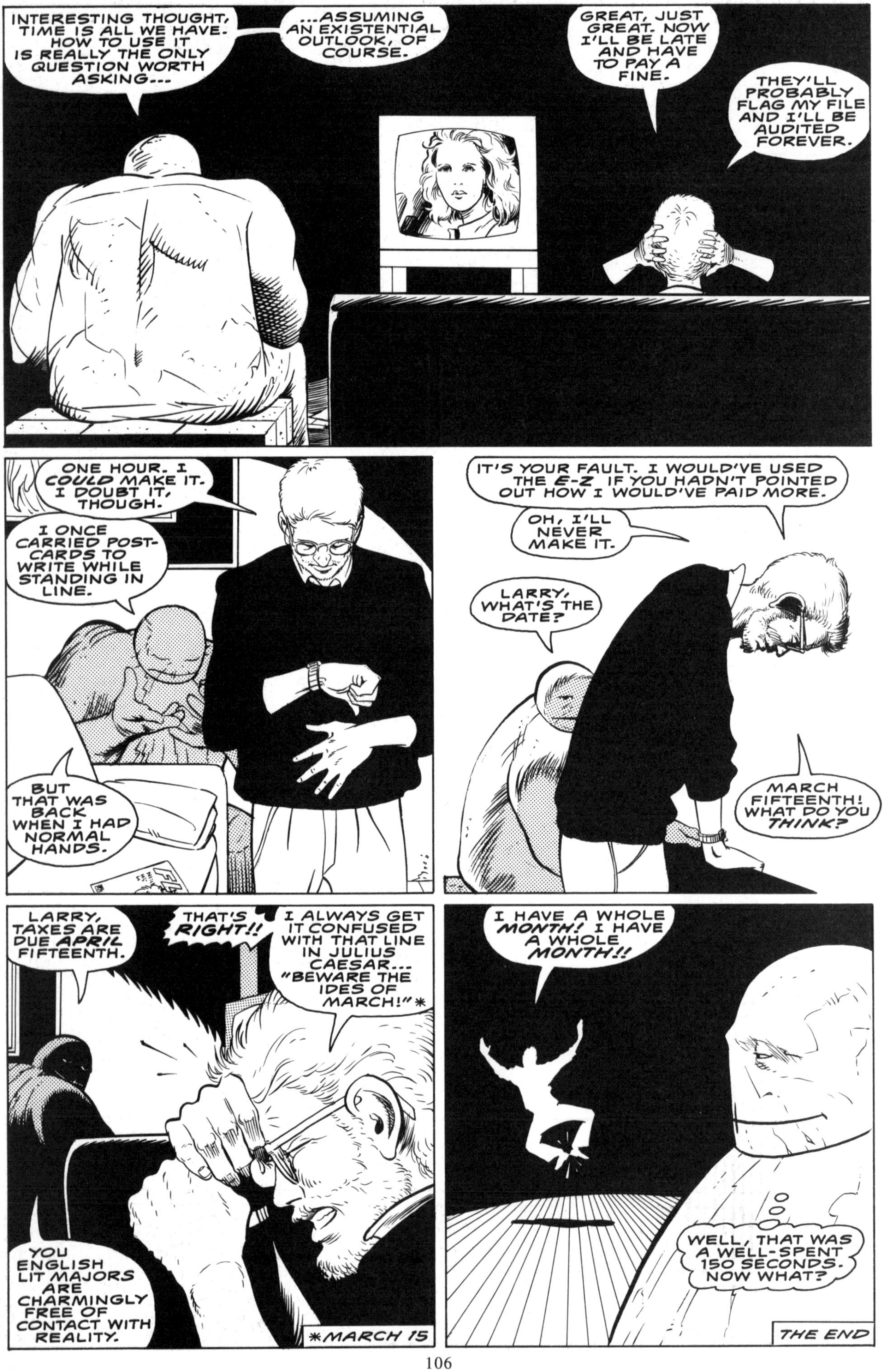
INTERESTING THOUGHT, TIME IS ALL WE HAVE. HOW TO USE IT IS REALLY THE ONLY QUESTION WORTH ASKING...
...ASSUMING AN EXISTENTIAL OUTLOOK, OF COURSE.
GREAT, JUST GREAT. NOW I'LL BE LATE AND HAVE TO PAY A FINE.
THEY'LL PROBABLY FLAG MY FILE AND I'LL BE AUDITED FOREVER.
ONE HOUR. I COULD MAKE IT. I DOUBT IT, THOUGH.
I ONCE CARRIED POST-CARDS TO WRITE WHILE STANDING IN LINE.
BUT THAT WAS BACK WHEN I HAD NORMAL HANDS.
IT'S YOUR FAULT. I WOULD'VE USED THE E-Z IF YOU HADN'T POINTED OUT HOW I WOULD'VE PAID MORE.
OH, I'LL NEVER MAKE IT.
LARRY, WHAT'S THE DATE?
MARCH FIFTEENTH! WHAT DO YOU THINK?
LARRY, TAXES ARE DUE APRIL FIFTEENTH.
THAT'S RIGHT!!
I ALWAYS GET IT CONFUSED WITH THAT LINE IN JULIUS CAESAR... "BEWARE THE IDES OF MARCH!"*
YOU ENGLISH LIT MAJORS ARE CHARMINGLY FREE OF CONTACT WITH REALITY.
*MARCH 15
I HAVE A WHOLE MONTH! I HAVE A WHOLE MONTH!!
WELL, THAT WAS A WELL-SPENT 150 SECONDS. NOW WHAT?
THE END

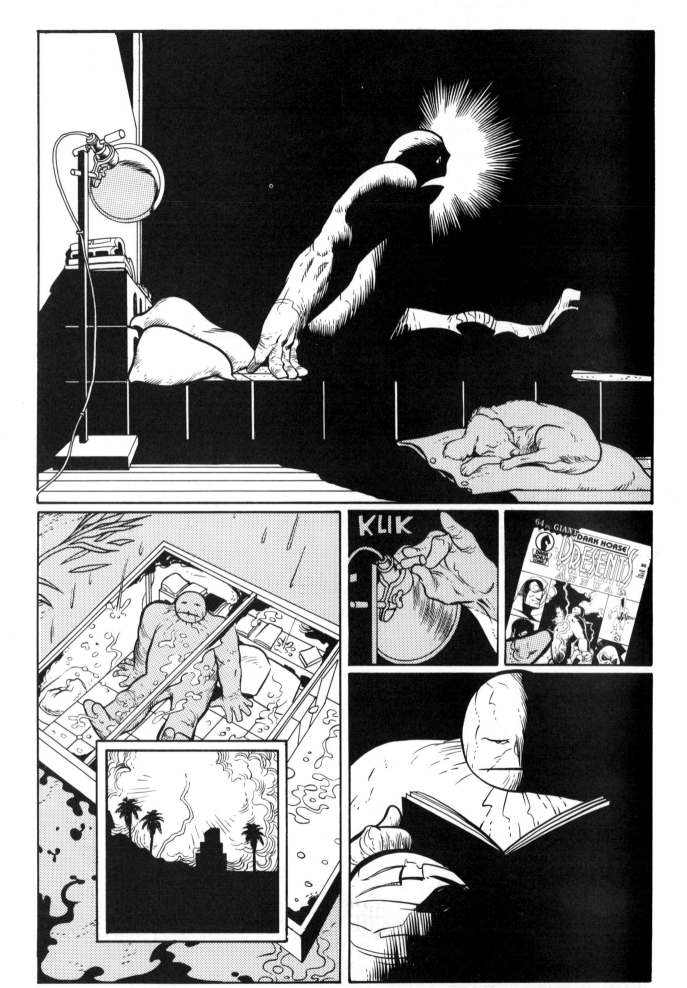

KLIK

64 pg GIANT

DARK HORSE

PRESENTS

ANNUAL

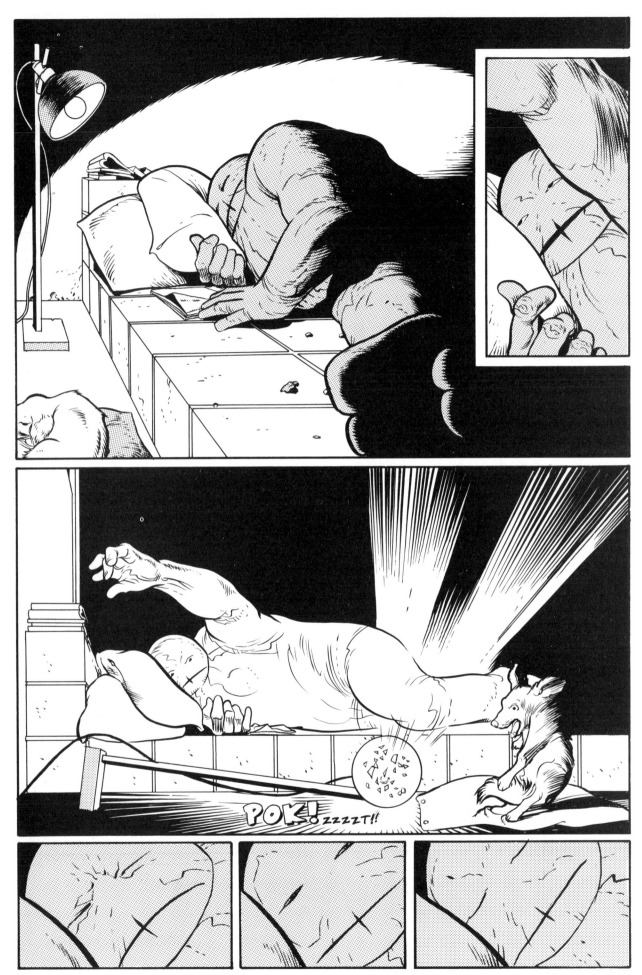

POK! ZZZZT!!

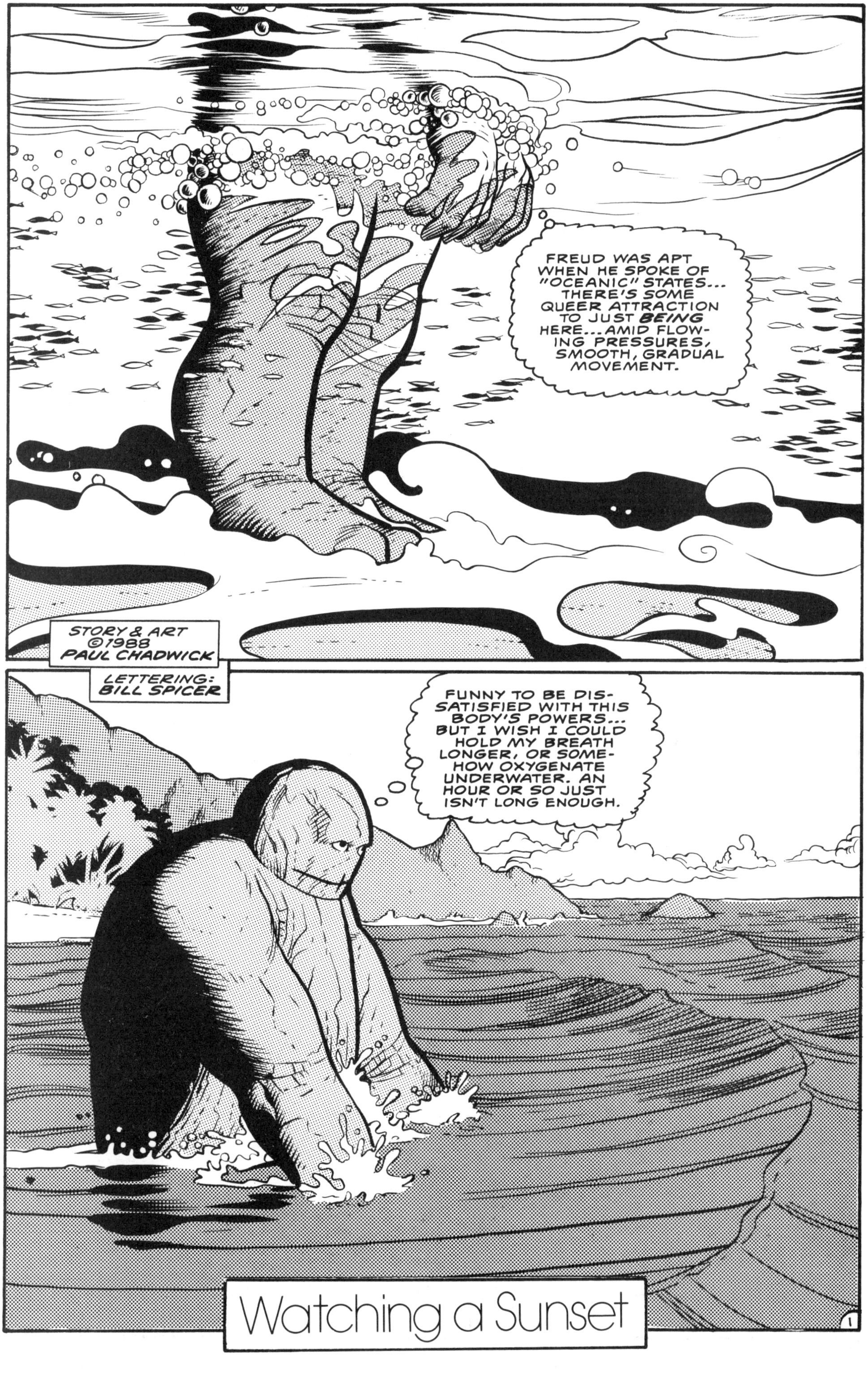
FREUD WAS APT WHEN HE SPOKE OF "OCEANIC" STATES... THERE'S SOME QUEER ATTRACTION TO JUST BEING HERE...AMID FLOWING PRESSURES, SMOOTH, GRADUAL MOVEMENT.
STORY & ART ©1988 PAUL CHADWICK
LETTERING: BILL SPICER
FUNNY TO BE DISSATISFIED WITH THIS BODY'S POWERS... BUT I WISH I COULD HOLD MY BREATH LONGER, OR SOMEHOW OXYGENATE UNDERWATER. AN HOUR OR SO JUST ISN'T LONG ENOUGH.
Watching a Sunset
1

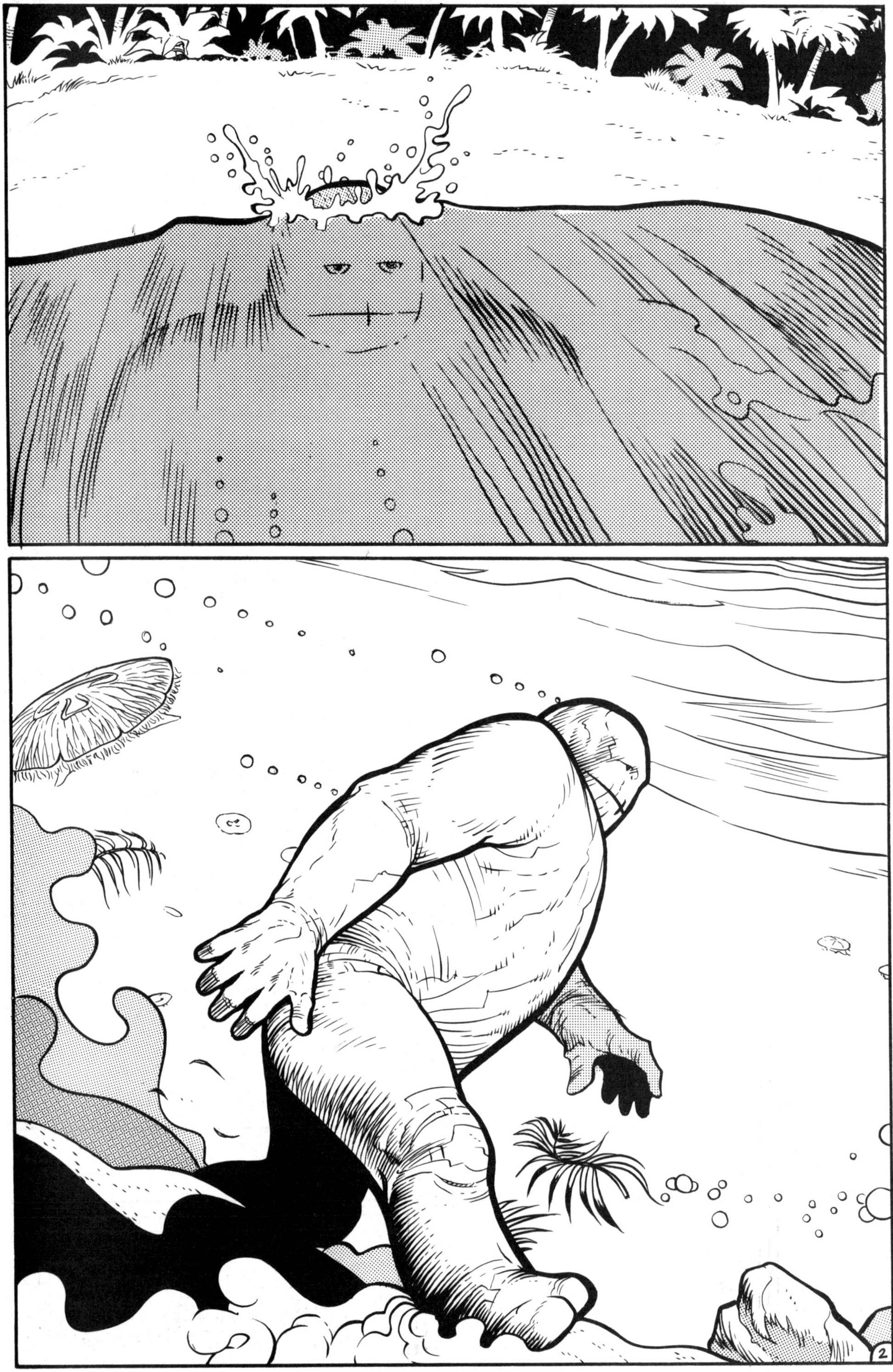
2

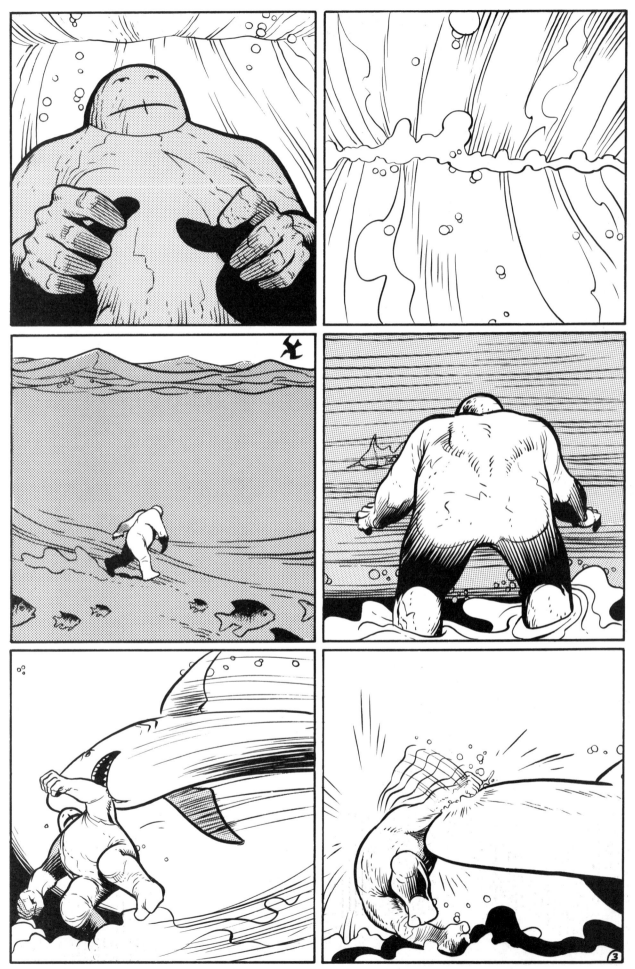

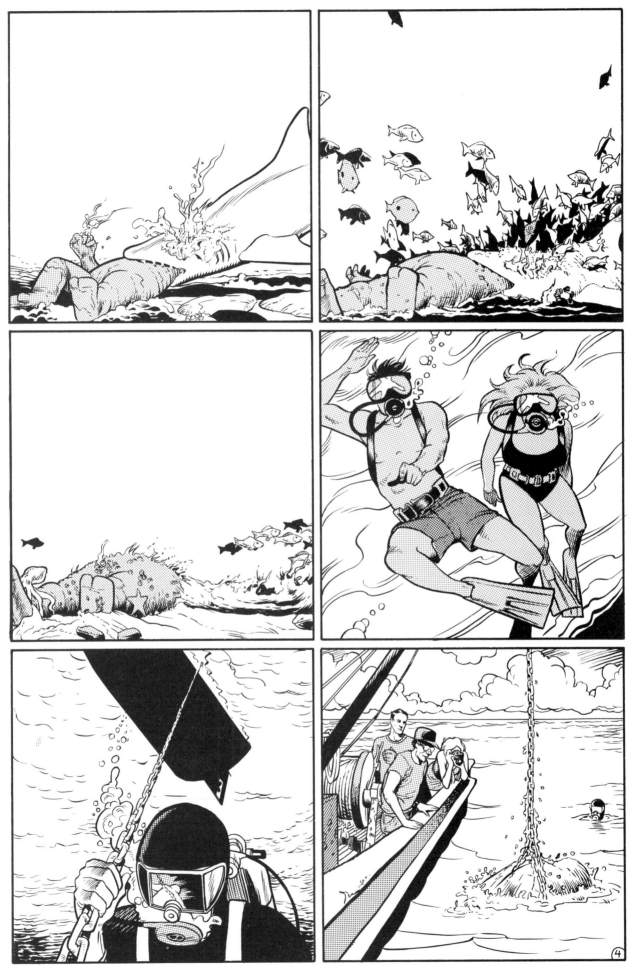

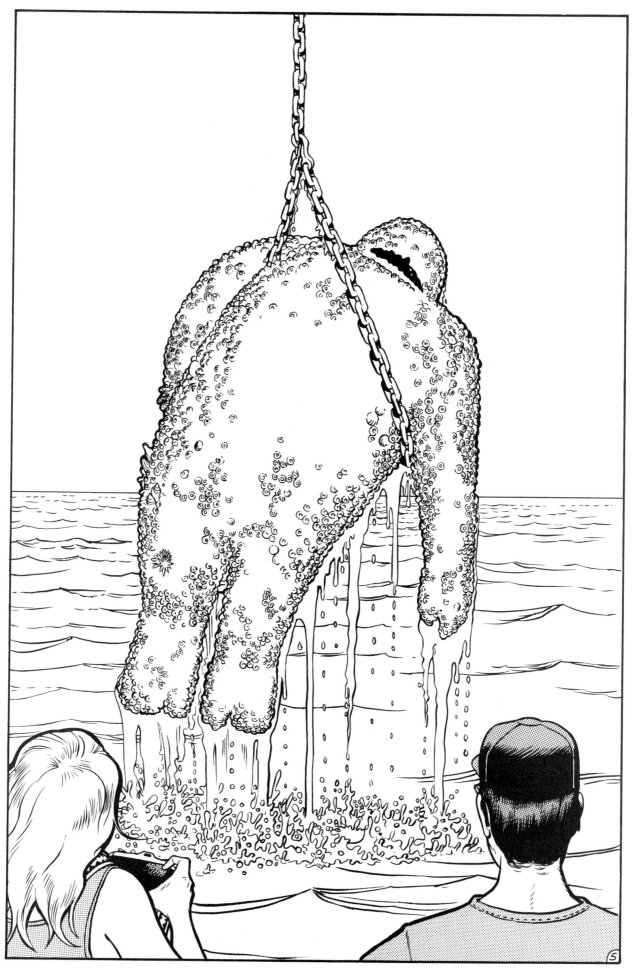

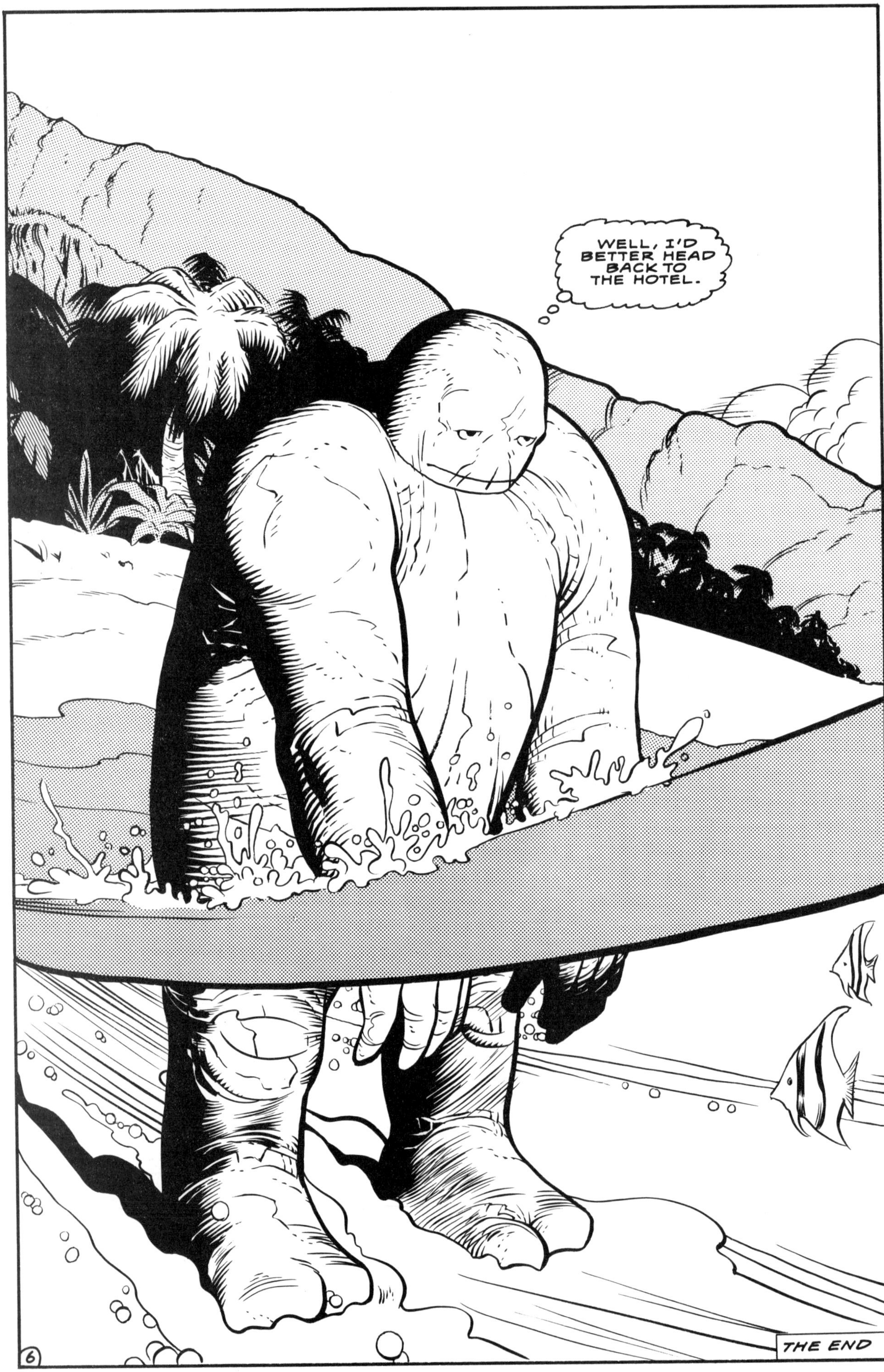
WELL, I'D BETTER HEAD BACK TO THE HOTEL.
6
THE END

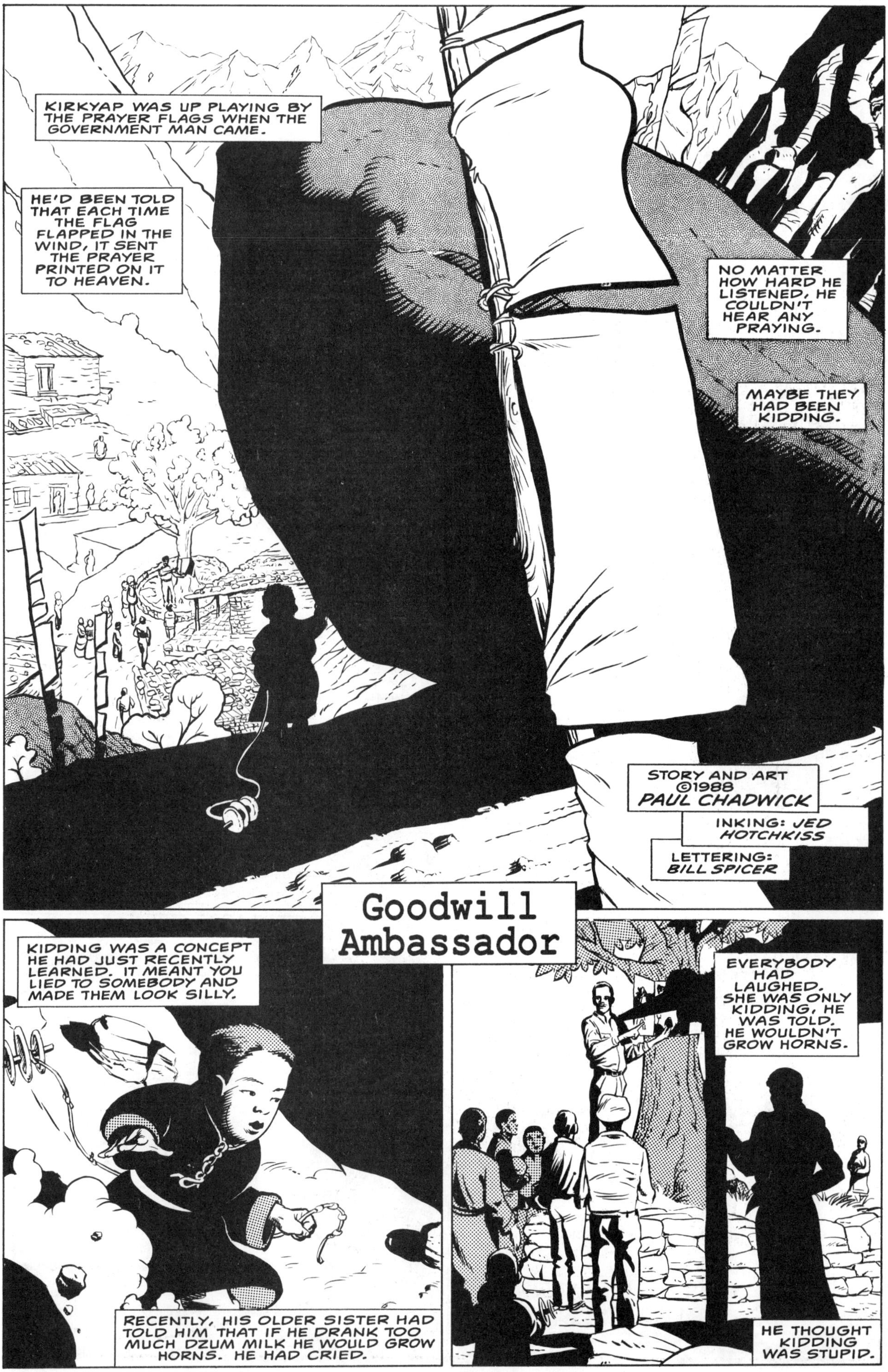
KIRKYAP WAS UP PLAYING BY THE PRAYER FLAGS WHEN THE GOVERNMENT MAN CAME.
HE'D BEEN TOLD THAT EACH TIME THE FLAG FLAPPED IN THE WIND, IT SENT THE PRAYER PRINTED ON IT TO HEAVEN.
NO MATTER HOW HARD HE LISTENED, HE COULDN'T HEAR ANY PRAYING.
MAYBE THEY HAD BEEN KIDDING.
STORY AND ART ©1988 PAUL CHADWICK
INKING: JED HOTCHKISS
LETTERING: BILL SPICER
Goodwill Ambassador
KIDDING WAS A CONCEPT HE HAD JUST RECENTLY LEARNED. IT MEANT YOU LIED TO SOMEBODY AND MADE THEM LOOK SILLY.
RECENTLY, HIS OLDER SISTER HAD TOLD HIM THAT IF HE DRANK TOO MUCH DZUM MILK HE WOULD GROW HORNS. HE HAD CRIED.
EVERYBODY HAD LAUGHED. SHE WAS ONLY KIDDING, HE WAS TOLD. HE WOULDN'T GROW HORNS.
HE THOUGHT KIDDING WAS STUPID.

THE MAN WAS SAYING AN AMERICAN NAMED "CONCRETE" WOULD BE PASSING THROUGH ON HIS WAY TO LHABARMA, WHERE HE WOULD BE BUILDING A BRIDGE.

THIS WAS A MOST UNUSUAL MAN, COVERED WITH ROCK. A ROCK MAN.

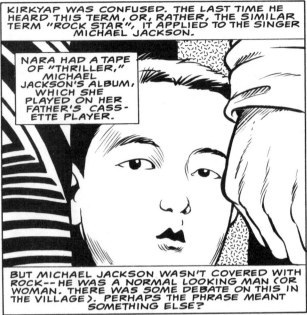

KIRKYAP WAS CONFUSED. THE LAST TIME HE HEARD THIS TERM, OR, RATHER, THE SIMILAR TERM "ROCK STAR", IT APPLIED TO THE SINGER MICHAEL JACKSON.

NARA HAD A TAPE OF "THRILLER," MICHAEL JACKSON'S ALBUM, WHICH SHE PLAYED ON HER FATHER'S CASSETTE PLAYER.

BUT MICHAEL JACKSON WASN'T COVERED WITH ROCK-- HE WAS A NORMAL LOOKING MAN (OR WOMAN). THERE WAS SOME DEBATE ON THIS IN THE VILLAGE). PERHAPS THE PHRASE MEANT SOMETHING ELSE?

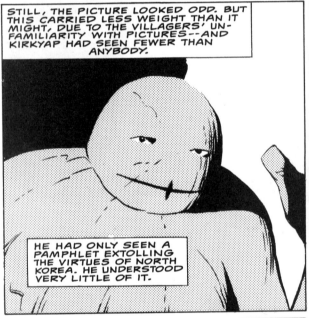

STILL, THE PICTURE LOOKED ODD. BUT THIS CARRIED LESS WEIGHT THAN IT MIGHT, DUE TO THE VILLAGERS' UNFAMILIARITY WITH PICTURES--AND KIRKYAP HAD SEEN FEWER THAN ANYBODY.

HE HAD ONLY SEEN A PAMPHLET EXTOLLING THE VIRTUES OF NORTH KOREA. HE UNDERSTOOD VERY LITTLE OF IT.

IT WAS HARD TO RELATE PICTURES TO REALITY. CONCRETE MIGHT BE THE SIZE OF A MONKEY OR THE SIZE OF A YAK FOR ALL HE KNEW.

THE PICTURES WERE BLACK AND WHITE. WHAT COLOR WAS CONCRETE? DID HE REALLY HAVE NO NOSE, OR WAS THAT A TRICK OF LIGHTING?

EVEN THESE QUESTIONS WENT UNFORMED. INSTEAD, THE PICTURES SIMPLY FAILED TO MAKE MUCH OF AN IMPRESSION ON KIRKYAP.

HE JUST DIDN'T KNOW HOW TO "READ" PHOTOGRAPHS.

WHAT WAS GOING ON?

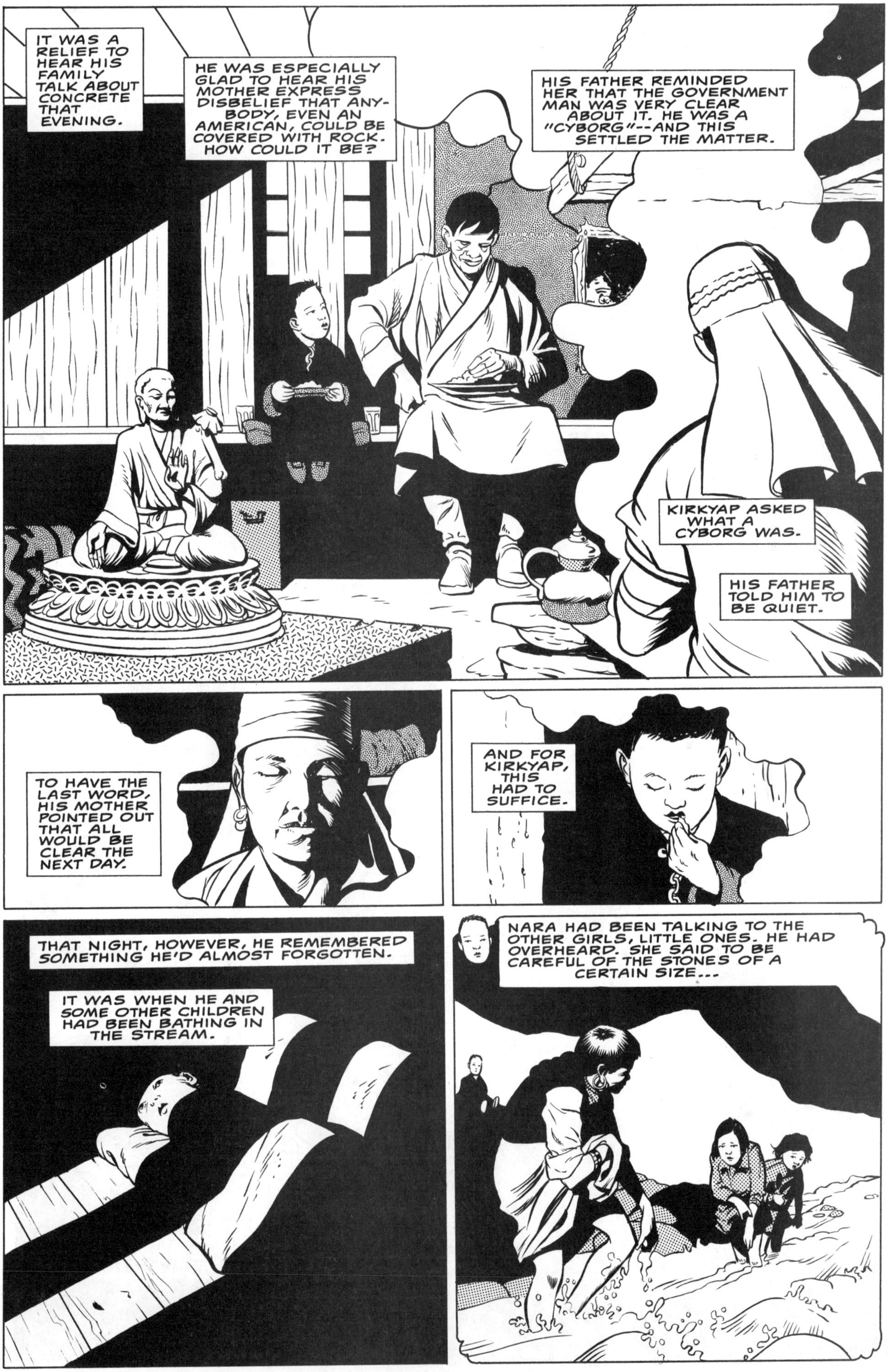
IT WAS A RELIEF TO HEAR HIS FAMILY TALK ABOUT CONCRETE THAT EVENING.
HE WAS ESPECIALLY GLAD TO HEAR HIS MOTHER EXPRESS DISBELIEF THAT ANY-BODY, EVEN AN AMERICAN, COULD BE COVERED WITH ROCK. HOW COULD IT BE?
HIS FATHER REMINDED HER THAT THE GOVERNMENT MAN WAS VERY CLEAR ABOUT IT. HE WAS A "CYBORG"--AND THIS SETTLED THE MATTER.
KIRKYAP ASKED WHAT A CYBORG WAS.
HIS FATHER TOLD HIM TO BE QUIET.
TO HAVE THE LAST WORD, HIS MOTHER POINTED OUT THAT ALL WOULD BE CLEAR THE NEXT DAY.
AND FOR KIRKYAP, THIS HAD TO SUFFICE.
THAT NIGHT, HOWEVER, HE REMEMBERED SOMETHING HE'D ALMOST FORGOTTEN.
IT WAS WHEN HE AND SOME OTHER CHILDREN HAD BEEN BATHING IN THE STREAM.
NARA HAD BEEN TALKING TO THE OTHER GIRLS, LITTLE ONES. HE HAD OVERHEARD. SHE SAID TO BE CAREFUL OF THE STONES OF A CERTAIN SIZE...

NARA SAID THE HEADS OF DEAD PEOPLE SOMETIMES TURNED TO STONE WHEN THEY WERE BURIED.

THESE HEAD-STONES LAY IN THE GROUND FOR A LONG, LONG TIME, BUT SOMETIMES WERE EXPOSED WHEN STREAMS WASHED THE DIRT AWAY.

AT NIGHT THE EXPOSED STONES GAZED UP INTO THE SKY, WONDERING ABOUT THE STARS AND FEELING SAD THEY WERE DEAD. THEIR CONVERSATION SOUNDED EXACTLY LIKE RUNNING WATER.

EVEN DURING THE DAY, THEY WATCHED. BUT AS SOON AS YOU LOOKED AT THEM, THEY TURNED TO ORDINARY STONES.

YOU COULDN'T SURPRISE THEM, NO MATTER HOW FAST YOU WERE.

"SO DON'T LET ANY STONES SEE UP YOUR SARONG," NARA TOLD THE GIRLS. THIS CAUSED BULGING EYES AND NERVOUS GIGGLES.

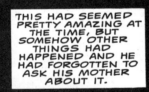

THIS HAD SEEMED PRETTY AMAZING AT THE TIME, BUT SOMEHOW OTHER THINGS HAD HAPPENED AND HE HAD FORGOTTEN TO ASK HIS MOTHER ABOUT IT.

COULD NARA HAVE BEEN KIDDING? SURELY...

BUT HE STILL HAD NIGHTMARES THAT NIGHT.

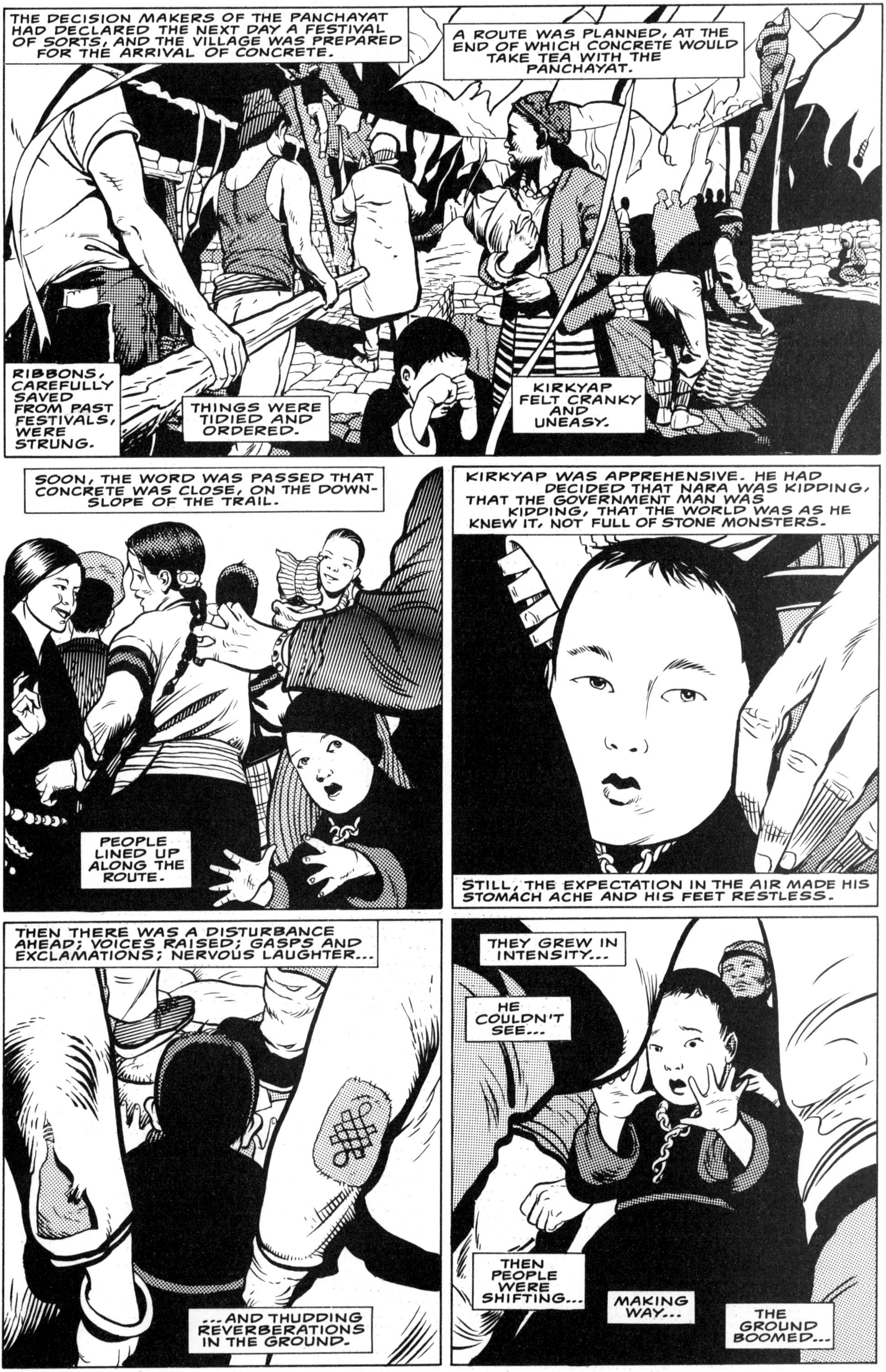
THE DECISION MAKERS OF THE PANCHAYAT HAD DECLARED THE NEXT DAY A FESTIVAL OF SORTS, AND THE VILLAGE WAS PREPARED FOR THE ARRIVAL OF CONCRETE.
A ROUTE WAS PLANNED, AT THE END OF WHICH CONCRETE WOULD TAKE TEA WITH THE PANCHAYAT.
RIBBONS, CAREFULLY SAVED FROM PAST FESTIVALS, WERE STRUNG.
THINGS WERE TIDIED AND ORDERED.
KIRKYAP FELT CRANKY AND UNEASY.
SOON, THE WORD WAS PASSED THAT CONCRETE WAS CLOSE, ON THE DOWN-SLOPE OF THE TRAIL.
PEOPLE LINED UP ALONG THE ROUTE.
KIRKYAP WAS APPREHENSIVE. HE HAD DECIDED THAT NARA WAS KIDDING, THAT THE GOVERNMENT MAN WAS KIDDING, THAT THE WORLD WAS AS HE KNEW IT, NOT FULL OF STONE MONSTERS.
STILL, THE EXPECTATION IN THE AIR MADE HIS STOMACH ACHE AND HIS FEET RESTLESS.
THEN THERE WAS A DISTURBANCE AHEAD; VOICES RAISED; GASPS AND EXCLAMATIONS; NERVOUS LAUGHTER...
...AND THUDDING REVERBERATIONS IN THE GROUND.
THEY GREW IN INTENSITY...
HE COULDN'T SEE...
THEN PEOPLE WERE SHIFTING...
MAKING WAY...
THE GROUND BOOMED...

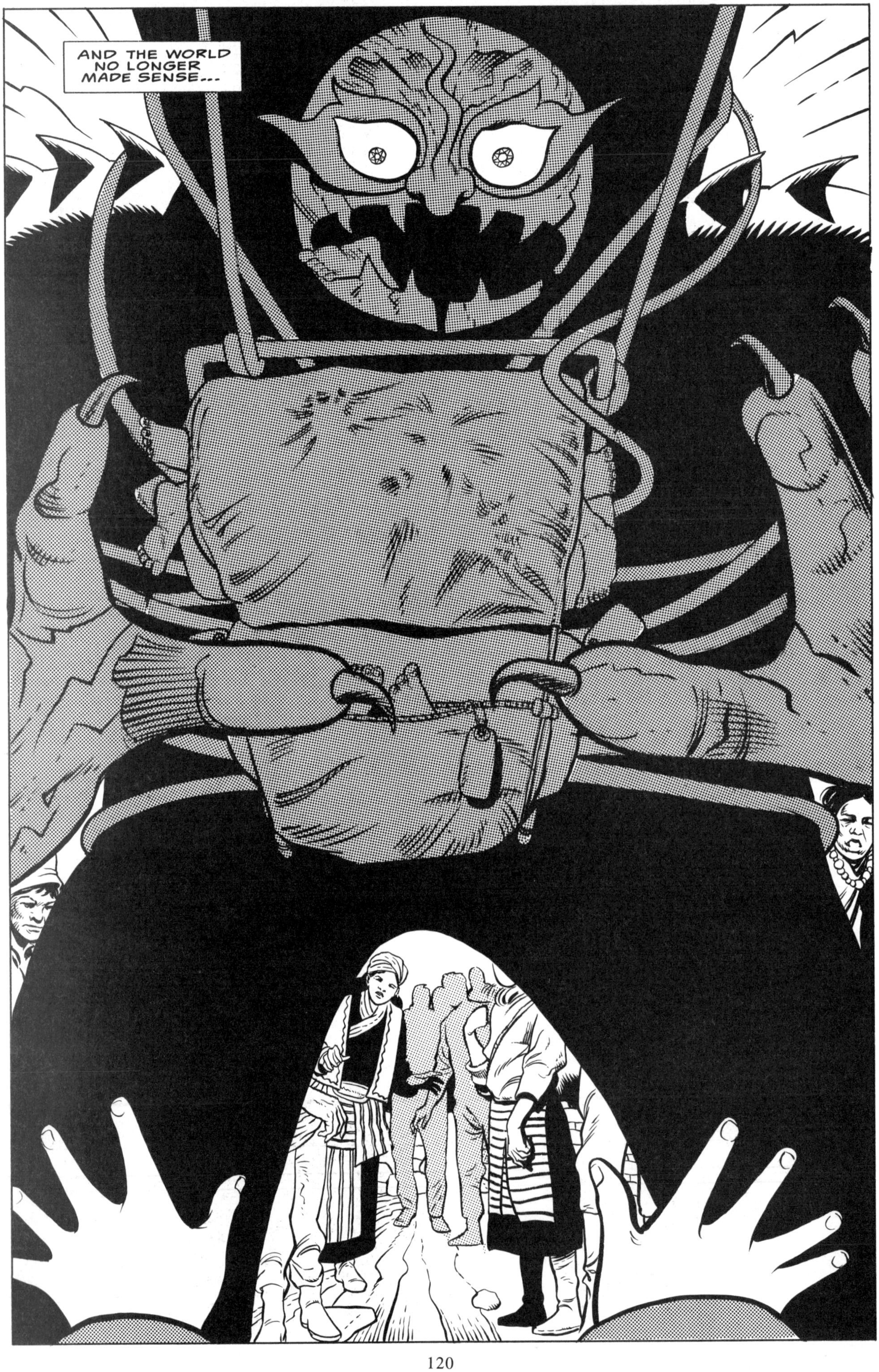
AND THE WORLD NO LONGER MADE SENSE...

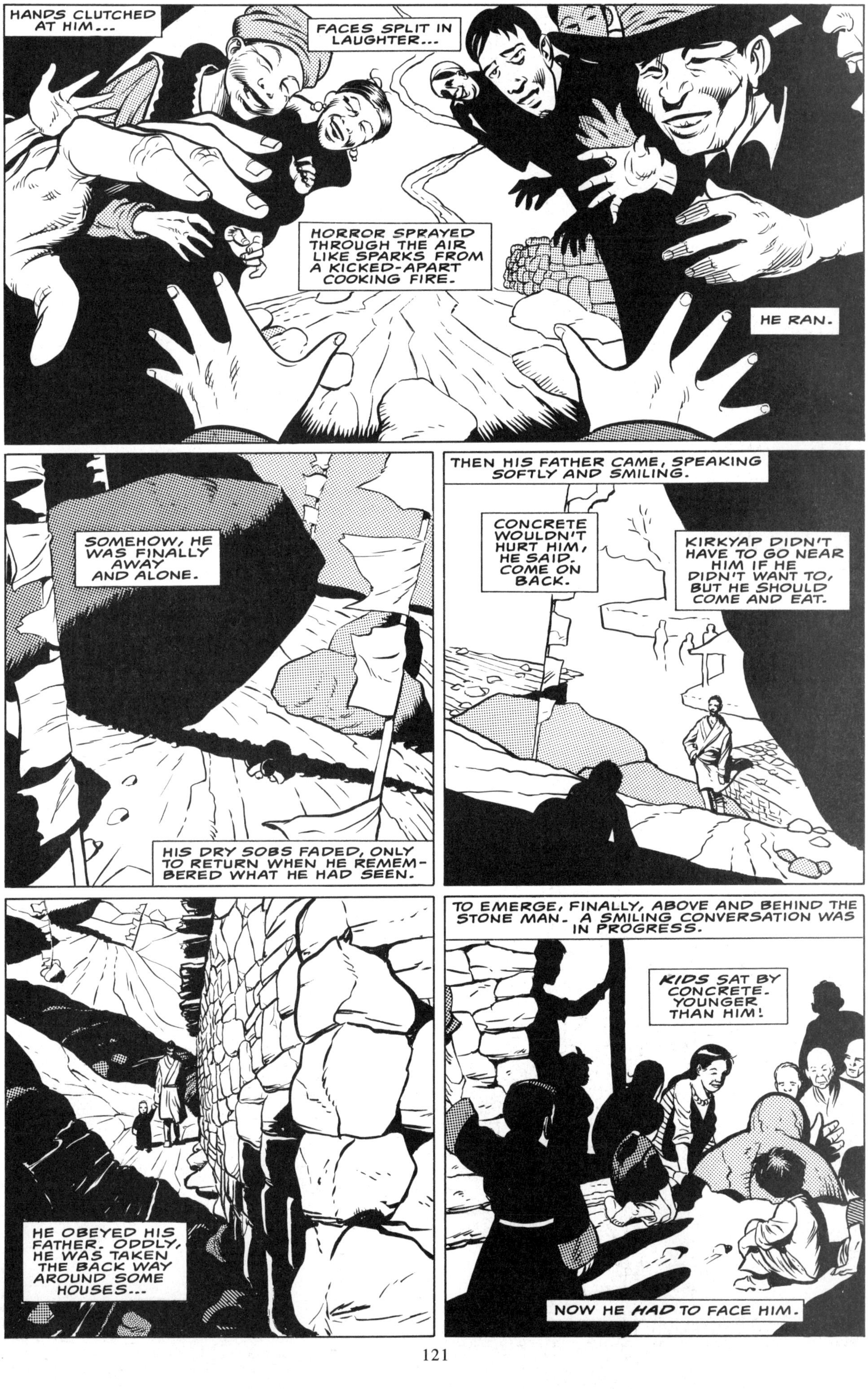
HANDS CLUTCHED AT HIM...
FACES SPLIT IN LAUGHTER...
HORROR SPRAYED THROUGH THE AIR LIKE SPARKS FROM A KICKED-APART COOKING FIRE.
HE RAN.
SOMEHOW, HE WAS FINALLY AWAY AND ALONE.
HIS DRY SOBS FADED, ONLY TO RETURN WHEN HE REMEMBERED WHAT HE HAD SEEN.
THEN HIS FATHER CAME, SPEAKING SOFTLY AND SMILING.
CONCRETE WOULDN'T HURT HIM, HE SAID. COME ON BACK.
KIRKYAP DIDN'T HAVE TO GO NEAR HIM IF HE DIDN'T WANT TO, BUT HE SHOULD COME AND EAT.
HE OBEYED HIS FATHER. ODDLY, HE WAS TAKEN THE BACK WAY AROUND SOME HOUSES...
TO EMERGE, FINALLY, ABOVE AND BEHIND THE STONE MAN. A SMILING CONVERSATION WAS IN PROGRESS.
KIDS SAT BY CONCRETE. YOUNGER THAN HIM!
NOW HE HAD TO FACE HIM.

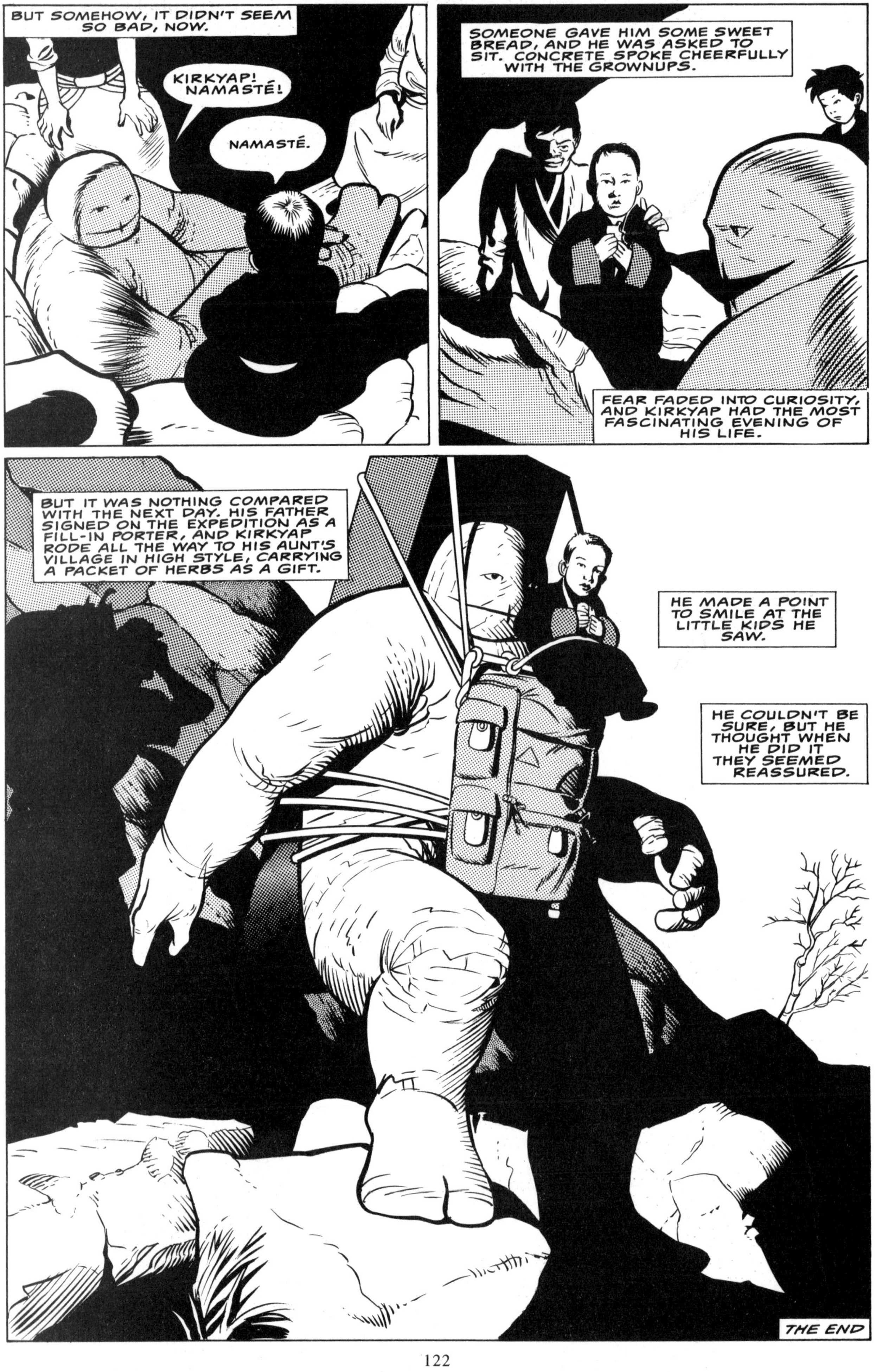
BUT SOMEHOW, IT DIDN'T SEEM SO BAD, NOW.
KIRKYAP! NAMASTÉ!
NAMASTÉ.
SOMEONE GAVE HIM SOME SWEET BREAD, AND HE WAS ASKED TO SIT. CONCRETE SPOKE CHEERFULLY WITH THE GROWNUPS.
FEAR FADED INTO CURIOSITY, AND KIRKYAP HAD THE MOST FASCINATING EVENING OF HIS LIFE.
BUT IT WAS NOTHING COMPARED WITH THE NEXT DAY. HIS FATHER SIGNED ON THE EXPEDITION AS A FILL-IN PORTER, AND KIRKYAP RODE ALL THE WAY TO HIS AUNT'S VILLAGE IN HIGH STYLE, CARRYING A PACKET OF HERBS AS A GIFT.
HE MADE A POINT TO SMILE AT THE LITTLE KIDS HE SAW.
HE COULDN'T BE SURE, BUT HE THOUGHT WHEN HE DID IT THEY SEEMED REASSURED.
THE END

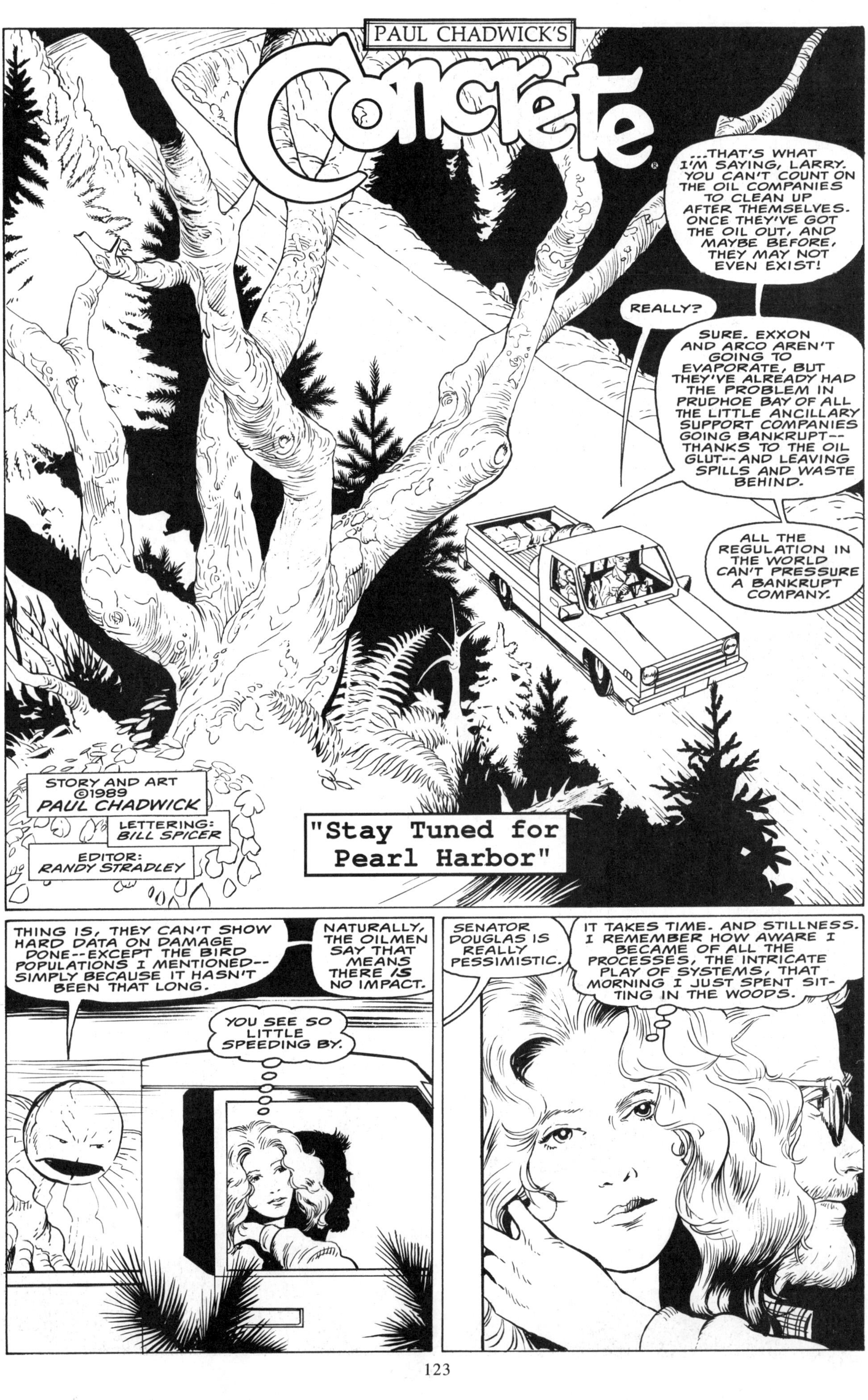
PAUL CHADWICK'S
Concrete
...THAT'S WHAT I'M SAYING, LARRY. YOU CAN'T COUNT ON THE OIL COMPANIES TO CLEAN UP AFTER THEMSELVES. ONCE THEY'VE GOT THE OIL OUT, AND MAYBE BEFORE, THEY MAY NOT EVEN EXIST!
REALLY?
SURE. EXXON AND ARCO AREN'T GOING TO EVAPORATE, BUT THEY'VE ALREADY HAD THE PROBLEM IN PRUDHOE BAY OF ALL THE LITTLE ANCILLARY SUPPORT COMPANIES GOING BANKRUPT--THANKS TO THE OIL GLUT--AND LEAVING SPILLS AND WASTE BEHIND.
ALL THE REGULATION IN THE WORLD CAN'T PRESSURE A BANKRUPT COMPANY.
STORY AND ART ©1989 PAUL CHADWICK
LETTERING: BILL SPICER
EDITOR: RANDY STRADLEY
"Stay Tuned for Pearl Harbor"
THING IS, THEY CAN'T SHOW HARD DATA ON DAMAGE DONE--EXCEPT THE BIRD POPULATIONS I MENTIONED--SIMPLY BECAUSE IT HASN'T BEEN THAT LONG.
NATURALLY, THE OILMEN SAY THAT MEANS THERE IS NO IMPACT.
YOU SEE SO LITTLE SPEEDING BY.
SENATOR DOUGLAS IS REALLY PESSIMISTIC.
IT TAKES TIME. AND STILLNESS. I REMEMBER HOW AWARE I BECAME OF ALL THE PROCESSES, THE INTRICATE PLAY OF SYSTEMS, THAT MORNING I JUST SPENT SITTING IN THE WOODS.

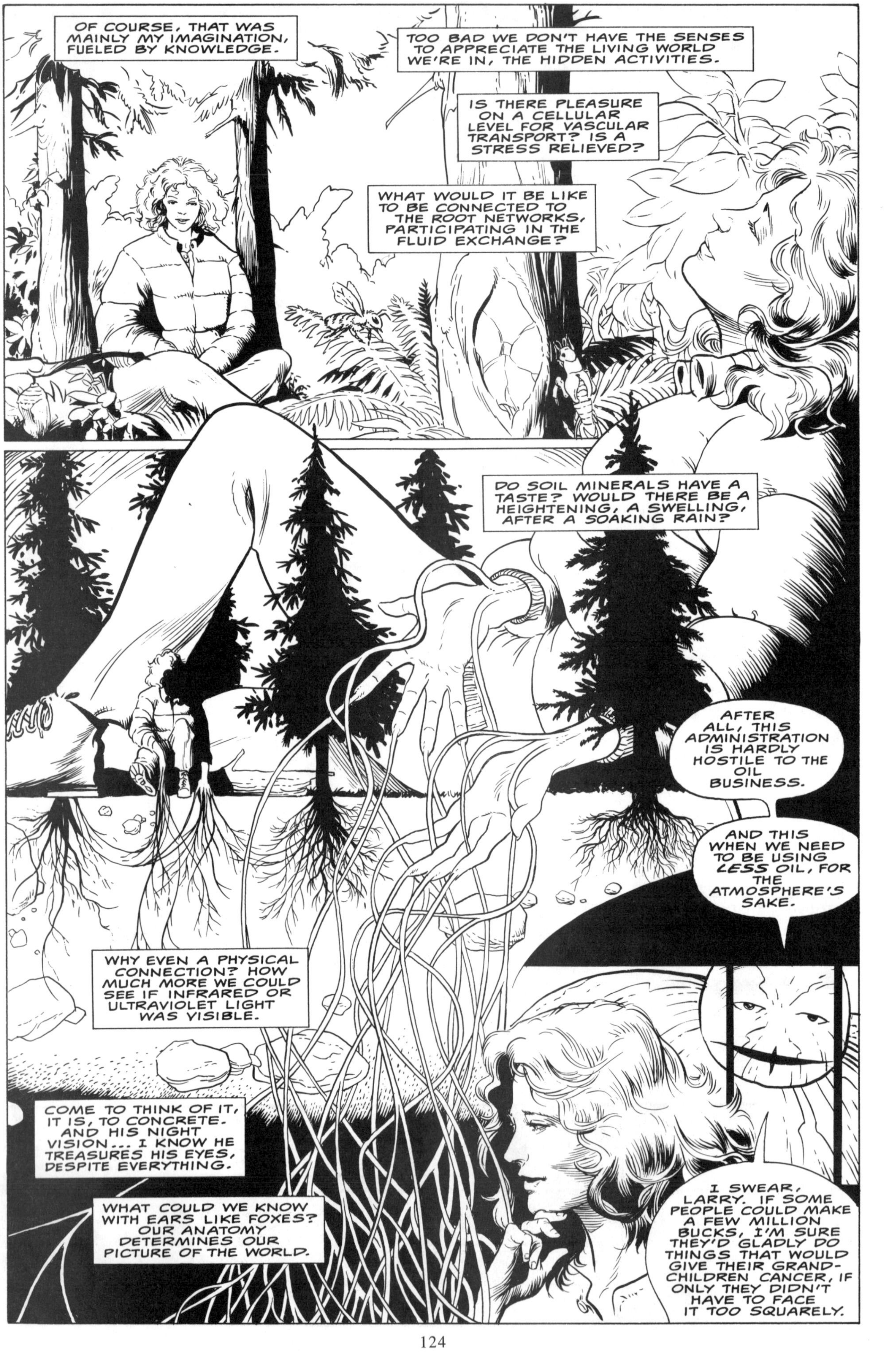
OF COURSE, THAT WAS MAINLY MY IMAGINATION, FUELED BY KNOWLEDGE.
TOO BAD WE DON'T HAVE THE SENSES TO APPRECIATE THE LIVING WORLD WE'RE IN, THE HIDDEN ACTIVITIES.
IS THERE PLEASURE ON A CELLULAR LEVEL FOR VASCULAR TRANSPORT? IS A STRESS RELIEVED?
WHAT WOULD IT BE LIKE TO BE CONNECTED TO THE ROOT NETWORKS, PARTICIPATING IN THE FLUID EXCHANGE?
DO SOIL MINERALS HAVE A TASTE? WOULD THERE BE A HEIGHTENING, A SWELLING, AFTER A SOAKING RAIN?
AFTER ALL, THIS ADMINISTRATION IS HARDLY HOSTILE TO THE OIL BUSINESS.
AND THIS WHEN WE NEED TO BE USING LESS OIL, FOR THE ATMOSPHERE'S SAKE.
WHY EVEN A PHYSICAL CONNECTION? HOW MUCH MORE WE COULD SEE IF INFRARED OR ULTRAVIOLET LIGHT WAS VISIBLE.
COME TO THINK OF IT, IT IS, TO CONCRETE. AND HIS NIGHT VISION... I KNOW HE TREASURES HIS EYES, DESPITE EVERYTHING.
WHAT COULD WE KNOW WITH EARS LIKE FOXES? OUR ANATOMY DETERMINES OUR PICTURE OF THE WORLD.
I SWEAR, LARRY. IF SOME PEOPLE COULD MAKE A FEW MILLION BUCKS, I'M SURE THEY'D GLADLY DO THINGS THAT WOULD GIVE THEIR GRAND-CHILDREN CANCER, IF ONLY THEY DIDN'T HAVE TO FACE IT TOO SQUARELY.

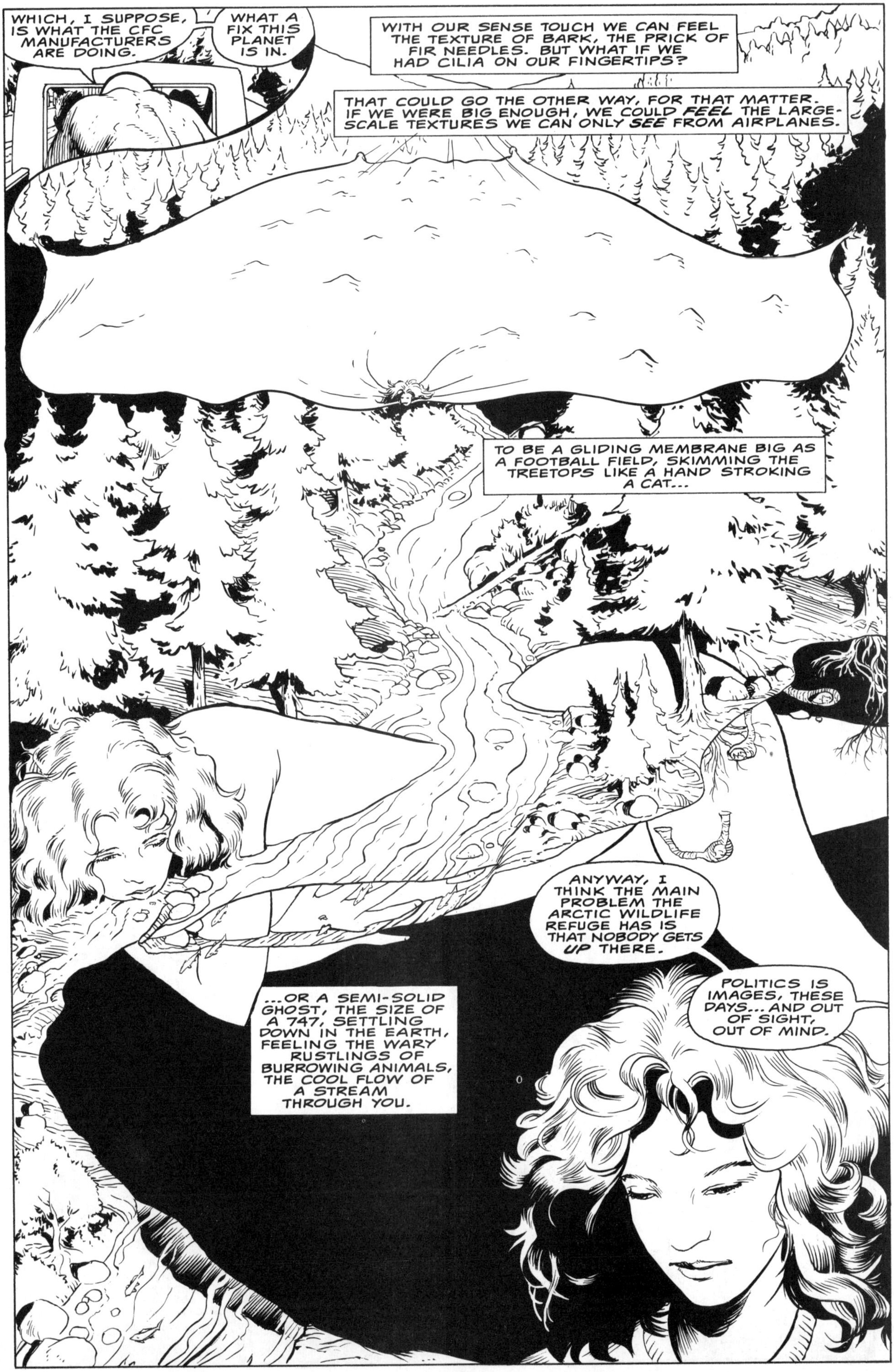
WHICH, I SUPPOSE, IS WHAT THE CFC MANUFACTURERS ARE DOING.
WHAT A FIX THIS PLANET IS IN.
WITH OUR SENSE TOUCH WE CAN FEEL THE TEXTURE OF BARK, THE PRICK OF FIR NEEDLES. BUT WHAT IF WE HAD CILIA ON OUR FINGERTIPS?
THAT COULD GO THE OTHER WAY, FOR THAT MATTER. IF WE WERE BIG ENOUGH, WE COULD *FEEL* THE LARGE-SCALE TEXTURES WE CAN ONLY *SEE* FROM AIRPLANES.
TO BE A GLIDING MEMBRANE BIG AS A FOOTBALL FIELD, SKIMMING THE TREETOPS LIKE A HAND STROKING A CAT...
...OR A SEMI-SOLID GHOST, THE SIZE OF A 747, SETTLING DOWN IN THE EARTH, FEELING THE WARY RUSTLINGS OF BURROWING ANIMALS, THE COOL FLOW OF A STREAM THROUGH YOU.
ANYWAY, I THINK THE MAIN PROBLEM THE ARCTIC WILDLIFE REFUGE HAS IS THAT NOBODY GETS *UP* THERE.
POLITICS IS IMAGES, THESE DAYS... AND OUT OF SIGHT, OUT OF MIND.

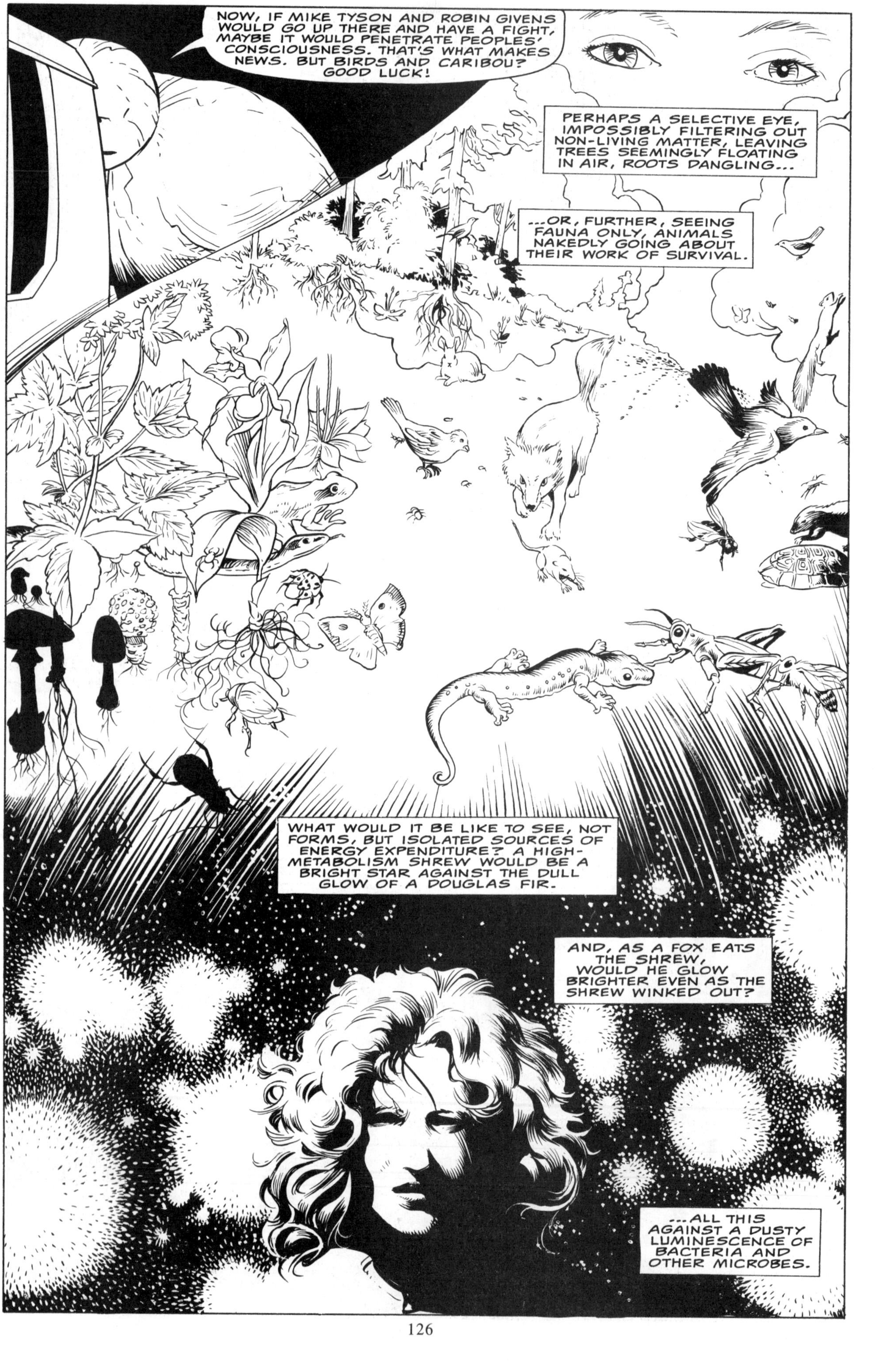
NOW, IF MIKE TYSON AND ROBIN GIVENS WOULD GO UP THERE AND HAVE A FIGHT, MAYBE IT WOULD PENETRATE PEOPLES' CONSCIOUSNESS. THAT'S WHAT MAKES NEWS. BUT BIRDS AND CARIBOU? GOOD LUCK!
PERHAPS A SELECTIVE EYE, IMPOSSIBLY FILTERING OUT NON-LIVING MATTER, LEAVING TREES SEEMINGLY FLOATING IN AIR, ROOTS DANGLING...
...OR, FURTHER, SEEING FAUNA ONLY, ANIMALS NAKEDLY GOING ABOUT THEIR WORK OF SURVIVAL.
WHAT WOULD IT BE LIKE TO SEE, NOT FORMS, BUT ISOLATED SOURCES OF ENERGY EXPENDITURE? A HIGH-METABOLISM SHREW WOULD BE A BRIGHT STAR AGAINST THE DULL GLOW OF A DOUGLAS FIR.
AND, AS A FOX EATS THE SHREW, WOULD HE GLOW BRIGHTER EVEN AS THE SHREW WINKED OUT?
...ALL THIS AGAINST A DUSTY LUMINESCENCE OF BACTERIA AND OTHER MICROBES.

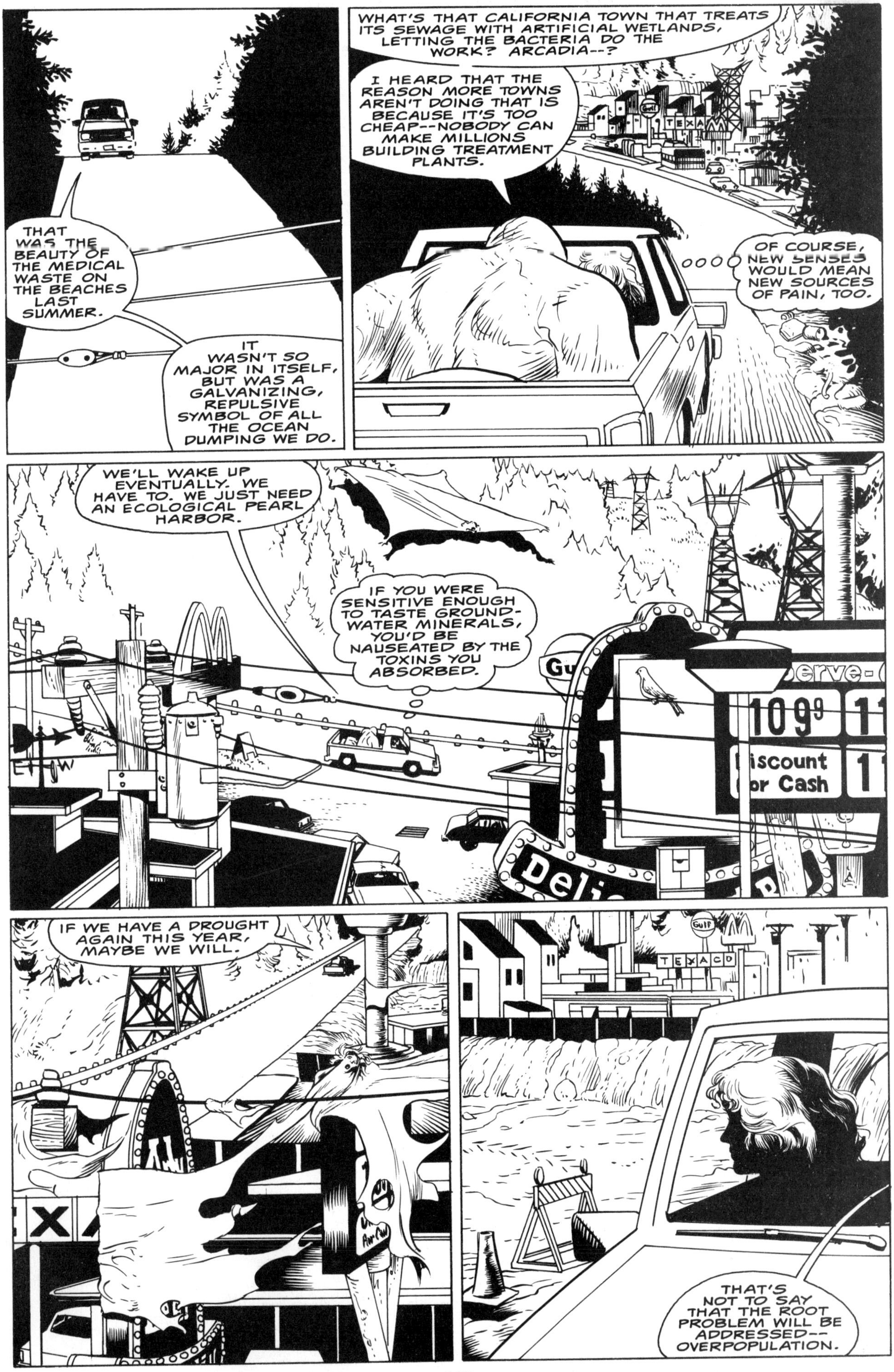
THAT WAS THE BEAUTY OF THE MEDICAL WASTE ON THE BEACHES LAST SUMMER.
IT WASN'T SO MAJOR IN ITSELF, BUT WAS A GALVANIZING, REPULSIVE SYMBOL OF ALL THE OCEAN DUMPING WE DO.
WHAT'S THAT CALIFORNIA TOWN THAT TREATS ITS SEWAGE WITH ARTIFICIAL WETLANDS, LETTING THE BACTERIA DO THE WORK? ARCADIA--?
I HEARD THAT THE REASON MORE TOWNS AREN'T DOING THAT IS BECAUSE IT'S TOO CHEAP--NOBODY CAN MAKE MILLIONS BUILDING TREATMENT PLANTS.
OF COURSE, NEW SENSES WOULD MEAN NEW SOURCES OF PAIN, TOO.
WE'LL WAKE UP EVENTUALLY. WE HAVE TO. WE JUST NEED AN ECOLOGICAL PEARL HARBOR.
IF YOU WERE SENSITIVE ENOUGH TO TASTE GROUND-WATER MINERALS, YOU'D BE NAUSEATED BY THE TOXINS YOU ABSORBED.
109⁹
Discount
or Cash
IF WE HAVE A DROUGHT AGAIN THIS YEAR, MAYBE WE WILL.
TEXACO
THAT'S NOT TO SAY THAT THE ROOT PROBLEM WILL BE ADDRESSED--OVERPOPULATION.

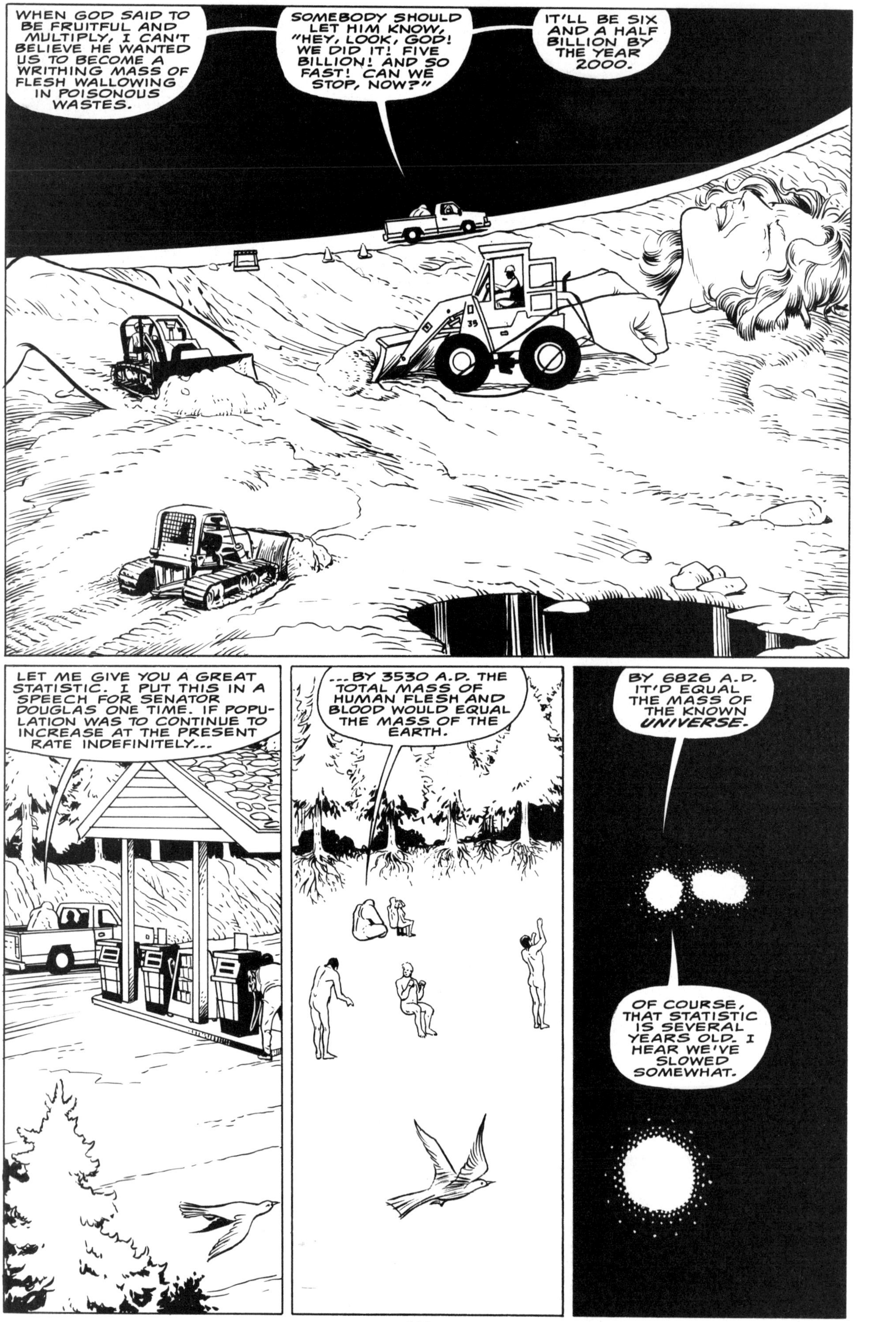
WHEN GOD SAID TO BE FRUITFUL AND MULTIPLY, I CAN'T BELIEVE HE WANTED US TO BECOME A WRITHING MASS OF FLESH WALLOWING IN POISONOUS WASTES.
SOMEBODY SHOULD LET HIM KNOW, "HEY, LOOK, GOD! WE DID IT! FIVE BILLION! AND SO FAST! CAN WE STOP, NOW?"
IT'LL BE SIX AND A HALF BILLION BY THE YEAR 2000.
35
LET ME GIVE YOU A GREAT STATISTIC. I PUT THIS IN A SPEECH FOR SENATOR DOUGLAS ONE TIME. IF POPULATION WAS TO CONTINUE TO INCREASE AT THE PRESENT RATE INDEFINITELY...
...BY 3530 A.D. THE TOTAL MASS OF HUMAN FLESH AND BLOOD WOULD EQUAL THE MASS OF THE EARTH.
BY 6826 A.D. IT'D EQUAL THE MASS OF THE KNOWN UNIVERSE.
OF COURSE, THAT STATISTIC IS SEVERAL YEARS OLD. I HEAR WE'VE SLOWED SOMEWHAT.

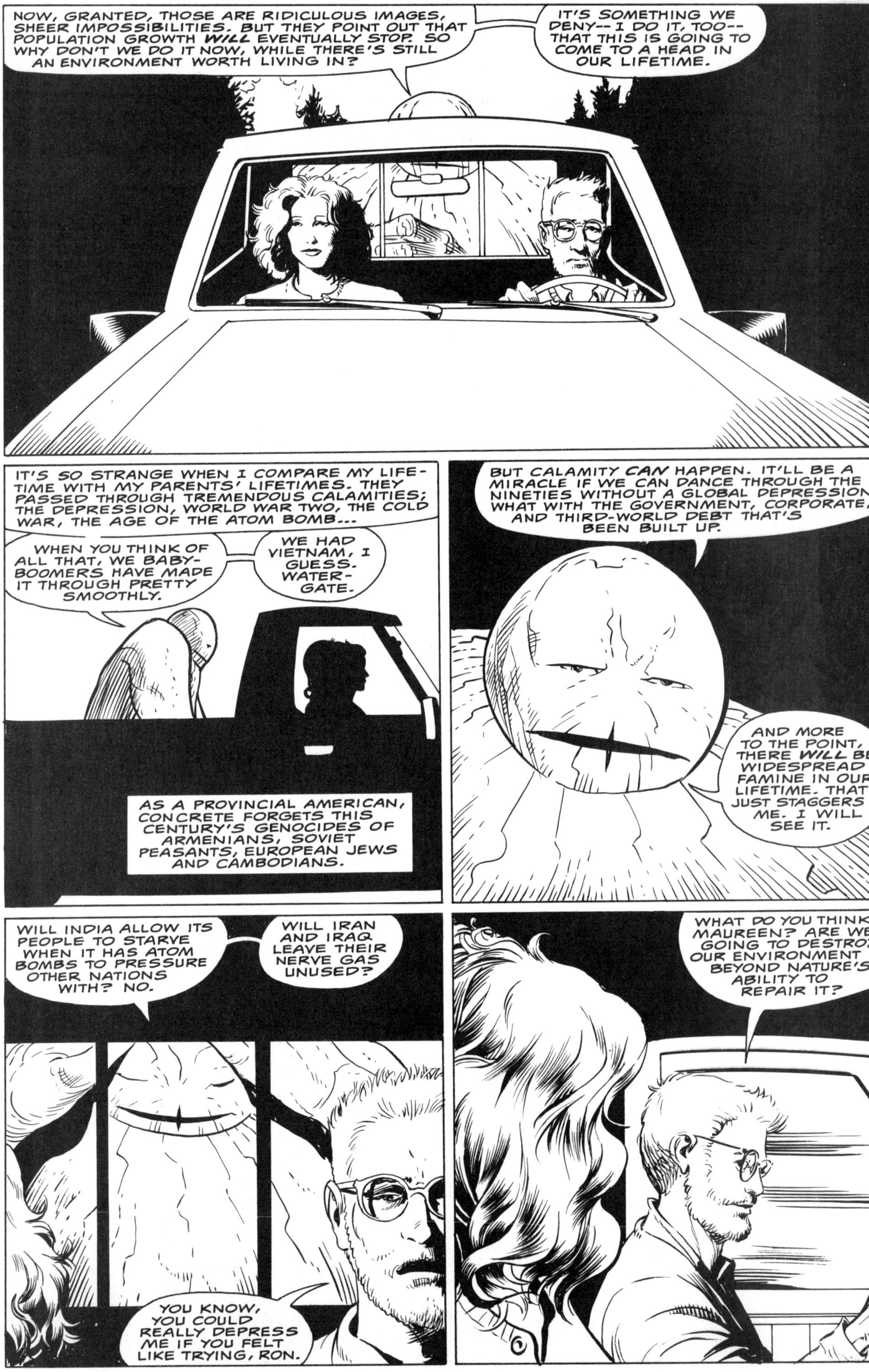
NOW, GRANTED, THOSE ARE RIDICULOUS IMAGES, SHEER IMPOSSIBILITIES. BUT THEY POINT OUT THAT POPULATION GROWTH WILL EVENTUALLY STOP. SO WHY DON'T WE DO IT NOW, WHILE THERE'S STILL AN ENVIRONMENT WORTH LIVING IN?
IT'S SOMETHING WE DENY-- I DO IT, TOO-- THAT THIS IS GOING TO COME TO A HEAD IN OUR LIFETIME.
IT'S SO STRANGE WHEN I COMPARE MY LIFETIME WITH MY PARENTS' LIFETIMES. THEY PASSED THROUGH TREMENDOUS CALAMITIES; THE DEPRESSION, WORLD WAR TWO, THE COLD WAR, THE AGE OF THE ATOM BOMB...
WHEN YOU THINK OF ALL THAT, WE BABY-BOOMERS HAVE MADE IT THROUGH PRETTY SMOOTHLY.
WE HAD VIETNAM, I GUESS. WATERGATE.
AS A PROVINCIAL AMERICAN, CONCRETE FORGETS THIS CENTURY'S GENOCIDES OF ARMENIANS, SOVIET PEASANTS, EUROPEAN JEWS AND CAMBODIANS.
BUT CALAMITY CAN HAPPEN. IT'LL BE A MIRACLE IF WE CAN DANCE THROUGH THE NINETIES WITHOUT A GLOBAL DEPRESSION, WHAT WITH THE GOVERNMENT, CORPORATE, AND THIRD-WORLD DEBT THAT'S BEEN BUILT UP.
AND MORE TO THE POINT, THERE WILL BE WIDESPREAD FAMINE IN OUR LIFETIME. THAT JUST STAGGERS ME. I WILL SEE IT.
WILL INDIA ALLOW ITS PEOPLE TO STARVE WHEN IT HAS ATOM BOMBS TO PRESSURE OTHER NATIONS WITH? NO.
WILL IRAN AND IRAQ LEAVE THEIR NERVE GAS UNUSED?
YOU KNOW, YOU COULD REALLY DEPRESS ME IF YOU FELT LIKE TRYING, RON.
WHAT DO YOU THINK, MAUREEN? ARE WE GOING TO DESTROY OUR ENVIRONMENT BEYOND NATURE'S ABILITY TO REPAIR IT?

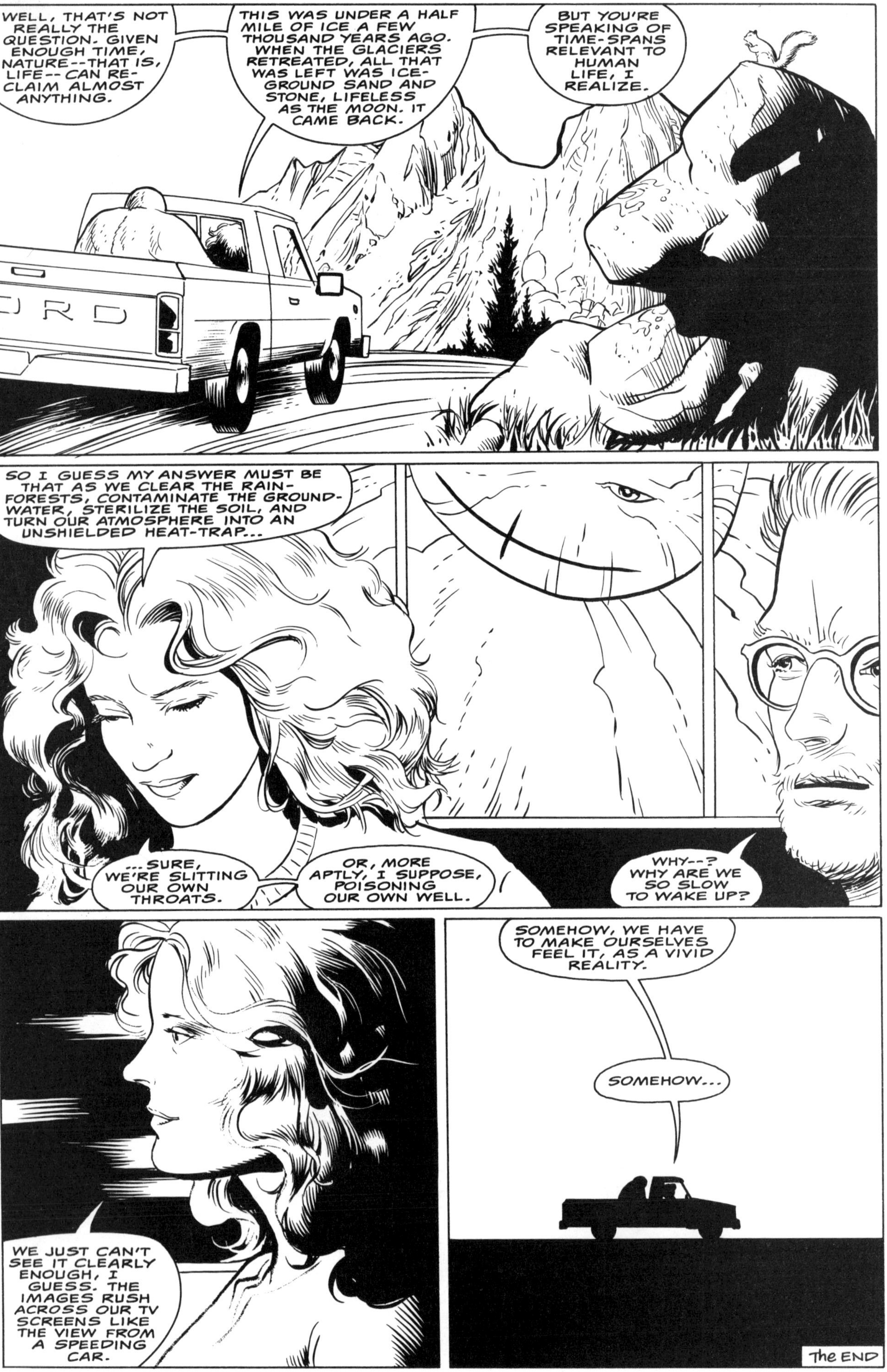
WELL, THAT'S NOT REALLY THE QUESTION. GIVEN ENOUGH TIME, NATURE--THAT IS, LIFE-- CAN RE-CLAIM ALMOST ANYTHING.
THIS WAS UNDER A HALF MILE OF ICE A FEW THOUSAND YEARS AGO. WHEN THE GLACIERS RETREATED, ALL THAT WAS LEFT WAS ICE-GROUND SAND AND STONE, LIFELESS AS THE MOON. IT CAME BACK.
BUT YOU'RE SPEAKING OF TIME-SPANS RELEVANT TO HUMAN LIFE, I REALIZE.
SO I GUESS MY ANSWER MUST BE THAT AS WE CLEAR THE RAIN-FORESTS, CONTAMINATE THE GROUND-WATER, STERILIZE THE SOIL, AND TURN OUR ATMOSPHERE INTO AN UNSHIELDED HEAT-TRAP...
...SURE, WE'RE SLITTING OUR OWN THROATS.
OR, MORE APTLY, I SUPPOSE, POISONING OUR OWN WELL.
WHY--? WHY ARE WE SO SLOW TO WAKE UP?
WE JUST CAN'T SEE IT CLEARLY ENOUGH, I GUESS. THE IMAGES RUSH ACROSS OUR TV SCREENS LIKE THE VIEW FROM A SPEEDING CAR.
SOMEHOW, WE HAVE TO MAKE OURSELVES FEEL IT, AS A VIVID REALITY.
SOMEHOW...
The END

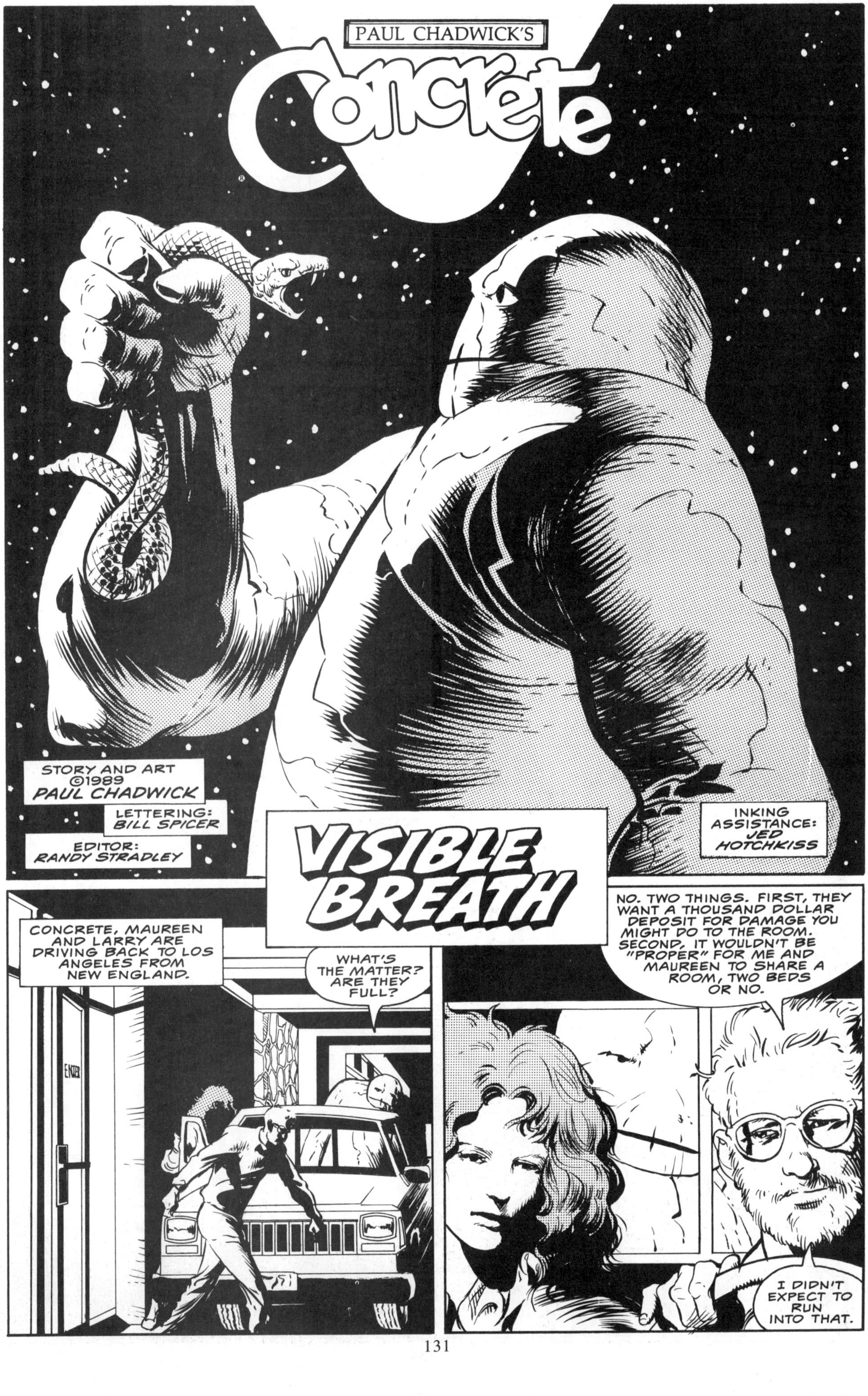
PAUL CHADWICK'S
Concrete
STORY AND ART ©1989 PAUL CHADWICK
LETTERING: BILL SPICER
EDITOR: RANDY STRADLEY
VISIBLE BREATH
INKING ASSISTANCE: JED HOTCHKISS
CONCRETE, MAUREEN AND LARRY ARE DRIVING BACK TO LOS ANGELES FROM NEW ENGLAND.
WHAT'S THE MATTER? ARE THEY FULL?
NO. TWO THINGS. FIRST, THEY WANT A THOUSAND DOLLAR DEPOSIT FOR DAMAGE YOU MIGHT DO TO THE ROOM. SECOND, IT WOULDN'T BE "PROPER" FOR ME AND MAUREEN TO SHARE A ROOM, TWO BEDS OR NO.
I DIDN'T EXPECT TO RUN INTO THAT.

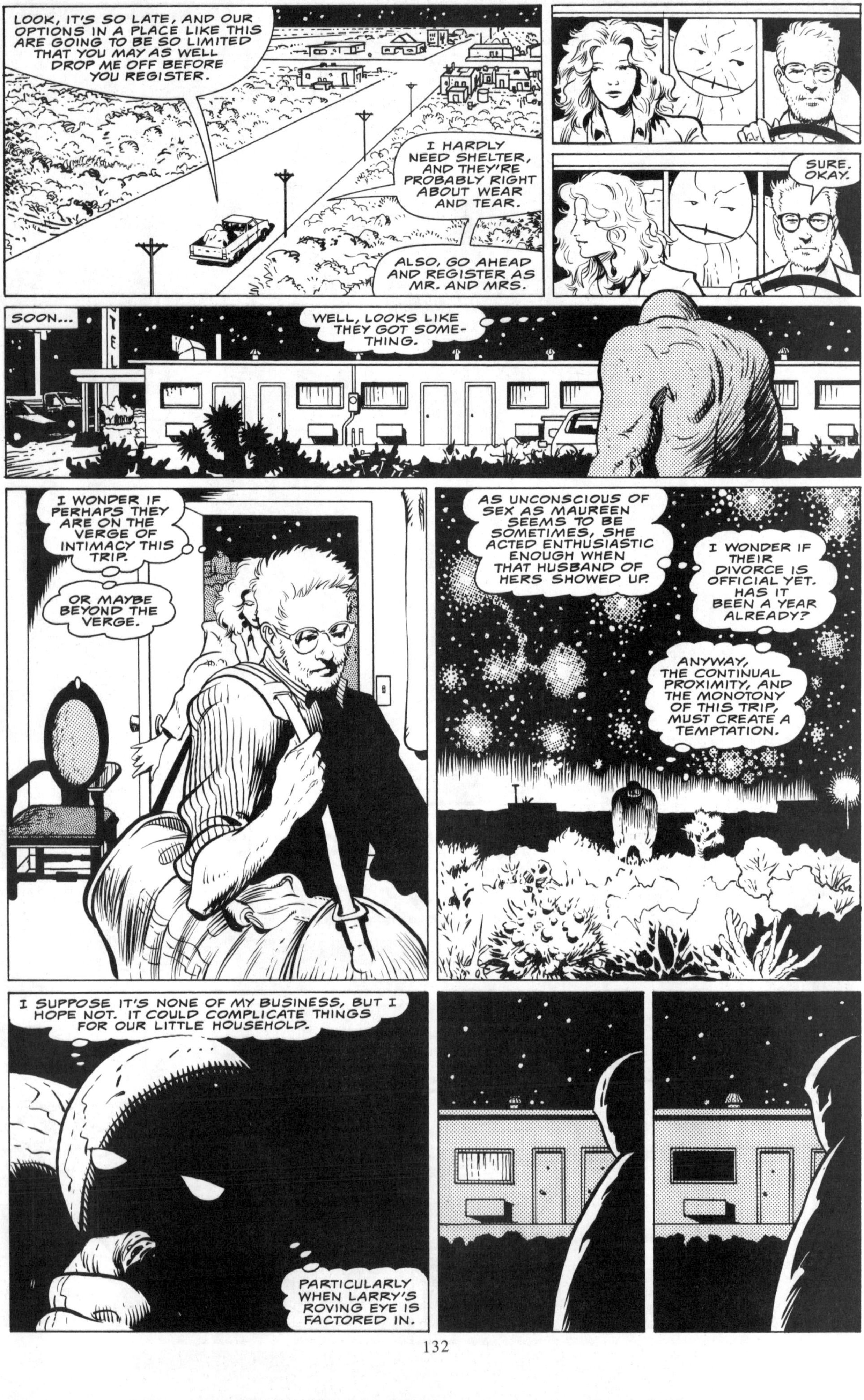

LOOK, IT'S SO LATE, AND OUR OPTIONS IN A PLACE LIKE THIS ARE GOING TO BE SO LIMITED THAT YOU MAY AS WELL DROP ME OFF BEFORE YOU REGISTER.
I HARDLY NEED SHELTER, AND THEY'RE PROBABLY RIGHT ABOUT WEAR AND TEAR.
ALSO, GO AHEAD AND REGISTER AS MR. AND MRS.
SURE. OKAY.
SOON...
WELL, LOOKS LIKE THEY GOT SOME-THING.
I WONDER IF PERHAPS THEY ARE ON THE VERGE OF INTIMACY THIS TRIP.
OR MAYBE BEYOND THE VERGE.
AS UNCONSCIOUS OF SEX AS MAUREEN SEEMS TO BE SOMETIMES, SHE ACTED ENTHUSIASTIC ENOUGH WHEN THAT HUSBAND OF HERS SHOWED UP.
I WONDER IF THEIR DIVORCE IS OFFICIAL YET. HAS IT BEEN A YEAR ALREADY?
ANYWAY, THE CONTINUAL PROXIMITY, AND THE MONOTONY OF THIS TRIP, MUST CREATE A TEMPTATION.
I SUPPOSE IT'S NONE OF MY BUSINESS, BUT I HOPE NOT. IT COULD COMPLICATE THINGS FOR OUR LITTLE HOUSEHOLD.
PARTICULARLY WHEN LARRY'S ROVING EYE IS FACTORED IN.

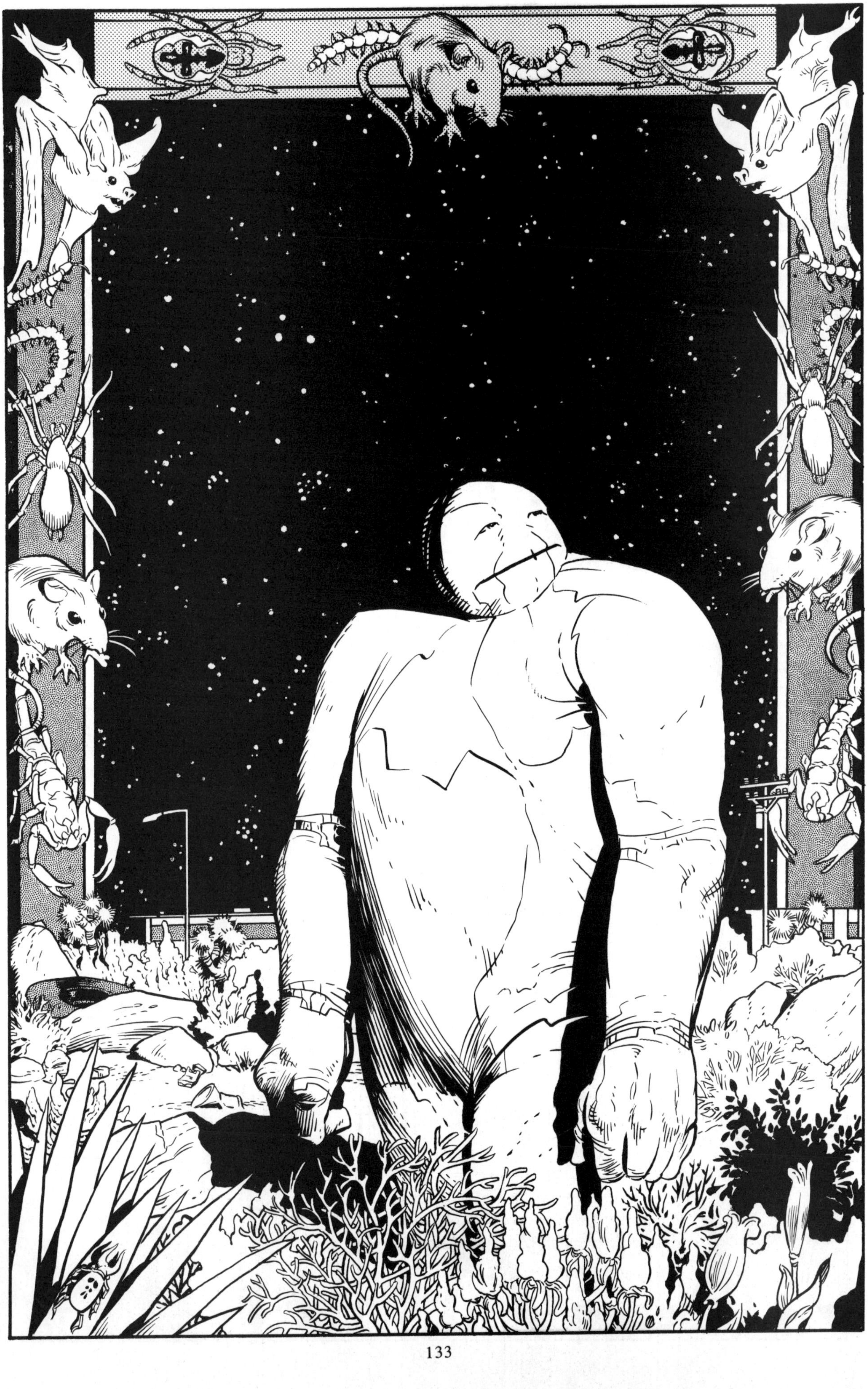

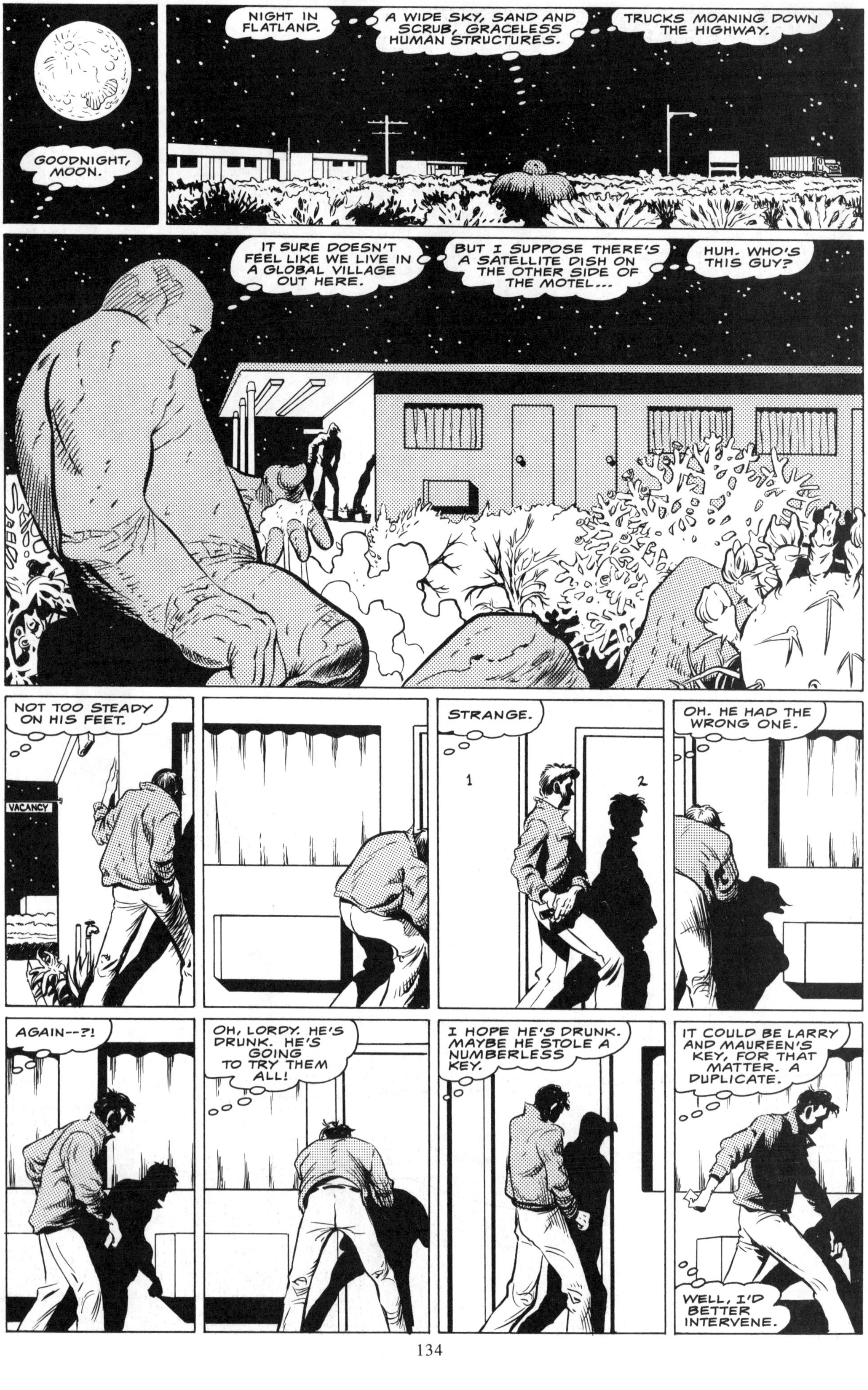
GOODNIGHT, MOON.
NIGHT IN FLATLAND.
A WIDE SKY, SAND AND SCRUB, GRACELESS HUMAN STRUCTURES.
TRUCKS MOANING DOWN THE HIGHWAY.
IT SURE DOESN'T FEEL LIKE WE LIVE IN A GLOBAL VILLAGE OUT HERE.
BUT I SUPPOSE THERE'S A SATELLITE DISH ON THE OTHER SIDE OF THE MOTEL...
HUH. WHO'S THIS GUY?
NOT TOO STEADY ON HIS FEET.
VACANCY
STRANGE.
1
2
OH. HE HAD THE WRONG ONE.
AGAIN--?!
OH, LORDY. HE'S DRUNK. HE'S GOING TO TRY THEM ALL!
I HOPE HE'S DRUNK. MAYBE HE STOLE A NUMBERLESS KEY.
IT COULD BE LARRY AND MAUREEN'S KEY, FOR THAT MATTER. A DUPLICATE.
WELL, I'D BETTER INTERVENE.

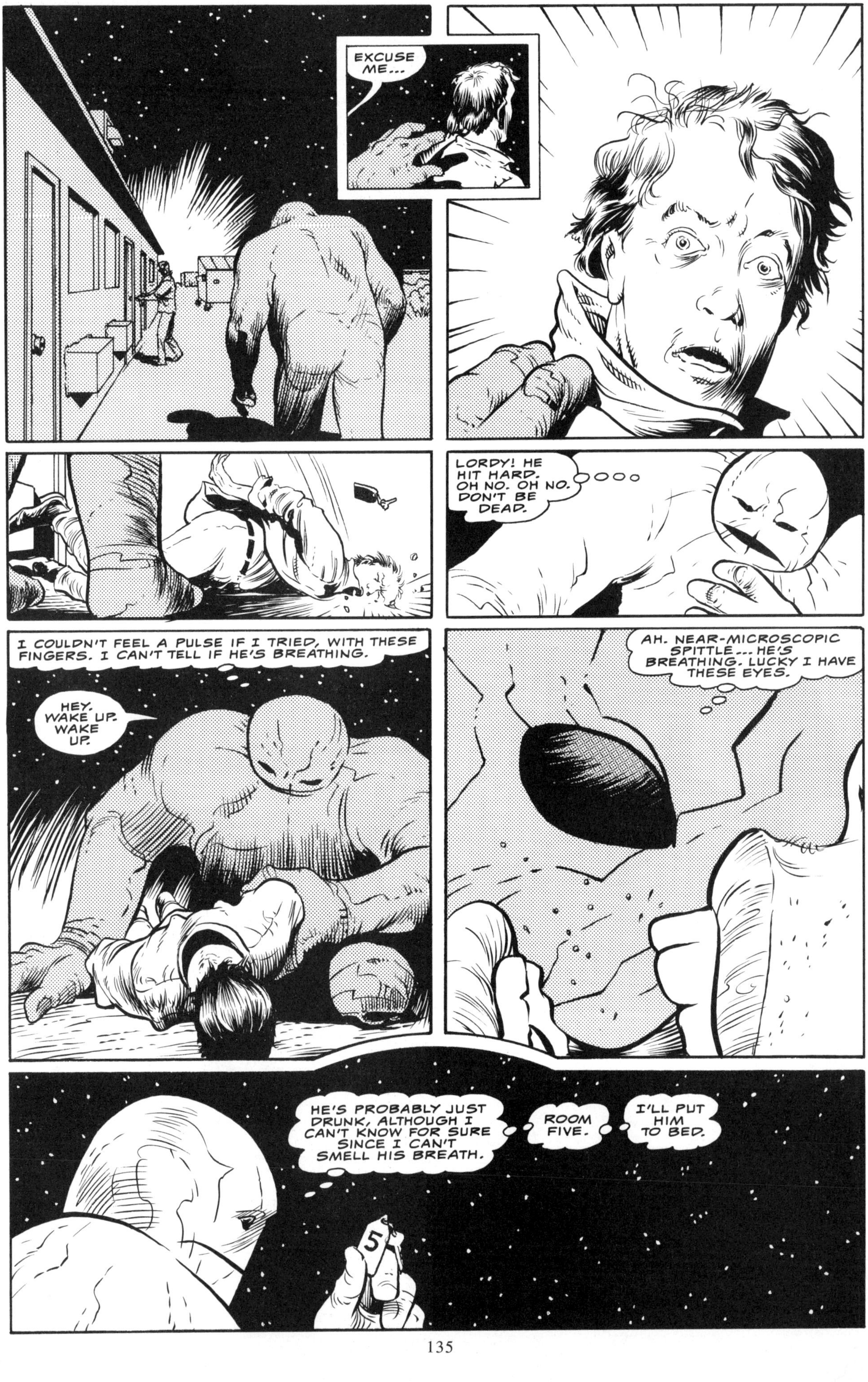
EXCUSE ME...
LORDY! HE HIT HARD. OH NO. OH NO. DON'T BE DEAD.
I COULDN'T FEEL A PULSE IF I TRIED, WITH THESE FINGERS. I CAN'T TELL IF HE'S BREATHING.
HEY. WAKE UP. WAKE UP.
AH. NEAR-MICROSCOPIC SPITTLE... HE'S BREATHING. LUCKY I HAVE THESE EYES.
HE'S PROBABLY JUST DRUNK, ALTHOUGH I CAN'T KNOW FOR SURE SINCE I CAN'T SMELL HIS BREATH.
ROOM FIVE.
I'LL PUT HIM TO BED.
5

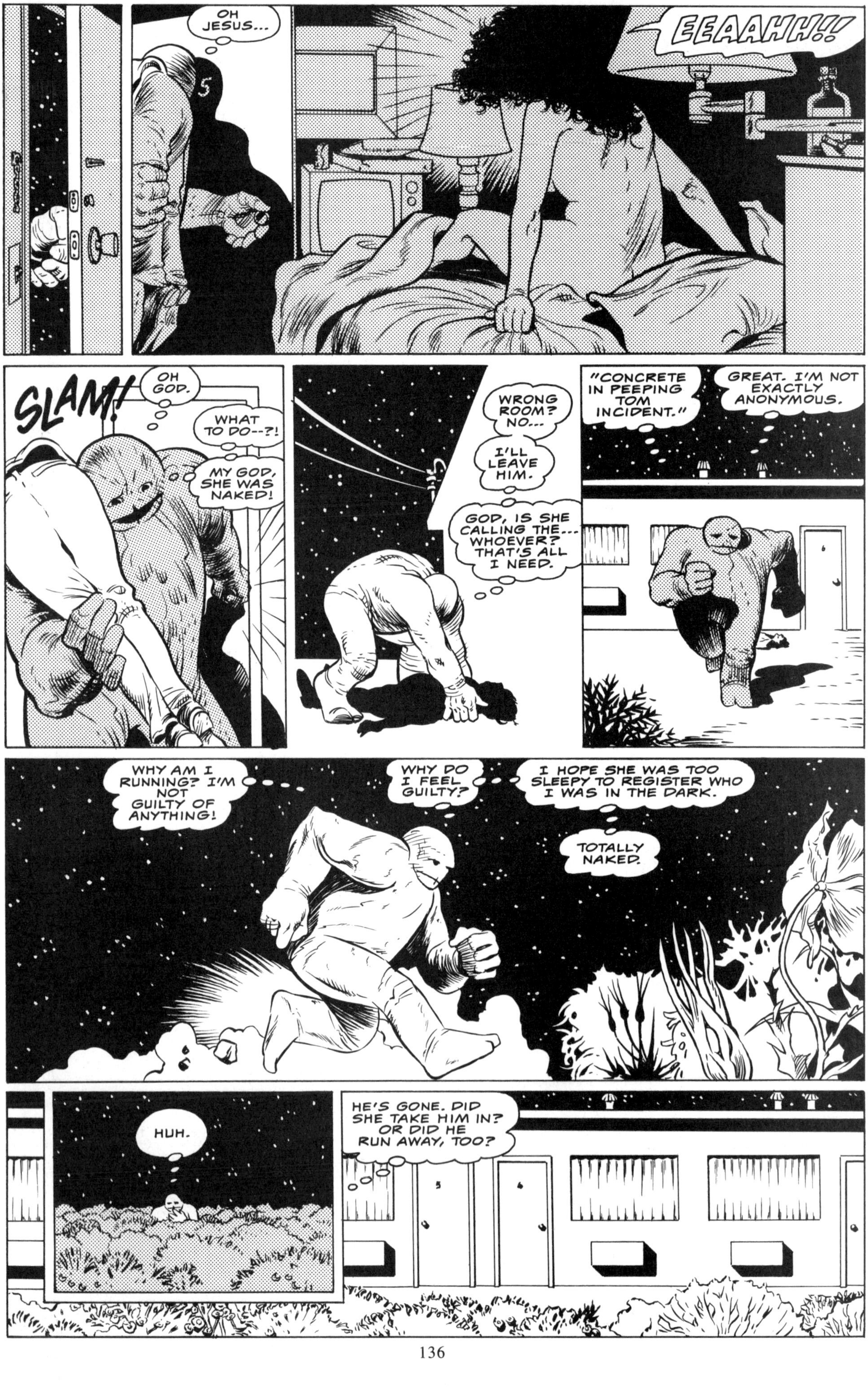
OH JESUS...
EEAAHH!!
SLAM!
OH GOD.
WHAT TO DO--?!
MY GOD, SHE WAS NAKED!
WRONG ROOM? NO...
I'LL LEAVE HIM.
GOD, IS SHE CALLING THE... WHOEVER? THAT'S ALL I NEED.
"CONCRETE IN PEEPING TOM INCIDENT."
GREAT. I'M NOT EXACTLY ANONYMOUS.
WHY AM I RUNNING? I'M NOT GUILTY OF ANYTHING!
WHY DO I FEEL GUILTY?
I HOPE SHE WAS TOO SLEEPY TO REGISTER WHO I WAS IN THE DARK.
TOTALLY NAKED.
HUH.
HE'S GONE. DID SHE TAKE HIM IN? OR DID HE RUN AWAY, TOO?

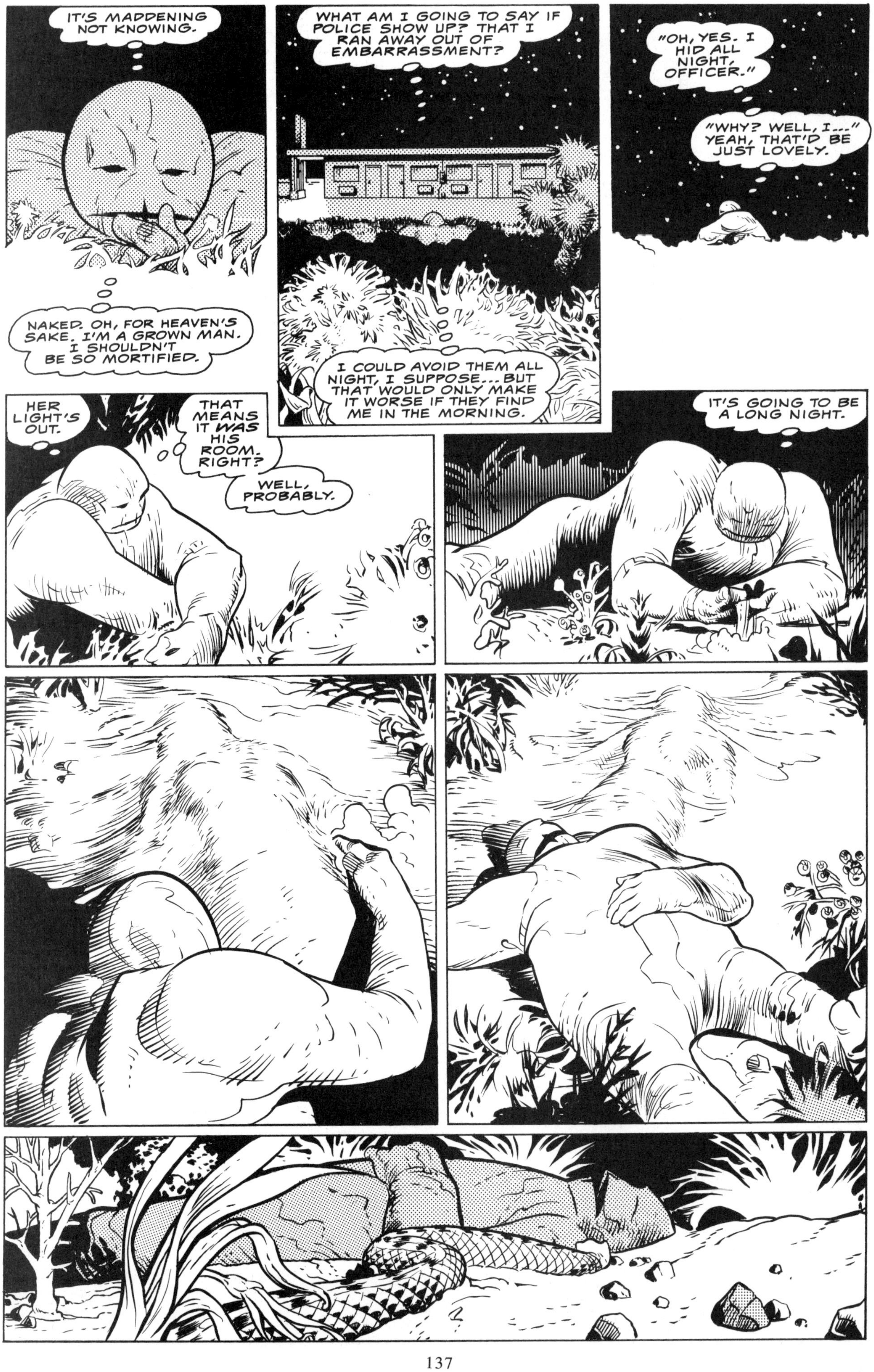
IT'S MADDENING NOT KNOWING.
NAKED. OH, FOR HEAVEN'S SAKE. I'M A GROWN MAN. I SHOULDN'T BE SO MORTIFIED.
WHAT AM I GOING TO SAY IF POLICE SHOW UP? THAT I RAN AWAY OUT OF EMBARRASSMENT?
I COULD AVOID THEM ALL NIGHT, I SUPPOSE... BUT THAT WOULD ONLY MAKE IT WORSE IF THEY FIND ME IN THE MORNING.
"OH, YES. I HID ALL NIGHT, OFFICER."
"WHY? WELL, I..." YEAH, THAT'D BE JUST LOVELY.
HER LIGHT'S OUT.
THAT MEANS IT WAS HIS ROOM. RIGHT?
WELL, PROBABLY.
IT'S GOING TO BE A LONG NIGHT.

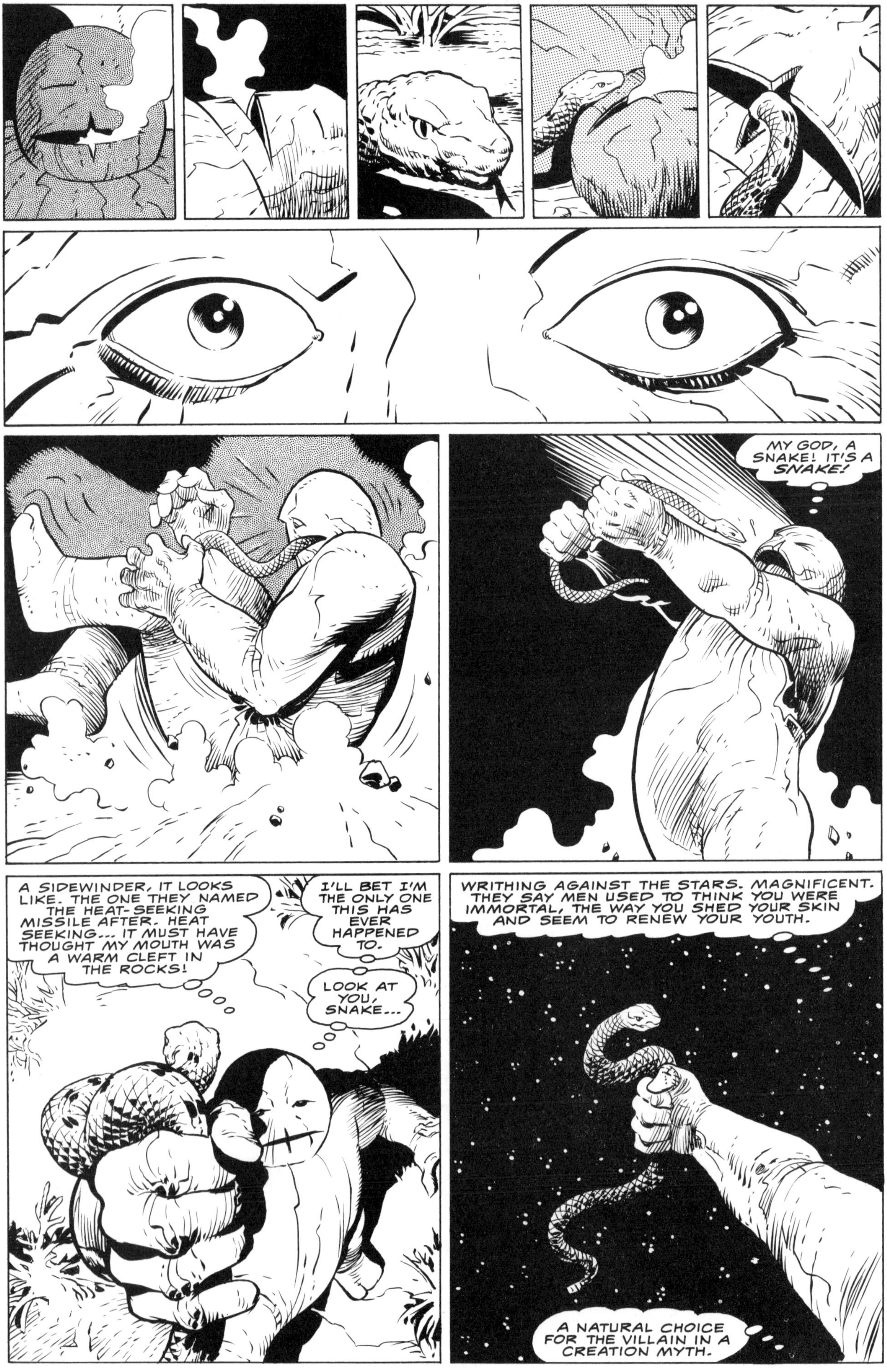
MY GOD, A SNAKE! IT'S A SNAKE!
A SIDEWINDER, IT LOOKS LIKE. THE ONE THEY NAMED THE HEAT-SEEKING MISSILE AFTER. HEAT SEEKING... IT MUST HAVE THOUGHT MY MOUTH WAS A WARM CLEFT IN THE ROCKS!
I'LL BET I'M THE ONLY ONE THIS HAS EVER HAPPENED TO.
LOOK AT YOU, SNAKE...
WRITHING AGAINST THE STARS. MAGNIFICENT. THEY SAY MEN USED TO THINK YOU WERE IMMORTAL, THE WAY YOU SHED YOUR SKIN AND SEEM TO RENEW YOUR YOUTH.
A NATURAL CHOICE FOR THE VILLAIN IN A CREATION MYTH.

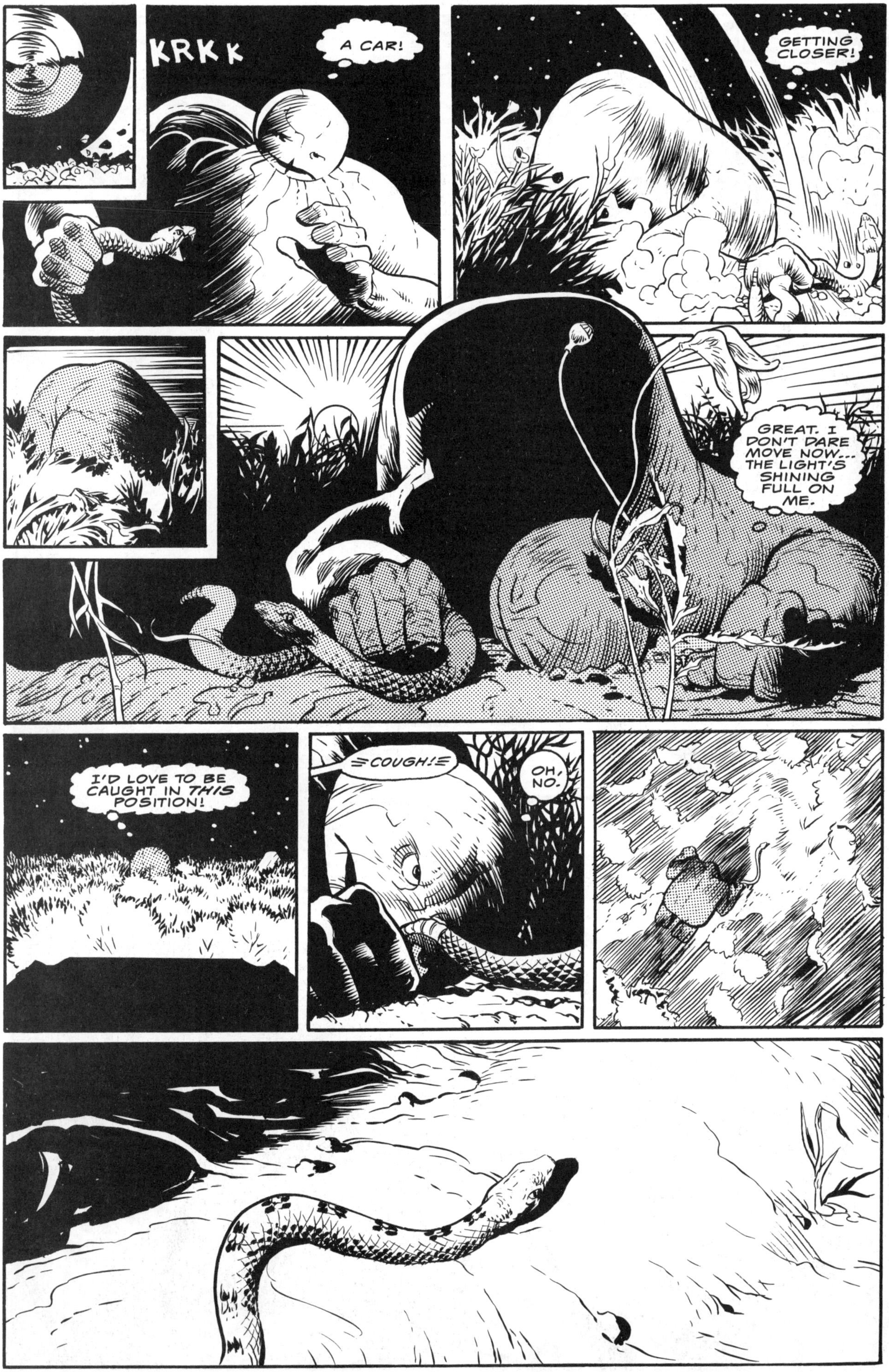
KRKK
A CAR!
GETTING CLOSER!
GREAT. I DON'T DARE MOVE NOW... THE LIGHT'S SHINING FULL ON ME.
I'D LOVE TO BE CAUGHT IN THIS POSITION!
COUGH!
OH, NO.

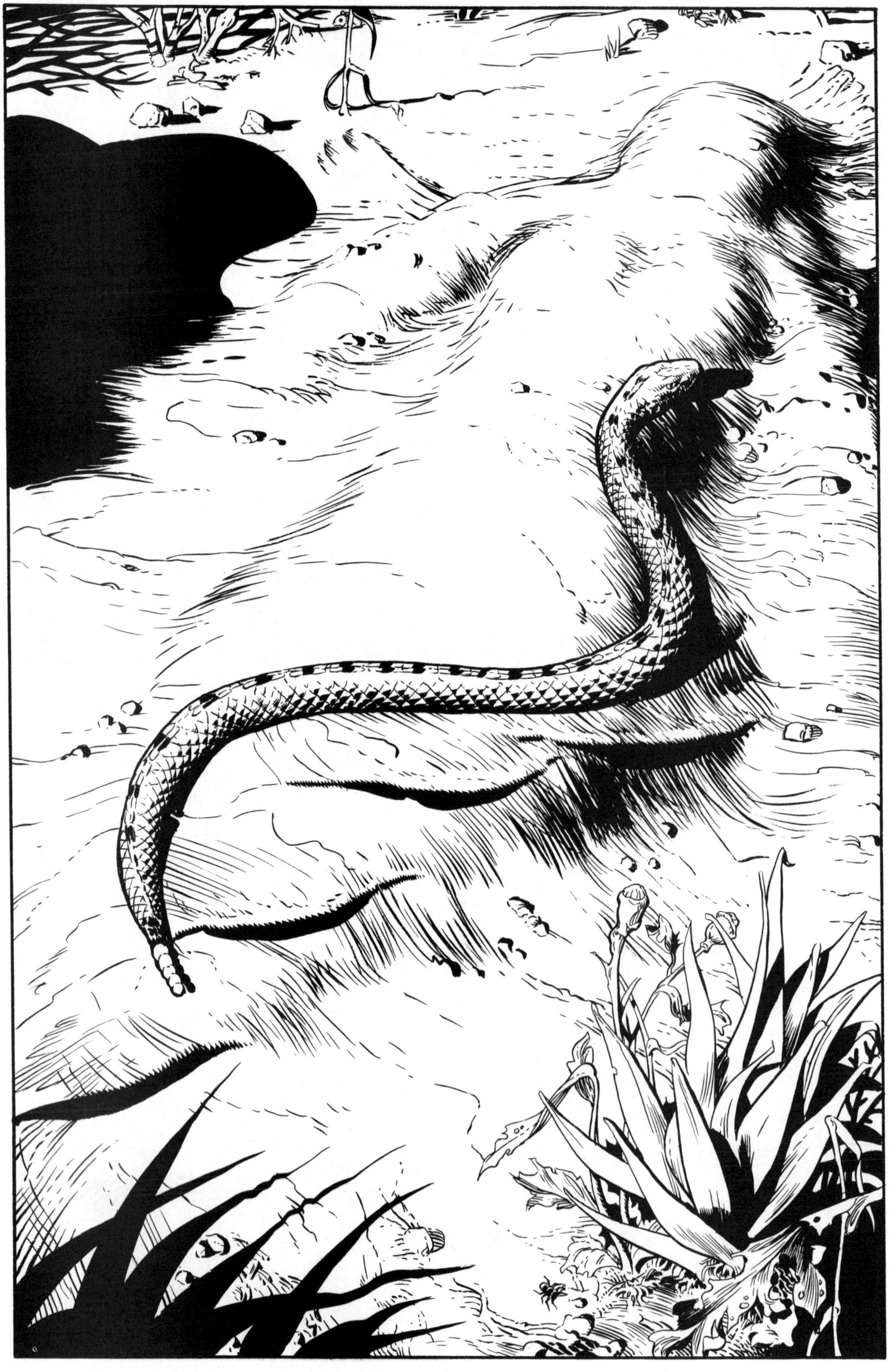

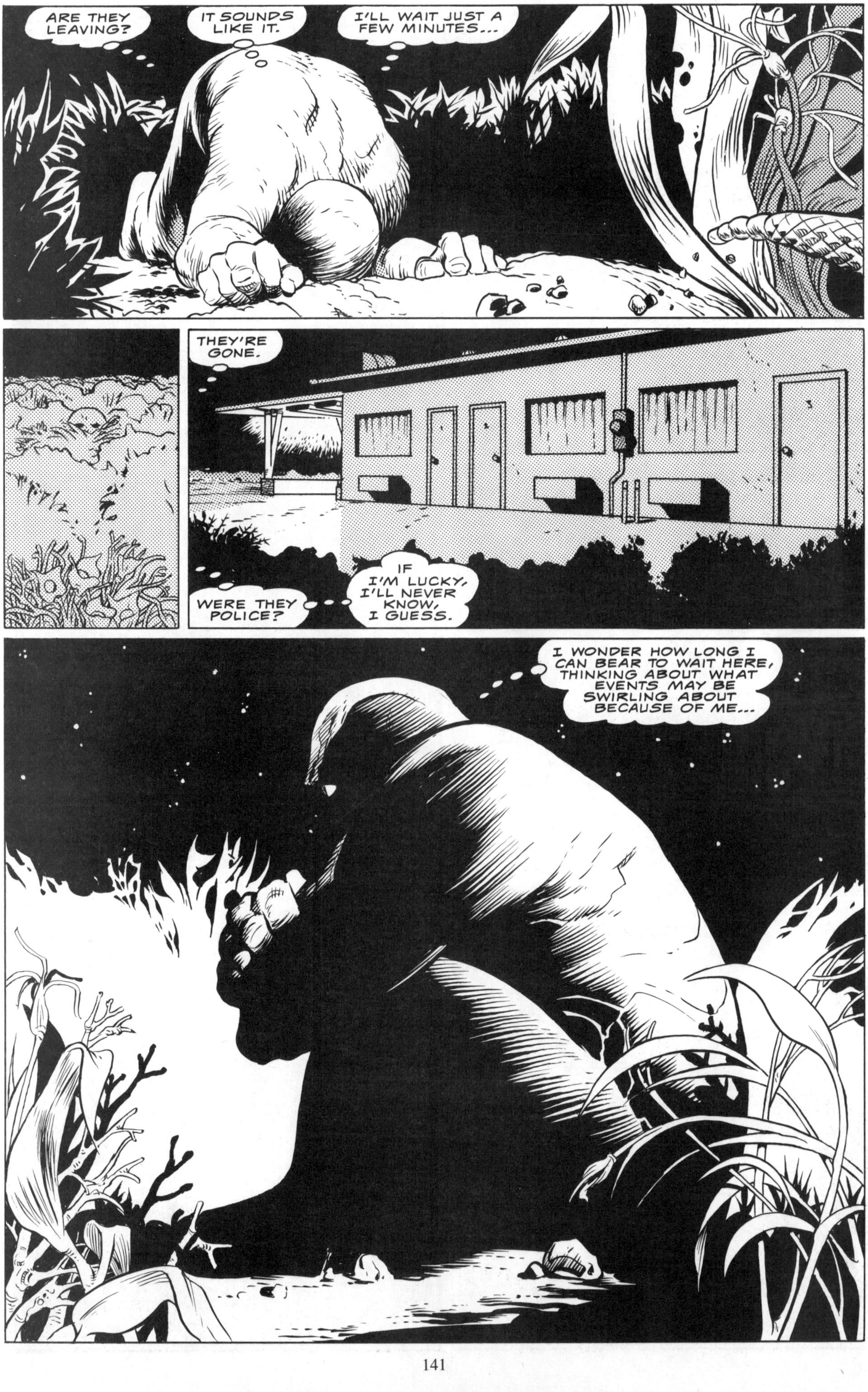
ARE THEY LEAVING?
IT SOUNDS LIKE IT.
I'LL WAIT JUST A FEW MINUTES...
THEY'RE GONE.
WERE THEY POLICE?
IF I'M LUCKY, I'LL NEVER KNOW, I GUESS.
I WONDER HOW LONG I CAN BEAR TO WAIT HERE, THINKING ABOUT WHAT EVENTS MAY BE SWIRLING ABOUT BECAUSE OF ME...

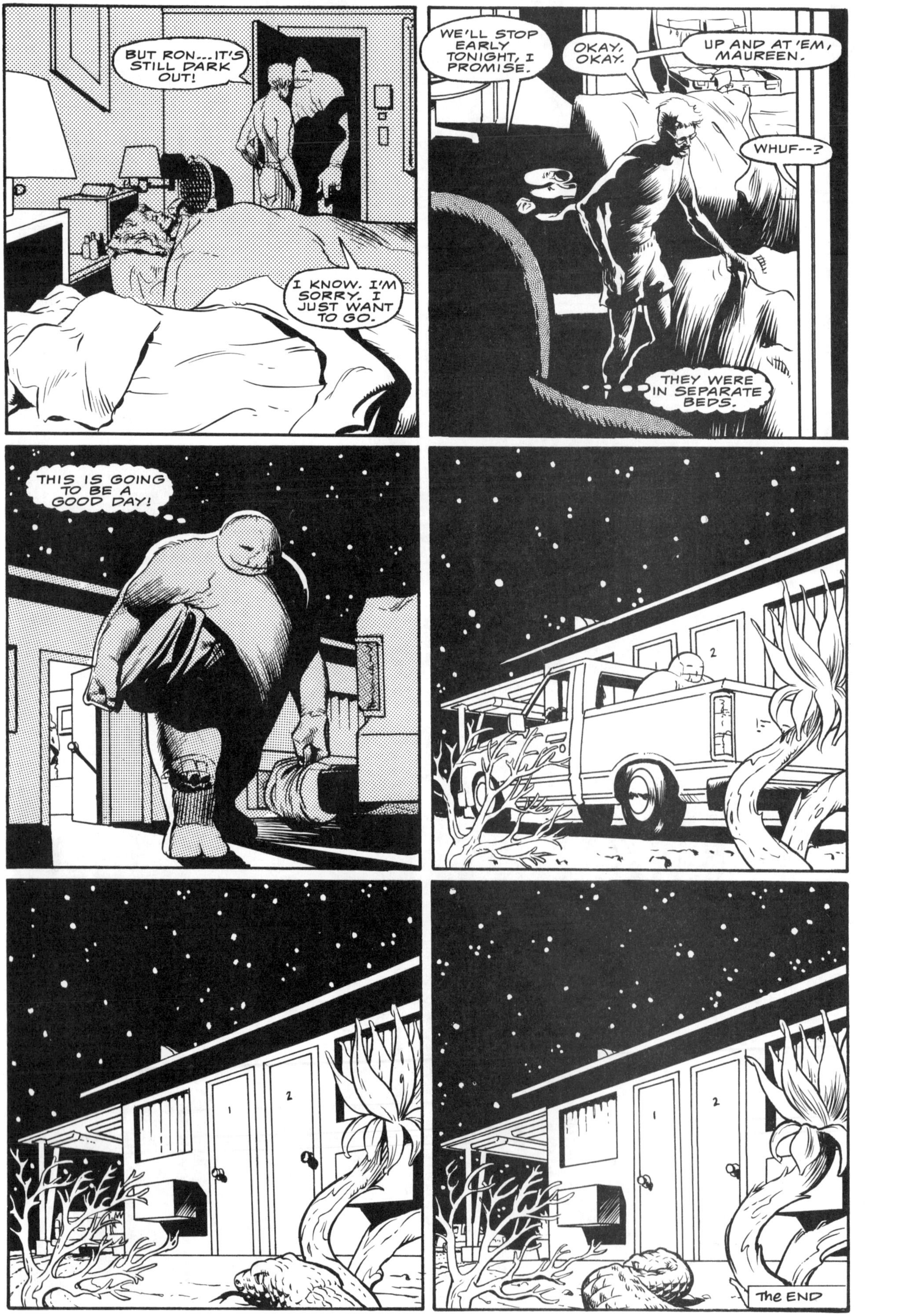
BUT RON... IT'S STILL DARK OUT!
I KNOW. I'M SORRY. I JUST WANT TO GO.
WE'LL STOP EARLY TONIGHT, I PROMISE.
OKAY, OKAY.
UP AND AT 'EM, MAUREEN.
WHUF--?
THEY WERE IN SEPARATE BEDS.
THIS IS GOING TO BE A GOOD DAY!
1
2
1
2
1
2
The END

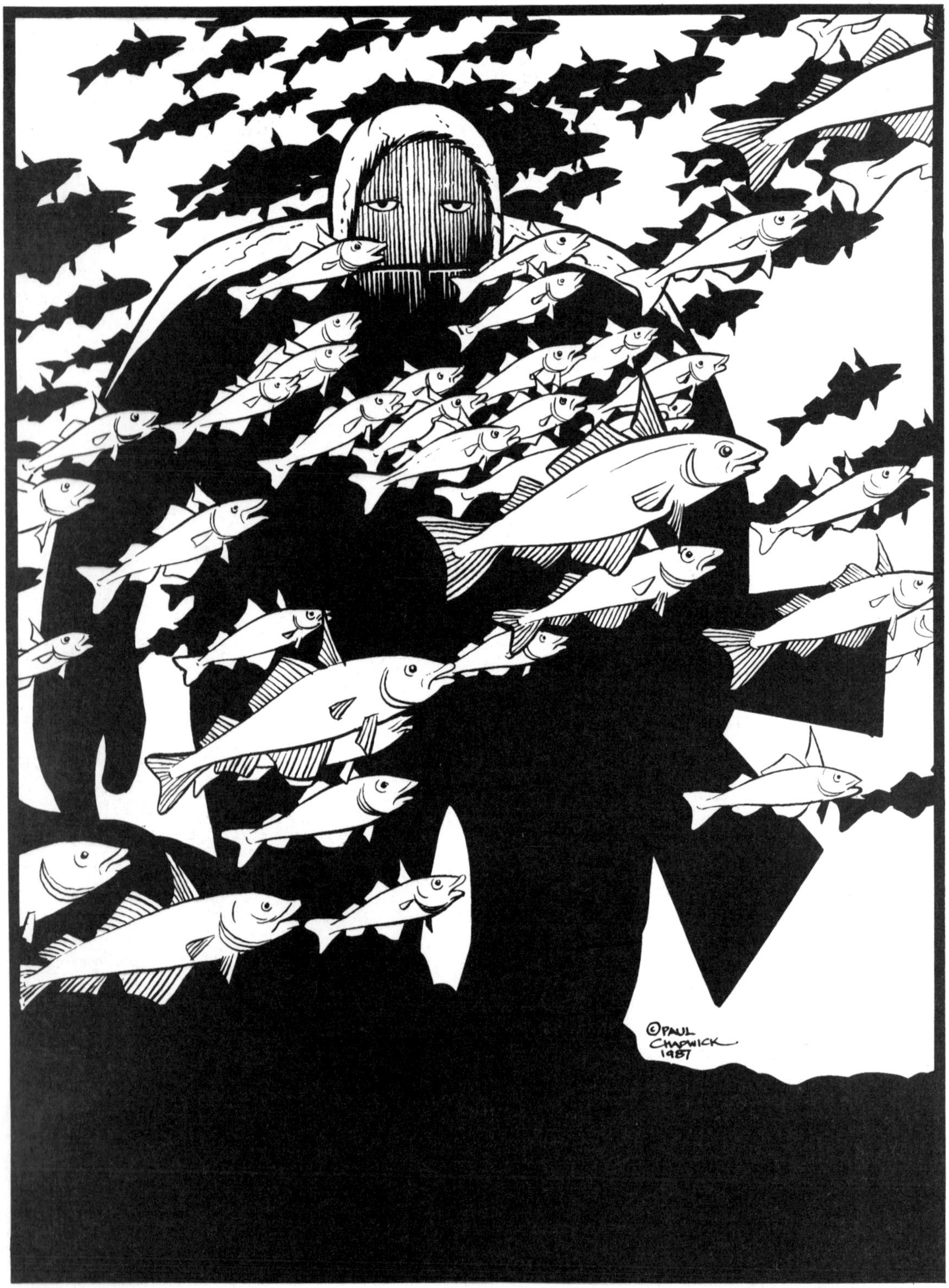
©PAUL
CHADWICK
1987